THE INDIAN ARMY

ITS CONTRIBUTION TO THE DEVELOPMENT OF A NATION

THE
INDIAN ARMY

ITS CONTRIBUTION TO THE
DEVELOPMENT OF A NATION

Stephen P. Cohen

UNIVERSITY OF CALIFORNIA PRESS
BERKELEY, LOS ANGELES, LONDON, 1971

University of California Press
Berkeley and Los Angeles, California
University of California Press, Ltd.
London, England
Copyright © 1971, by
The Regents of the University of California
Library of Congress Catalog Card Number: 77-111421
Standard Book Number: 520-01697-1
Printed in the United States of America

TO MY PARENTS
SAUL AND BESS COHEN

CONTENTS

ACKNOWLEDGMENTS

The research for this book was unusually extended in time and space. I have therefore incurred a heavy personal and intellectual obligation. It is a pleasure for me to mention some of the individuals and institutions whose assistance has been so helpful.

Professor Henry C. Hart of the University of Wisconsin made more than the usual advisory contribution to this study in its earlier incarnation as a dissertation. His continuing advice, encouragement, and intellectual stimulation are gratefully acknowledged. Deen and Eunice Gupta and Fritz and Jan Lehmann have been generous with their hospitality through the years, and have taught me much of what I know about India.

I have drawn on the facilities of the School of Oriental and African Studies, the India Office Library, the Indian Council of World Affairs, the United Services Institution of India, the Institute of Defense Studies and Analysis, New Delhi, and the Ministry of Defense, Government of India. I am grateful to the Ministry of Defense for enabling me to examine their archives and library and to visit several military institutions.

Throughout the book interview sources are not usually identified by name. However, I wish to especially thank the many Indian, Pakistani, and British officers, active and retired, who gave so freely of their time. During their interviews, and interviews with journalists, politicians, and administrators, outline notes were recorded and later expanded. Thus, quotations for these interviews are not always verbatim, except in a few instances where personal correspondence was involved or the interview was tape recorded. I have tried to remain faithful to the trust of these individuals by recording what I have seen and heard as accurately as possible.

I am grateful to the University of Wisconsin for timely support in 1962–1963 and 1965, to the American Institute of Indian Studies for research fellowships in India in 1964–1965 and 1968–1969, and to the University of Illinois for both financial assistance and that most precious commodity of all, time to think and write.

Finally, I wish to acknowledge a debt to my wife, Roberta, whose unfailing support and encouragement over three continents and four years considerably lightened my task.

Although the above individuals and institutions have made substantial contributions to this book, responsibility for any error of fact or interpretation is my own.

S. P. C.

INTRODUCTION

The Indian subcontinent contains nearly a fifth of the world's population. Although it is a recognizable geographical entity, the people of the region are divided into several thousands of castes, clans, and tribes, and comprise thirty different language groups, each of which encompasses several vernaculars. Its people are also organized into social systems of varying complexity and sophistication: from tribes living in stone-age isolation to the intermixed remnants of great Hindu and Muslim civilizations. There is something uniquely Indian about most of these systems, although they vary greatly. The analogy comes to mind of a Europe riven by linguistic, political, and economic differences, yet psychologically and culturally different from other great civilization-regions.

To this great reservoir of human wealth and skill came European adventurers of various nationalities: Dutch, French, Portuguese, and British. They all came to plunder and conquer, but only the British stayed to rule and transform the social and political institutions of the subcontinent—to the extent that these institutions were amenable to transformation. Certainly, one of the most impressive accomplishments of the British was the military integration of the land, without which nothing else could have been accomplished. Without political and military unity India would not have been safe for anything but haphazard exploitation. The British learned that for systematic economic gain, as well as for strategic security, an organized military establishment based in large part upon indigenous manpower was necessary. Later, the notion of a civilizing mission developed; this mission, too, benefited from the stability assured by a monopoly of reliable military power.

As important as its direct impact upon British rule in India, the development of an Indian army has had lasting effects on the social and especially the political life of the people of the subcontinent. Long after the British have departed, their military imprint can still be seen in the villages of the Punjab, the cantonments of the great and small urban centers, and even in the politics of both successor states. This influence is most obvious in Pakistan where British-trained officers have long dominated that nation's government, but is also important in India where democratic politics are burgeoning behind the protective shield of the world's fourth-largest army. In both states the existence of a powerful, unified army places limits on political behavior. Groups which would otherwise incline toward revolutionary strategies are forced to stay within the "legal" parliamentary system, and politicians know that severe civil disorder or political vacillation which disrupts the routine of the military may well cause the latter to intervene in politics. The existence of these powerful, well-armed armies may insure national integrity *vis a vis* external threats, but it may also mean that major social change through revolutionary activity or radical political activity will be difficult to achieve; modernization will come to South Asia, but only at the pace tolerated by the military.

Not surprisingly, the impact of almost three hundred years of British military presence in India is most apparent in the two successor military establishments. It is visibly so in the cantonments and on the frontiers in matters of badge, dress, and drill, but it also remains in more fundamental ways. The greatest military legacy of the British was a sense of organizational integrity; the armies of India and Pakistan certainly have the capacity to form and reform themselves in the face of changing military tasks, with a considerable degree of efficiency, and despite the handicap of a relatively narrow resource base. The strength of these two armies lies ultimately not in their hardware, where they compare unfavorably, say, to Indonesia or Egypt, but in the intelligent use of manpower.

This book is not a history of the Indian military, although many of its data are drawn from that history. It is a study of the development of a modern army in South Asia, and its relationship to its own political and social environment. For such a study historical data are necessary, but we shall treat them from a perspective which is, we hope, informed by contemporary theories of military organization and nation-building. Conventional military history usually confines itself to the study of warfare *per se* and to organizational problems, and the perspective of such an approach is relatively narrow. We are interested in the development of the Indian Army in a broader sense. The Indian Army underwent a two-fold process of modernization, first as its own officer corps became highly professionalized, and secondly as it established a relationship between that officer corps and indigenous personnel recruited for the ranks. Conventional political history—especially in India—has virtually ignored the military as a factor in the process of nation-building. This is surprising, for the military had a profound impact on the course of nationalist politics, and also upon politics after 1947. This book will show what the Indian and Pakistani armies have been, so that we may better understand what they might be.

1
BRITISH INDIAN MILITARY ORGANIZATION

The British struggle to develop an efficient and loyal military organization was a long and difficult effort, which did not cease until the transfer of power in 1947. This chapter will describe some of the problems they faced in developing and controlling their own officer corps, and will examine some of the theories of civilian control which comprise part of the British military legacy to India and Pakistan. We shall stress the creation of a professional officer corps, because the Indian Army has always relied on its commissioned officers for leadership and direction. This reliance means that civilian-military relations will be a critical issue, because civilians cannot readily approach the masses of soldiers without going through their officers.

FROM COMPANY TO RAJ

The first hundred years of British presence in India saw a desperate two-fold struggle. First, the British were only one of several foreign powers competing with each other and with indigenous Indian power centers for markets, territory, and influence. Second, they were attempting to build up and

4

control their own military resources and eliminate internal dissension.

The earliest British forces in India were largely private, raised by the forerunners of the United East India Company. The Royal charters of these companies were at first limited, in keeping with the limited commercial aims of the companies. Royal forces, especially naval forces, were often attached for duty with private companies, and the first serious incident between the military and civilians grew out of such an attachment. The "Keigwin Rebellion" of 1683 struck a surprisingly modern note: the most professional of all British services, the navy, resented civilian bungling in the management of Bombay's defenses and finances.[1] Richard Keigwin, a Royal Navy captain, seized control over Bombay in the face of Company opposition, claiming that he was acting in the higher interests of the King. He defended Bombay's neutrality, the first time this had been done in years, and improved the finances of the then minor outpost to such an extent that when the rebellion ended after eleven months, there was more money in the treasury than when it began.

In the course of the rebellion several important issues were raised. First, did a King's officer serving in the Company or on attached duty owe allegiance to his immediate superiors, or did he have a higher allegiance to the Crown, from which both military and Company authority derived? Second, was an officer justified in disobeying his superiors in order to carry out his duty to *their* superiors, or was he to obey, and by his obedience do harm to that higher authority? Keigwin and his fellow mutineers placed their loyalty to the Crown above their loyalty to the Company, and took matters in their own hands.[2] Whatever the moral or legal implications of the mutineers' actions, they were politically secure, for rather than being punished, they were granted complete pardons; Keigwin was given a bag of gold, and assigned to his old ship, the *Assistance* where he later died a sailor's death in combat.

[1] See Ray and Oliver Strachey, *Keigwin's Rebellion, 1683–1684* (Oxford: Clarendon Press, 1916), for a general history.

[2] Keigwin to King Charles II, September 15, 1684. India Office Library. Home Misc. Series, Vol. 52, No. 1, ff. 206–209.

The Company, however, could not afford to take the mutiny lightly, and Keigwin was labeled a "new Cromwell," the "Oliver of the Rebells and Protector of Bombay."[3] The Secret Committee sought and received enhanced powers from the Crown, and the new charter of James II gave the Company power to appoint their own admirals and other sea-going officers in Company ships, relieving them of the necessity of relying upon Royal officers (such as Keigwin).[4] The Company was also given the power of martial law at sea.

Some of these enhanced powers were necessary because the Company had embarked upon a more militant policy. In 1661 the Company of Merchants (a forerunner of the United East India Company) was given power to send armed ships and men to India to make war against non-Christians "in the place of their trade."[5] In a later renewal of the charter the Company was given the power to declare war and make peace with any of the "heathen nations" of Asia, Africa, and America.[6] It took advantage of these provisions by making war on the entire Moghul empire.

The war was a military failure, but illustrated some of the limitations of British power in South Asia. Ever-reluctant to trust their soldiers, the Company appointed only a lieutenant to command the ten ships and 600 men it deployed against Aurangzeb. Even then, this force was urged to go cautiously: it could hire an Indian army, providing it did not recruit too heavily from one "nation" (perhaps the earliest example of the principle of a mixed rather than homogeneous army). The force was urged not to kill too many people, and always be careful lest "ye crafty Dutch" interfere.[7] The Company was highly suspicious of its own military establishment: it not

3 Letter to Charles II from John St. John, September 20, 1684. Home Misc. Series, Vol. 52, No. 1, fo. 225. St. John had been sent to examine the situation and found the Company free from blame.

4 The Secret Committee, *Transactions,* Letter to Charles II, August 15, 1684. Home Misc. Series, Vol. 42, No. 39, fo. 330, and the Charter of April 12, 1686, India Office Library.

5 "The East-India Companies Charter," April 13, 1661, India Office Library.

6 A. Berriedale Keith, *A Constitutional History of India* (reprint of 1937 ed.; Allahabad: Central Book Depot, 1961), p. 10.

7 "Instructions for our Agent and Councill of Bengall." Court of Directors, East India House, Jan. 14, 1686. Home Misc. Series, Vol. 803, No. 18, ff. 480–87.

only feared a repetition of the Keigwin Rebellion, but did not trust the loyalty of its own officers, who were prone to sell their services to the highest bidder.[8] The Company attempted to unite military and political functions in the hands of its own personnel; lacking any effective code of civilian control and any significant standard of professionalism, this unification was probably the best course of action, but only feasible when both the level of military action and the degree of organizational sophistication were low.

In the first half of the eighteenth century a heightened political and military competition with the French forced the British to reassess their position in India. Although they later became the dominant European power in the subcontinent, they were first forced to overhaul radically their military establishment. Two discoveries were central to the ultimate success of the British: first, a few disciplined British troops could defeat large but disorganized Indian armies; second, Indians were themselves amenable to discipline. Ironically, both discoveries had been made by the French, but were exploited by the British to defeat both French and indigenous Indian armies.[9] Earlier (1721–1729) the French had employed Indian troops in a struggle with the British on the West Coast of India.[10] Termed "cypayes," they partly replaced the Indian auxiliaries until then used by all European powers. The sepoy (derived from sipahii=soldier) differed from other Indian troops in that he was trained and organized according to European military standards, and was led in the field by European officers. H. H. Dodwell's history of early recruit-

---

[8] Lieut.-Col. W. J. Wilson, *History of the Madras Army* (5 vols.; Madras: The Government Press, 1882–1889), I, 4.

[9] Sir J. R. Seeley argued this point in the late nineteenth century, but he notes James Mill had developed it much earlier. Seeley, *The Expansion of England*, 2nd ed. (London: Macmillan, 1905), pp. 233 ff.

[10] H. H. Dodwell, *Sepoy Recruitment in the Old Madras Army* (Calcutta: India Historical Records Commission, 1922), pp. 3 ff. Other histories of the early presidency armies include: Lieut.-Col. Sir Wolesley Haig, "The Armies of the East India Company," in H. H. Dodwell, ed., *The Indian Empire*, Vol. VI of *The Cambridge History of India* (reprint ed.; Delhi: S. Chand & Co., 1964), *Recruiting in India Before and During the War of 1914–1918* (India: Army H.Q., October, 1919) [an unclassified printed volume in the Archives of the Ministry of Defense, Government of India], and the various official and unofficial histories of individual presidency armies and military regiments.

ment practices indicates that the sepoy was introduced on the East Coast by Dumas around 1740.[11] In 1748 Captain Stringer Lawrence copied the French system and established regular permanent companies which were led by British officers. The sepoys demonstrated their effectiveness against, among others, the French, and Lawrence won himself the title "Father of the Indian Army." The British recruited additional sepoy units until a total of 9,000 were in use in 1765, grouped into at least seven battalions, and divided into numerous companies of about a hundred men.

Although units were created and disbanded many times, the fundamental organizational principle of these units did not change, and the present structure of both the Indian and Pakistani armies reflect their origin. The British allowed Indian officers to command the companies. Each was led by a *subedar* assisted by a *jamedar* and several noncommissioned officers. Although an Indian officer was in charge of each battalion, the real power, as well as responsibility for training, rested in the hands of several British officers permanently appointed to the battalion. The extraordinary merit of this system is obvious: it gave an opportunity for ambitious and able Indian soldiers in the service of the British to achieve promotion to at least the battalion level, yet it maintained an element of direct British control over all Company troops. The Indian officer (later given the title Viceroy's Commissioned Officer) provided the link between the indigenous Indian sepoy and the professional British officer; the link proved to be so strong that it was rarely broken.

The sharpening of conflict in India necessitated additional support to the East India Company from the British government. This support gave rise to considerable difficulties in Company-Crown relations, difficulties similar to those encountered when the Crown backed the Company in its struggle with the Dutch in the previous century.[12]

One material expression of government support of the Com-

---

11 Dodwell, p. 3.
12 Lucy Sutherland, *The East India Company in Eighteenth Century Politics* (Oxford: Clarendon Press, 1952), p. 77.

pany was the arrival of Royal troops in India in 1754 for the first time since the previous century. At the same time the Company's own military organization was further professionalized. The Company's army was placed under contemporary standards of discipline, and rules governing the relationship between King's officer and Company's officer were laid down.[13] Company troops were now fully covered by British military law, and many minor as well as major crimes—such as mutiny —were punishable.[14]

There was good cause for the Crown to enact such a statute, for only two years earlier the Company had had difficulty in maintaining military discipline in Madras. The Council there had to send home rebellious officers, for when it had tried to court-martial some offenders, they banded together and intimidated their fellow officers to evade punishment.[15] Although the Royal legislation strengthened the hand of the Company's civil servants, discipline problems recurred in later years.

The arrival of Royal troops created new discipline difficulties in the Company's armies. New questions of precedence and command developed, for each army tended to view the other as a competitor for military honor and status, as well as the more material rewards of plunder.

The difficulty of relating King's officer to Company's officer was compounded by the existence of three different presidency governments in British India, each with its own army under separate and unrelated command. These armies were raised and financed by the presidency governments of Bengal, Madras, and Bombay, but Royal troops were often assigned to the presidencies, and obeyed a different chain of command. Conflict arose when Company and Royal officers disagreed over responsibility for joint military action, when pay differentials arose between Royal and Company officers (and be-

13 See "An Act for Punishing Mutiny and Desertion of Officers and Soldiers in the Service of the United Company of Merchants of *England* trading to the *East Indies*; and for the Punishment of Offences committed in the East Indies, or at the Island of *Saint Helena*," 1753–1754.

14 *Ibid.*, Section I.

15 President and Council of Fort St. David to Directors, August 6, 1751. Home Misc. Series, Vol. 93, No. 7, ff. 18–19.

tween Company officers of different presidencies), and when different promotion policies placed younger officers of one army in command of older or more experienced officers from another army. Such conflicts occurred often, and most notably before the Battle of Plassey when a King's officer refused to serve under the Company representative Robert Clive, Deputy Governor of Madras, and leader of the expedition against Siraj-ud-daulah, the Nawab of Bengal. A compromise had to be arranged in which Clive was placed under the over-all authority of a Royal Navy admiral. Even so, during the battle, at a moment of great uncertainty, the rivalry between Company and Crown again emerged when King's officers demanded precedence over Company officers.[16]

Clive's position in the expedition against the Nawab was unique, for he had been granted both political and military responsibility by the Madras Council.[17] Yet, he was neither a professional soldier nor a representative of the Bengal Council, for whose relief the expedition was ostensibly fighting. He was an able military commander and an astute political leader, and was ideally suited to deal with the next major crisis in British-Indian military history.

Robert Clive and Army Reform

When Clive returned to India for his second term as Governor-General in May, 1765, he was faced with two major problems: one external and one internal. The first was the settling of the political relations between the Company and

[16] Clive would not have led the expedition had it not been for three senior officers who were disqualified for one reason or another: Lord Pigot, Governor of Madras, had no military experience; Colonel Stringer Lawrence, a KCO (but loyal to the Company), was ailing; and Colonel Aldercron "would have had it if he had not made the most extravagant and absurd claims for himself as a King's officer and showed a complete disregard for the Company's rights and interests." A. Mervyn Davies, *Clive of Plassey* (London: Nicholson and Watson, 1939), p. 152.

[17] The professional soldiers, all King's officers, were bitter that Clive, a gifted amateur, was made senior to all of them except Admiral Watson. Clive had to wage a continuous battle of nerves with the King's officers, including Watson, to retain direction of the expedition. At one point (after Clive occupied Fort William) the tension was so great that Watson threatened to fire on Clive and his men. Clive refused to yield, and the officers gave in to him. Davies, pp. 160 ff.

the Emperor and nawabs of Oudh and Bengal in the light of the vastly improved military position of the British. The second was the overhaul of the Company's administrative procedures, a task which proved more difficult. Part of this overhaul was a reduction in military expenditures, and the resistance of the military was so strong that the officers broke out in open revolt.

The crux of the problem was the need to restore the military to a peacetime basis. A widespread practice of the day was to pay the officers a *batta*, or field allowance, when they were in the hinterlands, as their expenses were presumably greater. This form of danger pay was also received by the troops when they fought outside of Company territory.[18] The Company had made several attempts before 1766 to reduce Bengal batta to the level in Madras, but every time renewal of warfare or pressure by the military frustrated the Bengal Council. The directors charged Clive with the task of reducing the batta, which since Plassey had doubled in Bengal.

Clive tried to cut the extra batta, but softened the blow by creating a pension fund out of a huge legacy he had received from Siraj's successor as Nawab of Bengal, Mir Jafar (The legacy may have been a gift, and illegal under the directors' new regulations).[19] The promise of a pension fund of uncertain legality was unsatisfactory to most officers and the cut in batta was especially threatening to junior officers who relied on it to maintain a grossly inflated standard of living.

Clive's reduction of the batta led to an open revolt. British civilians in Bengal were already angry with Clive, and they supported the freshly enraged military. The officers resigned en masse, forty from one brigade alone.[20] A subscription fund

---

[18] Batta had originated in the Carnatic with the payment to French and English officers in the employ of, respectively, Chanda Sahib and Muhammad Ali. The Company eventually took over payment of the *batta* in the Carnatic, and later in Bengal, directly. H. H. Dodwell ed., "Bengal, 1760–72," in *British India*, Vol. V of *Cambridge History of India* (reprint ed.; Delhi: S. Chand, 1963), p. 179.

[19] Davies, p. 366.

[20] They agreed to stay on for one month as volunteers to keep the defenses of Bengal from disintegrating, since the Marathas at that moment were moving to invade Bengal.

of £16,000 was raised among the civilians of Calcutta, and each officer bound himself by a bond of £500 not to reaccept his commission until double batta was restored. Clive correctly diagnosed this defiance as a bluff, and insisted that officers who had resigned retire from their positions. He also called up loyal officers from Madras, and confronted the discontented European troops with the still loyal Indian sepoys. These vigorous actions successfully ended the mutiny.

After he had suppressed the 1766 mutiny, Clive received only indifferent support from the East India Company. While it did acknowledge the right of the President and Council to delegate their authority to whom they wished—and to place the military under the control of their civilian agent—the Company balked at Clive's proposals for detailed involvement of civilians in military affairs. Clive was warned that although the Company wanted the military to be under the authority of the civil servant, they did not mean that the "Civil Servant is to control the Military Officer in the Execution of Military Operations which is his proper Department."[21]

Robert Clive had a consistent philosophy concerning the Company's military in India. Most of his reforms were designed to make it easier for the military themselves to limit their interests in politics. The establishment of the Clive Fund, mentioned earlier, was an important step in the development of professionalism in the military. Clive also drastically reduced the number of troops collecting revenue. This reduction removed to a great extent a source of temptation to the officers and gave them fewer opportunities to interfere in matters outside their normal sphere of activity. Clive was convinced that the state of Company interests and British honor would not be improved until there was a revolution in the morals of the British in India, and the "rich and factious" were removed.[22] Nearly everyone realized the need for in-

---

21 Extract of Court's Letter to Lord Clive, May 17, 1766. Home Misc. Series, Vol. 78, No. 13, ff. 642–643. The directors were at this time themselves divided on the issue, and were subject to pressure from the King's officers, who had their own lines of communication from India to the Crown, and to fellow officers in Britain.

22 For Clive's reasoning, see "Clive to Verelst," April 19, 1766. Home Misc. Series, Vol. 739, No. 5, fo. 68.

creasing the ability of the Company's officers and quelling
their defiant attitude, but finding a feasible solution was another matter.[23]

Difficulties in Madras

The difficulties of the British East India Company with
recalcitrant officers continued. Another serious conflict arose
in Madras in 1780 between the Council and King's officers
serving in the South. In this instance the problem was not pay
or batta, but a disagreement over the nature and degree of
civilian direction of the war against the ruler of Mysore, Hyder Ali, and his son Tipu Sultan. The war was too much for
the incompetent Madras army to manage, and Sir Eyre Coote
(the second Commander-in-Chief of the Company's army, and
the first officer to serve in more than one presidency) was sent
to Madras in 1780. The Madras Council sought to retain some
control over military affairs. Coote's goal was prompt victory;
the Council was more worried about driving Hyder Ali into
an alliance with the French. When the Council asked Coote
to attempt a negotiated peace, he refused to cooperate, claiming that his original orders came from Calcutta, not from
Madras.[24] However, the Madras Council eventually pressured
Coote into resigning and then dismissed his successor, Major-
General James Stuart, as well.

Stuart's dismissal alienated the King's officers serving in
Madras, and in a mood of noncooperation the next senior
King's officer, Sir John Burgoyne, refused to take Stuart's

[23] Warren Hastings once wrote to the Court warning of the growing need
for European soldiers in India. The deficit was due to the temporary flow of
military men from India to America. Hastings suggested that officers who had
returned from India be used for recruitment in England. Since most of these
men were returning for health or disciplinary reasons, the suggestion seems
ill-advised. Hastings to chairman of the Court of Directors, April 2, 1777
(original). Home Misc. Series, Vol. 134, No. 23, ff. 647–649.
[24] This whole dispute parallels an earlier quarrel Coote had with the Madras
Council. In 1770 he was appointed Commander-in-Chief of the Madras Army;
on arrival he wanted to issue orders in his own name. The Council refused,
maintaining that in order to preserve the supremacy of civilian authority
orders should be given in the name of the Governor, who also had the title of
Commander-in-Chief. Coote refused, and went home to England. He returned
to India in 1779 as Commander-in-Chief of all Indian forces. See E. W. Shep-
pard, *Coote Bahadur* (London: Werner Laurie, 1956), pp. 100–102.

place.[25] The Madras Governor, Lord Macartney, had to get a young lieutenant to arrest Stuart and expel him from Madras. (Macartney and Stuart later fought a duel in Hyde Park but neither was killed.) Since no King's officer would serve, Macartney obtained a Company officer to serve as commander of *both* King's and Company troops in Madras. The appointment caused all the King's officers to withdraw their services, but they did allow their subordinates to serve on.

Although Macartney had achieved a limited victory in dealing with recalcitrant officers in Madras, his position was undercut from London. Civilian friends of the deposed Stuart put pressure on the Company to remove Macartney. The Governor-General, Hastings, withdrew his support from Macartney, who then resigned. Exhausted by the whole affair, the Company agreed to replace Macartney with anyone the King's ministers wanted and, in fact, a King's officer did succeed Macartney as Governor of Madras.[26]

During this period the Company was not strong enough to maintain its position when confronted by King's officers who were united and who had the firm support of the Home government. There were still no clear lines of authority defining the proper relationship between the presidencies, between Company representatives in the civil government and its military commanders, and between the two types of commissioned officer in India.

STEPS TOWARD REFORM

For almost a hundred years the British East India Company had been plagued by a series of conflicts between military and civilian leadership. It is always difficult to draw a precise line between military and civilian functions, or to allocate respon-

---

[25] Burgoyne was thanked by the younger Pitt's Home Secretary for not yielding to Macartney by succeeding Stuart. Viscount Sydney (Thomas Townshend, 1733–1800) to Burgoyne, April 24, 1784. Home Misc. Series, Vol. 178, No. 14, ff. 477–482.

[26] East India Company, Memo., n.d. (1784?). Home Misc. Series, Vol. 178, No. 49, f. 1033.

sibility when policy problems are not exclusively civilian or military. This was as true in the late eighteenth century as it had been during the early years of Company expansion. Attempts were made, however, to regularize these matters in India. The Home government saw no reason why India should be different from England or other parts of the Empire in the thorny area of civil-military relations.[27]

Pitt's India Act finally brought the affairs of the East India Company under the general control and direction of the government, and located responsibility in the House of Commons. The Board of Commissioners (Board of Control) was given jurisdiction over all civil and military matters in the British East Indies. A Committee of Secrecy was appointed from the Board of Directors of the British East India Company, who were responsible to the Board of Control and who could not inform other directors of their actions. The principle of civilian control was maintained in India by specifying that the Governor-General and Commander-in-Chief were to be two different persons, and although the head of the military was second to the head of the civilian government, and one of his three councilors, he could not succeed to the governor-generalship in the case of a vacancy. This rule had to be modified shortly afterwards, over Edmund Burke's strong objections, to permit Lord Cornwallis to hold a joint appointment.[28]

The relations between the minor presidencies (Bombay and Madras) and the Governor-General in Bengal were also clarified, and the latter's powers of war and diplomacy were greatly strengthened. He was given control over the minor presidencies in these matters, and the minor presidencies were compelled to obey the Governor-General unless they had different or secret orders from the directors. But even then the councils of the minor presidencies were instructed to inform the Governor-General and Council, who were then to

[27] Sir George Yonge (Secretary at War) to Company (original), May 6, 1784. Home Misc. Series, Vol. 84, No. 20, ff. 501–524.
[28] Keith, p. 99.

issue the instructions to the presidency. It was a cumbersome arrangement, especially when communications were slow, but this obstacle made central control even more important in preventing two presidencies from working at opposite purposes.

An attempt was also made in the act to improve the quality of the Company's army by regularizing promotion on the basis of seniority. Although such a system did not necessarily bring the ablest men to the highest ranks, it did prevent the worst kind of jobbery and favoritism. Minimum and maximum ages (15 and 22) were also set for cadets in the army to help in weeding out the very young or the very old, although fifteen is very young indeed.

Perhaps no one better epitomized the spirit of the military reform during this period than Lord Cornwallis, one of Britain's most distinguished soldier-statesmen. Cornwallis had what was probably the unique distinction of being thrice sworn in as Governor-General of India, although he served only twice in that position, during 1786–1793 and part of 1805 (he died shortly after his second arrival in India). Before his first term as Governor-General he demanded and received a special constitutional change which also gave him the military rank of Commander-in-Chief. Ordinarily, he said, he would prefer to be either a soldier or a politician, but in India both positions were necessary to make any progress.[29]

In India Cornwallis was preoccupied with various important diplomatic, military, and administrative tasks. He found the military establishment in India in great turmoil and unrest, and the particular weakness was the Company's officer corps. Company officers had no official government support and no strong regimental traditions to support them in time of need. Their health was in perpetual peril, and if they could not manage to save money they were condemned to a life which could verge upon beggary after they returned to Britain. "Under these circumstances," Cornwallis wrote to the Duke of York, "the most rigid General must relax a little, and

---

[29] Cornwallis to Lord Sydney, August 4, 1784. Charles Ross ed., *Correspondence of Charles, First Marquis Cornwallis* (3 vols; London: John Murray, 1859), I, 173.

suffer practices that are in some degree repugnant to the nice feelings of a soldier."[30]

Upon his return to England in 1794 Cornwallis was requested to draft a plan for the reorganization of the Company's entire military establishment. In a lengthy letter to Henry Dundas, Chairman of the Board of Directors, Cornwallis outlined his "New Model" Indian Army. He proposed that all officers serving in India be put under the King's jurisdiction, although King's commissioned officers commanding native soldiers would form a distinct and separate cadre.[31] They would be assured of regular promotion and the opportunity to fill the highest military posts in India. They would also be recruited directly in London, and their pay and status would be equivalent to that of officers commanding British troops. Cornwallis also emphasized the need for strengthening civilian control over the military in India, and proposed that the Governor-General and Council be given the authority to send home or punish any officer, even a King's officer.[32]

Some of these reforms had been proposed in London by Dundas in 1785–1787.[33] At that time they were rejected by the directors. Cornwallis' proposals were equally unacceptable to the directors and to the officers of the Bengal Army. His plan would have reduced the number of patronage appointments of the Directors and the officers were not willing to shift to a radically different system. Lack of the discipline was virtually the norm in Bengal, and although the officers' situation was uncertain and chaotic, they preferred it to an uncertain but ordered future. Distance, climate, and the lack of close ties with the home country had made the Company's officers difficult to deal with—they were eager to get as much as possible as quickly as possible.

Some reforms were carried out in the years directly following Cornwallis' proposals. The two armies were not fused but

[30] Cornwallis to H. R. H. the Duke of York, November 10, 1786. *Ibid.*, I, 225–226.

[31] Cornwallis to Dundas, November 7, 1794. *Ibid.*, II, 567–577.

[32] *Ibid.*

[33] C. H. Philips, *The East India Company, 1784–1834* (Manchester: Manchester University Press, 1940), pp. 90–91.

the opportunities for promotion for Company officers were somewhat expanded and their pay was increased. It was not until 1799 that a new recruitment system was established in which the King's recruiting officers provided the Company with officers. These reforms were only marginal in preventing further conflicts between civilian and military authorities. In this manner the Crown acquired *de facto* authority in India, and some of the problems which led to conflicts between Company and King's officers were removed, but clashes of prestige and jurisdiction still occurred. The notion of absolute civilian control was not even accepted in England, and military professionalism was still a long distance away. In India the military was central to the British for maintaining and expanding their power. Although the Cornwallis reforms had clarified the situation somewhat, a minor squabble in Madras in 1797 had to be resolved by the directors, and indicated that the system was still unstable and easily upset.[34] Its instability was again demonstrated in 1809, and again in the Madras presidency.

THE WHITE MUTINY

The "White Mutiny" of 1809 represented in many ways a turning point in the development of British control over their own officer corps, because it was the last open break between the officer corps and civilian authorities.[35] Although civilian-military disputes occurred later, various social, organizational, political, and technological developments were already underway which were to alter considerably the character of British rule in India.

[34] The Board followed a flexible theory of civilian control: " . . . there are situations rather of a political than of a military nature on the selection of officers for which, however necessary it may be to pay a due attention to professional merit, the choice must turn upon points not exclusively military and therefore within the peculiar consideration and province of Government." Extract of Military Letter to Fort St. George, May 17, 1800. Home Misc. Series, Vol. 86, No. 23, ff. 735–754.

[35] For a fuller account see Philips, *op. cit.*, Ainslie T. Embree, *Charles Grant and British Rule in India* (London: George Allen and Unwin, 1962), and Alexander Cardew, *The White Mutiny: A Forgotten Episode in the History of the Indian Army* (London: Constable, 1929).

The mutiny itself was a rather insignificant affair and amounted to only a few acts of open defiance in the interior. It's antecedents and aftermath were more important. The mutiny grew out of the alienation of the Company's Madras officer corps from the Madras presidency's civilian leadership. The Governor of Madras, Sir George Barlow, had quarreled with the Madras Commander-in-Chief over the abolishment of the tent contract system which enabled officers to make large profits on supply purchases in the field. The Commander-in-Chief, Sir Hay Macdowall, had ordered the arrest of an officer who had written a report on the system which Barlow had accepted. Barlow attempted to punish the officers who carried out the arrest, and removed Macdowall from his post, *in absentia* (Macdowall and his predecessor had both resigned and gone back to England).

The Madras officers corps opposed the elimination of the tent contract system and resented the wording of the report, which they regarded as a slur on their honor. When Barlow ordered the punishment of the officers who had arrested the author of the report they rebelled, discussed the possibility of a coup, refused to obey some orders, and delayed the execution of maneuvers. Governor-General Minto came to Barlow's assistance, and the mutiny was quelled. Significantly, both the sepoys and King's officers serving in Madras failed to come to the assistance of the mutineers, and the revolt quickly fizzled out.

Although Governor Barlow and Governor-General Minto had suppressed the White Mutiny, much of their work was undone during the following years. Lack of support from the British government and the Board of Directors was a political weakness which no amount of argument could overcome.[36] The Company officers had their own political allies, notably a private citizen in Madras, Charles Marsh. He and a few others had complaints against Barlow and Minto, and served as the spokesmen for the officers at first in Madras, and later in London. For a few years after the mutiny a fierce struggle

[36] For details of the maneuvering among the directors, and the close voting which determined policy at the time, see Philips, pp. 170 ff.

was waged within the Board of Directors for a reversal of their support of Barlow and Minto's actions in 1809. Marsh and others lobbied the Board, publicly and privately. In 1810 Charles Grant—Barlow's chief protector—lost the chairmanship of the Board, and the strength of the anti-Barlow group increased until, in April 1912, four of Barlow's supporters left the Board on rotation. Since the government did not take an active interest in the question, nothing stood in the way of a reversal of the Board's support for Barlow. In 1812 the dismissed officers were restored to service, and Barlow himself was recalled from Madras. Barlow's humiliation was completed with the announcement that his successor would be a military man, and another military man, the Earl Moira, was appointed both Governor-General of India and Commander-in-Chief.

REFORM AND THE
MODERN INDIAN ARMY

The White Mutiny was not the last rupture in civilian-military relations in British India, although no other struggle of equivalent magnitude occurred until the Kitchener–Curzon dispute of 1905. The years between 1809 and 1905 were dotted with clashes between British officers and British civilians, just as they were bloodily stained with sepoy mutinies. Many problems which emerged during the course of the White Mutiny again confronted the British in these later disputes. The old clash between Home and Indian viewpoints, and between a King's officer and a Company officer was an essential part of a bitter struggle between a Governor-General, Lord Dalhousie, and his Commander-in-Chief, the irascible Charles Napier. Napier, the self-styled "Conqueror of Sind" fought with Dalhousie over a series of personal, political, and military issues. Napier, a renowned soldier, resented Sir Henry Lawrence and other former military men who were attempting to establish British authority in the newly acquired territories, and derided them as "beardless civilians." Napier was forced to resign, after narrowly missing turning the Home government against Dalhousie.[37] A few years later, after the sepoy Mutiny of 1857 the Royal Army, under the Duke of Cambridge, Queen Victoria's illustrious cousin, attempted to gain control over all military forces in India, which resulted in another confrontation of Home and Indian perspectives.[38]

Yet, despite these later episodes, the White Mutiny was a turning point, and there was never again open mutiny against civilian authority. In view of the distance, importance, and size of their Indian colony, and in view of the frequent mutinies up to 1809, this stability was a major accomplishment of the British. Several factors brought about this stability and control.

First (though least important) technological developments after 1809 had the effect of changing the nature of the decision-making process. Steam power, first in ships and then in the railroads, brought all concerned parties closer together and had the effect of speeding up decisions. The Governor-General was more closely watched from abroad, while he in turn had better control over his subordinates. The net effect of technological progress was not to *remove* sources of conflict but to improve the means of resolution of conflict.

A second development which began to take effect after 1809 was the increasing professionalization of the officer corps. Although the Company's army, and later the Indian Army, always lagged behind Western armies in technological sophistication, it did overcome its mercenary, freebooting origins and developed considerable organizational integrity. After 1804 officers were chosen for promotion from a general list. Cavalry and infantry regimental lists were kept separate, and

---

[37] A good source for many important minutes and documents is *Discussions Between the Marquis of Dalhousie and Lieut.-Gen. Sir C. J. Napier, G.C.B.* (London: Printed by Order of the Court of Proprietors of the East India Company, 1854).

[38] See *Copies of Correspondence during the year 1858 . . . on the subject of placing the Armies of India under the Horse Guards,* House of Commons, July 20, 1860, Gt. Britain, Parliamentary Papers, Vol. 50, No. 467 (East India, Army). The Duke was also attempting to make the Indian Army a dumping ground for his favorite British Army generals. The Duke claimed that British Army generals should command the Indian Army because it was largely British. Duke of Cambridge to Sir C. Wood, Secretary of State for India, December 22, 1859. *Copies of Correspondence,* p. 3.

officers were guaranteed promotion up to the rank of major. Furlough and pension regulations were introduced by 1804, and the regimental system was continually adjusted in a search for a more practical structure. However, increased professionalism does not necessarily mean increased civilian control, for as the sense of corporateness grew, the British officers obtained a sense of identity and enhanced status which at times enabled them better to resist civilian demands.

A final development in British India which contributed to increasingly effective civilian control was the introduction of several administrative and financial checks upon the military. One major step was taken in the Charter Act of 1833 which placed the responsibility for both "civil and military government" in the hands of a Governor-General-in-Council. Hitherto the Commander-in-Chief alone had served as the military advisor on the Council. After 1834 a "military member" was added, to give the Governor-General-in-Council the benefit of additional military advice. This new position enabled the Governor-General to obtain expert military advice from another source than the Commander-in-Chief, and at times proved a source of conflict. Other steps were taken to improve the quality of financial control over military affairs, especially after the army grew in size in the late nineteenth century. The roll of the Military Member (who did not hold an active military command) to scrutinize and pass upon financial and administrative proposals of the Commander-in-Chief was gradually increased. The dissatisfaction of one Commander-in-Chief, Lord Kitchener, with this arrangement was in part the cause of the most significant civilian-military clash ever to occur in India.

THE KITCHENER–CURZON DISPUTE

The savage struggle for power, in 1904–1905, between the Viceroy of India, Lord Curzon of Kedleston, and his Commander-in-Chief, Kitchener of Khartoum, was the last, but the most important civilian-military dispute in the long history of British India.[39] The conflict began on a low level but, fueled by a combination of high principle and even higher ambition, rapidly developed to a point where neither Kitchener nor Curzon could back down, and Curzon was eventually forced out of India. The affair attracted much attention in Britain as well as in India, and ruined several important careers.

The clash was unnecessary, which makes it all the more interesting. Kitchener was no booty-seeking adventurer but a thoroughly professional career soldier, who had in fact been asked by Curzon to come to India. Curzon was one of the most versatile, brilliant, and well-connected men ever to serve as Viceroy. He had behind him a large, well established civilian bureaucracy and a fully developed (if antiquated) system of financial control over the military budget. Curzon and Kitchener were not far apart politically for both were closely linked to the inner councils of the Conservative party. There was, in short, no obvious reason why they should quarrel and become locked in a struggle which eventually led to Curzon's total political defeat.

The overt point of disagreement between the two men was the relative power and influence of the Military Member of the Viceroy's Council. Kitchener wanted to abolish the position and centralize organizational and command powers in his own hands. He especially resented the power of the Military Member to criticize his own proposals, for the Military Member was a junior officer, who in addition had direct access to the Viceroy. Curzon at first persuaded Kitchener to drop his demand for the abolishment of the Military Member's position but Kitchener revived the idea in correspondence with the Home government. When the Home government proposed a compromise solution which would have retained the Member but drastically reduced his power, Curzon resisted, and was finally forced to resign. The issue of

[39] For a full description and interpretation of the dispute see Stephen P. Cohen, "Issue, Role, and Personality: The Kitchener-Curzon Dispute," *Comparative Studies in Society and History*, X (April, 1968), 337–355.

the Military Member was important in itself, but it is clear that it was not sufficient cause for Curzon's resignation. Curzon resigned because the Military Member issue was a test case for at least two other issues of greater significance: the disagreement between Kitchener and Curzon over the nature of the Empire, and over the role of the military within that Empire, and particularly within India.

Before his dispute with Kitchener, Curzon had difficulties with the Home government over his interpretation of his powers and the place of India in the imperial scheme. He had been told quite bluntly by Prime Minister Balfour and Secretary of State for India Sir Arthur Godley that he was responsible to the Home government, and that "the real government of India is in the House of Commons."[40] Curzon was neither temperamentally nor intellectually ready to accept this British doctrine of ministerial responsibility. Curzon acknowledged ultimate Home government supremacy, especially in foreign affairs, but in internal Indian matters he insisted the man on the spot should decide, and he regarded military administration as primarily an internal matter. He viewed his historical task as raising India from the level of a dependency to the position of "the greatest partner in the Empire" and fostering the development of India's own "constitution," or set of norms and rules, which was to guide the conduct of Indian affairs.[41]

By sharp contrast Kitchener viewed India's imperial role as less central. He had served the Empire in South Africa, Egypt, and the Sudan, and hardly thought of these territories as mere guardians of the route to India. They were important in their own right, and his concern for centralized direction of all imperial policy led him to argue that Indian military policy should be controlled by the Committee for Imperial Defence, not the government of India.[42] Thus Kitchener sidestepped

40 Godley to Curzon, January 8, 1904. Kilbracken Collection, India Office Library, MSS Eur. F. 102./60.
41 Curzon to Godley, January 27, 1904. Kilbracken Coll.,/60.
42 See Kitchener's "A Note on the Military Policy of India," July 19, 1905. Kitchener Papers, Public Records Office (London), PRO 30/57. Also Philip

an open struggle for power between himself and Curzon, and put the dispute on a theoretical level where he pushed for broader imperial control. This was a great strength in his position, for it put him on the side of Curzon's superiors.

Despite these divergent views on the nature of the Empire, British administration in India had worked fairly well, for other viceroys had had the same argument with their secretaries of state and Home governments. Yet in the Kitchener-Curzon dispute none of the participants was willing to compromise on the basic question of the distribution of imperial power, in part because they were unwilling to yield ground in the parallel debate over the exercise of that power.

Kitchener and Curzon disagreed sharply over the role of the military in India. They both attempted to reconcile civilian control with military efficiency, but proceeded to argue from very different assumptions.

Curzon claimed that by destroying the position of Military Member without substituting a civilian in his place Kitchener's plan was in reality "not one to disestablish an individual or even a department, but to subvert the military authority of the Government of India as a whole, and to substitute for it a military autocracy in the person of the Commander-in-Chief."[43] His supporters, including the distinguished former Commander-in-Chief of the Indian Army, Lord Roberts, amplified Curzon's argument and cautioned Kitchener that India could not be run like Egypt. In fact, Roberts argued, India was more like Britain than Egypt, and required a separation of civilian and military powers, and the retention of civilian control over fiscal aspects of military administration.[44]

This argument was dismissed by Kitchener. He agreed he wanted to establish an autocracy, but only "the autocracy exercised in his own sphere by every commander of a regiment, a brigade, or a division. I desire . . . to put an end to the exist-

Magnus, *Kitchener: Portrait of an Imperialist* (London: Gray Arrow Books, 1961), p. 223. [Reprint of 1958 ed. published by John Murray].

[43] "Minute of Lord Curzon," *Gazette of India Extraordinary*, (Simla: June 23, 1905).

[44] Roberts to Kitchener, June 18, 1903. Kitchener Papers, /28/GG 14.

ing divorce between responsibility and control."[45] Kitchener would not become an autocrat, he argued, for the ultimate check of the Secretary of State for India would always be retained. (This argument reflects his view of imperial politics.) He ridiculed Curzon's fears of a military "bogey" and persisted in his belief that the military should be under the control of civilian authority in Britain, not India.

There is no reason to doubt Kitchener's sincerity. His obsession for control over military matters derived not from political ambition but from what he termed "efficiency." It was Kitchener's ambition to gain a good reputation for himself in India by reforming the antiquated Indian military organization. For this he needed, he thought, absolute authority in military matters. While Curzon was more concerned with obtaining several military opinions on any particular issue (and hence wanted to retain the Military Member), Kitchener felt that there was only one military opinion, the right one, and that he was the man best able to deliver that opinion. Kitchener had a faith in the ability of a military organization to produce the right answer, a faith which was not shared by Curzon, who held a low opinion of the Indian Army and of military men in general.[46] The harder he was pressed, the clearer this attitude became to the officers of the Indian Army, who largely rallied behind Kitchener.

Had the Kitchener-Curzon dispute been merely a disagreement over the role of the Military Member, it undoubtedly could have been amicably compromised. However, when the broader issues were raised, the political stakes were increased. Even then the dispute might have been settled had not both

---

[45] Kitchener to Stedman (copy), March 8, 1905, p. 18. Curzon Coll., /400. Stedman was Military Secretary at the India Office. Through him Brodrick and others saw the letter, written "behind my back" according to Curzon's annotation of his copy.

[46] "I wonder if you feel as I do that from the business point of view soldiers with rare exceptions are the most impossible men. They seem to me to be congenitally stupid. Their writing is atrocious. . . . I have a few good men. But the majority fill me with despair: and as for a Military Committee—I would as soon remit a question of State to a meeting of Eton Masters." Curzon to Brodrick, March 16, 1902. Midleton Papers (British Museum), Add. MSS. 50,074. Both Curzon and Brodrick (Secretary of State for India, 1903–1905) had been to Eton.

men taken the conflict so seriously. Both Kitchener and Curzon were driven by personal and emotional pressures which had been building up for several years; these pressures included a heavy work load, physical illness, a difficult climate, and quite possibly neuroses which may have touched the psychotic level. It is difficult to disentangle personal and issue conflicts; they seem to have fed increasingly upon each other.[47]

The outcome of the dispute was clear: Curzon was placed in such a humiliating position that he had no option except to offer his resignation in a final effort to pressure the Home government. To his surprise the resignation was accepted. Kitchener remained in India to serve out his term as Commander-in-Chief, but fears that he would attempt to dominate the Indian government turned out to be unjustified. In the process of outmaneuvering Curzon he had made many enemies, and his later attempts at obtaining the position of Viceroy were turned aside. He died in a tragic sinking during World War I, a discarded figurehead with no real power.

The position of the Military Member was abolished in 1905, and the Commander-in-Chief was made directly responsible to the Viceroy's Council for organizational as well as command functions. A new Member of Council in charge of Military Supply was created, and some of the Military Member's responsibilities were given to him. But, crucially, financial control was not given to the Commander-in-Chief and the army. In 1906 the Military Finance Department was created under a "joint financial secretary," and placed under the overall control of the senior Financial Secretary (a civil servant) and the Member of Council in Charge of Finance. This arrangement was maintained until independence, when the position of Commander-in-Chief was abolished and the Cabinet member responsible for defense was a civilian. However, the Finance Ministry retains to this day a major share of the responsibility for fiscal control over military expenditures.

Despite the warnings of Curzon and his supporters, including some responsible Indian politicians concerned with defense

[47] See Cohen, "Issue, Role and Personality: The Kitchener-Curzon Dispute" for an elaboration of this argument.

matters, the increase in the power of the Commander-in-Chief did not lead to a military autocracy or even to a significant increase in the power of the military in India. This lack of a takeover by the Commander-in-Chief was in part due to the subsequent holders of this office. Although many of Kitchener's successors were his protégés, none brought to the position his overwhelming reputation. That reputation had suffered during World War I especially because of the adverse report on his Indian reforms by the Mesopotamian Commission.

More significantly, the civilian bureaucracy was itself growing and gaining competence in military affairs. There were further civilian-military disputes but they were restricted to the closed channels of Indian government, particularly the budgetary process. Financial control over the military was firmly in civilian hands. Kitchener had tried to take over all financial administration of military affairs, leaving only audit functions to the Finance Ministry. He failed, and tight civilian control over the military budget was retained through World War II. As one former Commander-in-Chief has stated:

The Kitchener tradition did not remain: it was not an autocracy. The Commander-in-Chief was tied down by the budget; I couldn't increase or decrease my forces without permission. As for operational control I had less than your Pentagon perhaps! In the Middle East, where there was direct contact with the Chief of the Imperial General Staff, orders had to be approved by the Viceroy.[48]

According to one civilian who held a high position in the Indian Defense Department, the military and the civilians—especially the civilians in the Finance Department—eyed each other suspiciously. They were bound together in a relationship parallel to that of Rajput warriors and their Brahmin advisors, or Moghul administrators and soldiers.[49] In each case a proud and aloof military feared encroachment by non-military elites, who were themselves suspicious of the simplicity and bluntness of the military.

---

[48] Interview with Field Marshal Sir Claude Auchinleck, London, 1963.
[49] Interview with Philip Mason, London, 1963.

THE LEGACY

The British legacy to the successor states was a theory of civilian-military relations which placed great stress upon "separate spheres" of military and civilian influence, while ultimate civilian control was always acknowledged. This theory was quite different from Clausewitz' theory of the conduct of war, with its stress upon the combination of political and military factors, a theory which was adapted and expanded by both Lenin and Mao Tse Tung.

The critical weakness in British civilian-military relations in India was the failure to set down firm guidelines defining the military sphere and the civilian sphere, and determining *who* is to indicate when the line between civil and military has shifted. The military certainly has the technical expertise, long experience with military affairs, and might be expected to know their own job better than anyone else. Yet, sometimes seemingly purely military matters are charged with political implications, as was the Kitchener-Curzon dispute over the Military Member. Recruitment of officers and sepoys in India became another political matter and deeply embittered the military. Should the civilians determine what is purely military and what is political? Should a politician or a civil servant, with little or no military expertise pass upon military problems, perhaps sacrificing military competence to political necessity?

The British East India Company on occasion solved the dilemma by appointing one man to both political and military commands, uniting the two functions. This unification partly explained Robert Clive's success, as well as the bitterness of the officer corps towards him. However, this solution became impractical as the military establishment grew and demanded highly specialized expertise and a permanent bureaucracy. In civilian affairs fiscal and diplomatic skills became increasingly important, and men who could combine military expertise and political ability were rare.

The solution of the British in India was a rough compromise: military organization and tactics were largely left to the military, as were questions of discipline, recruitment, training, and custom. The "military sphere" was gradually reduced in size as Indian political leaders took increasing interest in military affairs. Civilians did perform the audit function and carefully watched military expenditures (especially in the twentieth century), and, above all, the general size of the military budget was largely determined by civilians. Control of the military budget was particularly important, because the Indian Army was largely infantry and cavalry, and the size of the army could fluctuate as rapidly as its budget was increased or decreased.

Viceroys were generally chosen for their political, not military skill (the exception was Field Marshal Wavell, who served as Viceroy during World War II). India was not—as often charged by Indian politicians—a military autocracy run by and for the military. Although the military was always very visible in British-India—their cantonments were to be found in virtually every Indian city of any importance—the civilians held ultimate control. This control applied to most levels of military activity, from the extensive police activity undertaken by the army in times of civil disorder to the conduct of war in two world wars. As for police activity, detailed arrangements were developed for the discrete application of violence under the control of a local civilian magistrate or official; broad strategic decisions were always deferred to the British government, and the Indian Army then functioned as an extension of the British Army.

The legacy, in sum, was mixed. Although the military did have considerable autonomy in some areas, these areas were increasingly subject to civilian scrutiny. In general, Indian Army officers were content to concentrate on their job, and impatiently tolerated the strict financial controls to which they were subject.[50] With the exception of the Kitchener-Curzon

---

[50] "All British officers without exception felt that the Finance Department was completely unconcerned with the morale of the army, and continuously adopted a miserly unsympathetic and unrealistic attitude towards the officers in the army and the army in general. The balancing of the budget was their only concern. . . . The army was consistently starved of funds for vital equip-

dispute, the ultimate argument of the civilians—over-all civilian control applied to India as well Britain—was generally effective. Although in many instances civilian control was effectively applied to the detriment of the military, it was nevertheless a major accomplishment of the British that the doctrine of civilian control was generally accepted. The system can be and has been abused by ambitious politicians as well as ambitious military men in both modern India and Pakistan, but nevertheless does provide a reasonable base for dialogue between the two groups.

---

ment and grew up on a policy of having to 'make do' with second hand equipment. Luckily the officers of the army were so absolutely dedicated to their men that they did make-do, though at no time thanks to this cheese paring attitude." Personal communication to the author from a retired British Indian Army general, 1963.

2

RECRUITMENT AND IDEOLOGY

The military institutions of India present more features
for our imitation than those of any army or country in
Europe. . . . The value and economy of native troops
were early discovered, and nowhere in history has the
wisdom of a government been so signally rewarded as
in the organization of the native army.—*Major-General
Emory Upton (U. S. Army), 1876.*

Colonial powers traditionally rely heavily upon indigenous
manpower and brainpower. They must at least convince some
of the natives of the land that the service of the foreigner is
desirable; to be effective they must also convince them that
such service is respectable. In this chapter we will attempt to
show how the British obtained loyalty as well as obedience
in military matters, the supreme achievement of a colonial
power.

The sepoy system enabled the British to employ Indians as
they would their own manpower. These sepoys proved to be
so reliable, effective, and inexpensive that their numbers were
rapidly expanded. In 1794 there were 82,000 sepoys, in 1824
154,000, and on the eve of the great mutiny, in 1856, 214,000.[1]

[1] *Recruiting in India Before and During the War of 1914–1918* (India: Army
Headquarters, October 1919), p. 1 (an unclassified printed volume [192 pp.] in
the Archives of the Ministry of Defense, Historical Section, Government of
India, detailing the history of the army up to 1919).

Until about 1810 the sepoy regiments were raised haphazardly before each battle by an individual British officer who led the unit and frequently gave it his name. However, the great expansion of the Indian military establishment could not be carried out on a haphazard basis. Individualism gave way to regimental recruitment in the nineteenth century, and long-term military contracts with sepoys became common. The conditions of service were regularized, and military families slowly developed: son began to follow father in the service of the British. There are today soldiers in the Indian and Pakistani armies who can cite four generations of faithful service.

The three armies of Madras, Bombay, and Bengal without central direction, equal distribution of resources, and uniform traditions, developed different patterns of recruitment and slightly different principles of loyalty in the first half of the nineteenth century. The most significant difference was the recruitment of high-caste Hindus into the Bengal Army.[2] Before the Mutiny of 1857, Bengal had 74 regular infantry regiments, recruited mainly from Bihar, Oudh, and Agra, with a few Gurkha units. Madras had 57 infantry battalions, which were drawn entirely from the Presidency of Madras. Both in Madras and Bombay troops were of all castes, heterogeneously mixed together.

Bengal's recruitment pattern probably developed as a result of the different life-style of the Bengal officer corps. Eastern India was no longer a center of conflict and warfare. Its officers were physically and emotionally close to the center of power at Calcutta and were in a good position to secure desirable political appointments outside of their regiments. Bengal officers developed a style of their own. Leopold von Orlich, a German visitor in the 1850s commented:

I saw a Captain of the Bengal army, on his way to the army of reserve at Ferozepore, with two large wagons drawn by oxen full of geese, fowls, pigeons, wine, sugar, coffee, tea, and numberless

2 Amiya Barat, *The Bengal Native Infantry: Its Organization and Discipline 1796–1852* (Calcutta: Firma K. L. Mukhopadhyay, 1962), pp. 121 ff.

tin cases of delicacies, to say nothing of the goats, sheep, and the camels which carried his tents.[3]

Officers in the other presidency armies claimed that love for luxury and position had led the Bengal officers to deteriorate physically and mentally. They were accused of paying more attention to caste and status in recruitment and promotion than to ability and performance.[4] Comparing the officers and men of the three armies an observer claimed that

while in Madras and Bombay the troops become half-European through their association with the military, in Bengal the officers become "half-Hindoo" and become so pre-occupied with matters of caste and status that they lose their sense of professional "soldier-ship" and discipline.[5]

Henry Lawrence, writing in the *Calcutta Review* in the 1840s, frequently pointed out the growing danger of the Bengal Army's recruitment pattern. He suggested that "our sepoys come too much from the same parts of the country—Oude, the lower Doab, and upper Behar. There is too much of clanship among them, and the evil should be remedied."[6] He urged the recruitment of non-Indians, such as Malays, Chinese, and Burmese, and the application of strict standards of promotion to weed out malcontents. Low castes and "nonwarlike" races would be loyal and could be good soldiers: "Courage goes much by opinion; and many a man behaves as a hero or a coward, according as he considers he is expected to behave. Once two Roman Legions held Britain; now as many Britons might hold Italy."[7]

Lawrence also saw that even though an Indian army might be drawn from diverse regions, its composition alone was not a guarantee of its loyalty, let alone its competence. Promotion

[3] Leopold von Orlich, *The Military Mutiny in India*, trans. from the German original (London: T. & W. Boone, 1858). India Office Library Tracts, Volume 180.

[4] Brig.-Gen. John Jacob, *Tracts on the Native Army of India: Its Organization and Discipline* (London: Smith Elder, 1858), p. 106. India Office Library Tracts, Vol. 552.

[5] *Ibid.*

[6] Sir Henry Lawrence, *Essays Military and Political, Written in India* (London: W. H. Allen, 1859), pp. 24–25.

[7] *Ibid.*, p. 25.

by seniority, restrictions on the role of Brahmins as troops, and genuine loyalty to the British should be developed. The latter goal was not narrowly conceived: Colonel John Hodgson wanted to put the sepoys to work on public works projects and other nonmilitary tasks, not to save money, but because

it would be a grand political victory to induce the Sepahees to identify themselves, morally, with these noble undertakings of a paternal government. The development of this feeling would be the first and most important step towards the conversion of a mercenary into a *patriotic* army.[8] . . . We cannot hold India, save with the Indians.[9]

To talk of a patriotic army in India fifty or even seventy-five years after the Mutiny of 1857 might have seemed extraordinary to a Britisher at the time. Yet, once the excitement and recrimination which followed the mutiny subsided, the ideology of the paternalistic Punjab school came to dominate the Indian Army, and in British rule in India in general. This ideology lasted longer in the army than in the civilian sphere.

Before their view came to triumph, however, the "paternalists" had to meet and defeat a whole series of proposals which grew out of the mutiny, and even then not all their views were adopted.

THE MUTINY AND THE REORGANIZATION
OF THE INDIAN ARMY

The Mutiny of 1857 stands as one of the great turning points in Indian history, perhaps as much for its impact upon the British as its impact on the development of Indian nationalism. One source estimates that about 30,000 Indian sepoys remained loyal through the mutiny, an equal number were disarmed or deserted, and 70,000 joined the revolt at one time or another.[10] Had all of them mutinied at the same time British rule in India would have come to an end.

8 Col. John S. Hodgson, *Opinions on the Indian Army* (London: W. H. Allen, 1857), p. 53.
9 *Ibid.*, p. 199.
10 Surendra Nath Sen, *Eighteen Fifty-Seven* (New Delhi: Publications Division, Ministry of Information and Broadcasting, 1957), p. 406. This work is a good introduction to the mutiny and its literature.

The mutiny began in early 1857 with discontent over the introduction of greased cartridges, which were an affront to the religious scruples of both Muslims and Hindus. Open rebellion broke out at Meerut on May 10, 1857, and Delhi fell to the mutinous sepoys in two days. Ultimately, virtually all of Oudh and Rohilkhand—present-day Uttar Pradesh—was affected by serious uprisings. The Punjab and Bombay, however, remained relatively unaffected, and there was no loss of control in Madras. The mutiny was quelled after great loss of life on both sides, and after mutual atrocities, which have a history and mythology of their own.

The Mutiny of 1857 was politically and personally disastrous for many who were connected with British rule. The mutiny was carefully studied for the lessons it taught, and interpretations of the mutiny—even among the British—differed greatly.

The official body appointed to examine the military in India after the mutiny was the Peel Commission.[11] Although it was not instructed to examine the role of caste, it soon became aware that caste and the structure of Indian society would be a central problem.

Roughly three positions on reorganization emerged in the oral and written testimony of those examined by the commission. The first, generally advocated by officers and civilians more familiar with the Madras and Bombay systems, envisioned a balanced pattern of recruitment, drawing from all sections of a region's society. Sir Bartle Frere argued that only soldierly ability, and not caste, counted.[12] This guaranteed a natural heterogeneity in recruitment as some castes declined

[11] Great Britain, *Report of the Commissioners Appointed to Inquire into the Organization of the Indian Army; together with the Minutes of Evidence and Appendix,* Cmd. 2515, 1859. Also found in India Office Library, Parliamentary Branch (Records Dept.), Vol. 5, 1859, Session 1. Maj.-Gen. I. Peel, chairman of the commission was at the time Secretary of State for War. The commission also included the Duke of Cambridge and Lord Stanley who was Commissioner for Indian Affairs (later Secretary of State for India).

[12] *Papers Connected with the Re-Organization of the Army in India, Supplementary to the Report of the Army Commission.* n. d. (1859–1860?), p. 50. This volume was obtained from the Ministry of Defense, government of India, New Delhi. Frere was Commissioner and later Governor of Sind.

in soldierly ability. The important quality was not birth or origin but the ability to act independently and to be self-reliant.[13] Sir Bartle and others who argued this view emphasized the persistent military axiom, that there are no bad soldiers, only bad officers. However, in the shadow of the tragedies of the mutiny few were able to blame their fellow officers directly and openly.

The second position, diametrically opposed to the first, stated that some castes and classes should be eliminated from the Indian Army. Major-General J. B. Hearsey, one of the first Britishers to take note of the original uprising in Barrackpore in 1857, urged that the recruitment of all Brahmins and Muslims from "Hindustan" cease.[14] He further wanted to blacklist Oudh, the Doab of the Ganges, Jamuna, Shahabad, Bojhpur, and Rohilkhand. Hearsey and the others who advocated selective recruitment were hardly less emphatic over the need to refuse to cater to caste than those such as Frere. They were concerned with breaking down caste interests even among the selectively recruited groups: "Any soldier refusing to work, because it interfered with his caste was to be tried by court-martial and sentenced to be flogged, or transportation for life."[15] Out of a desire to smash the feelings and limitation of caste within the army, the idea of recruiting Christians was revived, and was popular at the time. In his written statement, for example, Hearsey urged the employment of Christians from foreign countries in the Indian Army: Nestorians, Karens, Malays, Christian Chinese, Christians from the Philippines and South America, "*all, all; but they must be Christians, and then* TRUST *can be reposed in them.*"[16]

According to a third, intermediate, position on the recruitment problem, no class should on principle be excluded from military service unless it was clearly unfit. Even recruitment in Bengal should use good available material; it would appear

[13] *Ibid.*, p. 105. The argument was echoed from Madras by Sir Mark Cubbon, Commissioner.
[14] *Ibid.*, pp. 169–170.
[15] *Ibid.*
[16] *Ibid.*, p. 173. Emphasis in original.

like a weakness in the government to exclude one caste (Brahmins) or one religion (Muslims) from the military.[17] Lawrence, Chamberlain, and Edwardes of the Punjab Committee urged extensive recruitment from their region, to counterbalance the soldiers from the United Provinces.[18] The three officials wanted Christians, Eurasians, Santals, Bhils, and other groups as well as Punjabis drawn into the army on the theory that these groups would counterbalance each other in religion and caste.[19] The Punjab trio placed more emphasis on the need to balance and separate castes within the army than did the Bombay and Madras spokesmen; this disparity in attitudes was made especially clear when the problem of untouchable and low-caste troops was raised.[20]

The Peel Commission eventually recommended that "the Native Army should be composed of different nationalities and castes, and as a general rule, mixed promiscuously through each regiment," although it based the latter suggestion on little official testimony.[21] In effect it evaded the task of specifying in detail the future composition of the army. Most of its recommendations dealt with army organization; how to strengthen control, and increase the number of qualified officers.

The commission followed the suggestions of the Punjab Committee and established a set of principles which became the guidelines for a whole generation of army reformers. These principles were confirmed twenty years later in another major examination of the army in India. It is worth quoting a concise statement of the Punjab viewpoint because of the persistence with which it remained official doctrine:

As we cannot do without a large Native army in India, our main object is to make that army safe; and next to the grand counterpoise of a sufficient European force, comes the counterpoise of

17 Testimony of Sir George Clark, I.C.S. in *Report of the Commissioners.* (Clark in 1858 became permanent Under Secretary of State for India).
18 *Papers Connected with the Re-Organization of the Army*, p. 27.
19 *Ibid.*
20 See Stephen P. Cohen, "The Untouchable Soldier: Caste, Politics and the Indian Army," *Journal of Asian Studies*, XXVIII, 3 (May, 1969).
21 *Report of the Commissioners*, p. xiv.

Natives against Natives. At first sight, it might be thought that the best way to secure this would be to mix up all the available military races of India in each and every regiment, and to make them all general service corps. But excellent as this theory seems, it does not bear the test of practice. It is found that different races mixed together do not long preserve their distinctiveness; their corners and angles, and feeling, and prejudice get rubbed off, till at last they assimilate, and the object of their association to a considerable extent is lost. To preserve that distinctiveness which is so valuable, and which, while it lasts, makes the Muhammadan of one country despise, fear or dislike the Muhammadan of another, corps should in future be provincial, and adhere to the geographical limits within which differences and rivalries are strongly marked. Let all races, Hindu or Muhammadan, of one province be enlisted in one regiment and no others, and having thus created distinctive regiments, let us keep them so against the hour of need by confining the circle of the ordinary service to the limits of their own province, and only marching them on emergency into other parts of the Empire, with which they will then be found to have little sympathy. By the system thus indicated, two great evils are avoided firstly, that community of feeling throughout the Native Army, and that mischievous political activity and intrigue which results from association with other races and travel in other Indian provinces; and secondly, that thorough discontent and alienation from the service which has undoubtedly sprung up since extended conquest has carried our Hindustani soldiers so far from their homes in India proper.[22]

The recommendations applied primarily to the Bengal Army, because the armies of Madras and Bombay already fulfilled the recommendation for mixed composition as well as most of the other recommendations. The armies of Madras and Bombay were organized on a "plum pudding" basis down to the company and squad level. The composition advocated by the Punjab Committee was adopted in the Bengal Army (which included the Punjab Frontier Force). In 1864 it consisted of twenty "mixed" regiments, sixteen regiments with ethnically homogeneous companies, and seven pure ethnic regiments (mostly Sikhs and Gurkhas). Recruiting in all three presidencies was localized, and troops rarely served outside of

[22] Punjab Committee quoted in the *Report of the Army Organization Commission* (Eden Commission), 1879, pp. 78–79. Great Britain, House of Commons. (East India [Army System] Return. London, November 11, 1884.)

the home presidency. The latter development had serious repercussions: without prospect of active duty, service in Bombay and Madras became increasingly unattractive to the able officer, and the quality of their units slowly declined.

The principles laid down in 1859 were reaffirmed in 1879 by the high-level Eden Commission appointed to reexamine the problems of the army in India.[23] The purpose of this commission was essentially that of its predecessor twenty years earlier:

Our main object has been to define the territorial formation of the army of India with due regard to the great principle of *divide et impera*. No one can study the history of the three armies of India, their organization, development, and distribution in times past, and at the present moment, without being struck with the fact that the present arrangements and distribution are based on an entire disregard of the above principle.[24]

The commission recommended that the three presidency armies be divided into four regional commands.[25] This division was designed to retain the geographic composition of the military and strengthen the hand of the central government in its efforts to prevent the Madras and Bombay armies from poaching recruits from the Punjab and Northwest India. The commission recommended strict recruiting by each presidency army only from its own area.

Although the Eden Commission tightened up the recruiting areas of the Bombay and Madras armies, it permitted the Bengal Army (and the Punjab units) to maintain their pure-caste regiments. Officers from these units appearing before the commission stressed the effectiveness of the homogeneous ethnic regiment, and the commission agreed, but not to the extent that they became more numerous than mixed regiments.

The growing illegal recruitment of northern Indians in the Bombay and Madras presidencies, could be dealt with in two ways. First, it could be legalized (a suggestion the com-

23 *Ibid.* Sir Ashley Eden, Lieutenant-Governor of Bengal was chairman of the commission. Lord Roberts (then a major-general) also served.
24 *Eden Commission,* p. 33.
25 This recommendation was not carried out for several years.

mission rejected because it interfered with the principle of divide and rule), or second, the size of those two armies could be reduced, making it easier to recruit soldiers from their own areas. The commission chose the latter course for the Madras Army and authorized small but important reductions. The commission argued that the internal security problem was considerably eased in Madras and that Madras soldiers were not effective enough to justify extensive recruitment. The decline of the Madras Army dates from this time, although this decline was slow because of the large number of officers, and because of protests from the presidency.

Both the Peel Commission in 1859 and the Eden Commission in 1879 based their recommendations on the premise that no major foreign expeditions were likely, and that the main problem was internal security. Army policy was not altered even after the second Afghan war, and only after the Russian scare of 1885 was the Eden Commission's assumption shattered that 60,000 men were the maximum necessary under any circumstances.[26] The Burma War of 1887–1889, followed the Russian scare and was used by many to prove the low fighting value of various classes, especially those from Madras. As external conflict grew more probable, and internal security problems lessened, newer notions of military efficiency took precedence over considerations of balance and the social composition of the military.

In a series of major reforms the entire base of recruitment was transformed from a territorial to a racial and caste basis. First, the system of linked battalions was revived. One battalion of a group was equipped for war, while other battalions supplied it with recruits.[27] This system expanded the base of recruiting in Bengal from one to three battalions, and spread the recruiting area for the other battalions as well. In 1887 each group of three battalions was given a regimental center,

<hr />

26 *Eden Commission*, p. 98.

27 *Indian Army, Recruiting In India Before and During the War of 1914–18*, p. 5. The principle had been rejected by the Army Commission of 1879, but was revived by the Secretary of State in 1883 and again in 1885 by Sir George Chesney. The principle was put into force in the Bengal Army in 1886. See Indian Army Circular, October, 1886, clause 170.

further stabilizing the system. But in 1892 this system was superseded by another one belonging to a different school of thought: the "class" recruiting center.[28] The earlier reforms of 1859, 1879, and even afterwards, were based on territorial recruiting (with the few exceptions of Sikh and Gurkha regiments), fixed depots, and periodical tours of local service for internal security purposes. The measures of 1892 introduced the long epoch of recruitment based on class and eliminated most territorial connections.

The distinction between "class regiment" and "class company regiment" also dates from this time.[29] Class regiments were composed entirely of the same ethnic or caste group; class company regiments had a different class in each of its three companies; the companies themselves were always "pure." Promotion for Indians to commissioned posts varied in the two types of regiment: in class regiments promotion was based on a general seniority list encompassing all companies, but in class company regiments promotion was made from the rolls of the particular class in which a vacancy occurred. No Indian officer of one class was permitted to command troops of another. This system guaranteed that the link between the unsophisticated sepoy and his British commander would be a solid, experienced Indian commissioned officer of the same class as the sepoy himself.

The internal organization of the Indian Army conceded a great deal to some important features of Indian—particularly Punjabi—society. The unique feature of the Indian Army was the rank of Viceroy's commissioned officer (VCO). The typical British Army company had a complement of six King's commissioned officers, (KCOs), usually Sandhurst graduates. The Indian Army company had only one KCO, a second-lieutenant

28 At about this time the British began to use the term "class" in referring to one particular ethnic group or caste which was recruited to the army. The term is not used in the sense of social level, but rather as a synonym for the cultural, ethnic, or caste groups which were recruited to the services. The more common meaning of "class" will be referred to as "social class."

29 Perhaps the clearest description of the difference between the two systems is to be found in the handbooks written for the instruction and guidance of the British officer. See any of the later editions of *Barrow's Sepoy Officer's Manual.*

or lieutenant who was first in command. The rest of the commissioned-officer positions were filled by VCOs. Some regimental positions were also held by VCOs. The VCO provided (and still provides) the link between the full commissioned officer, usually a graduate of a professional military academy, and the sepoy, whose language, customs, and outlook were utterly Indian. The Indian Army had a series of noncommissioned-officer positions as well: rifleman (private), lance-*naik* (corporal), *havildar* (sergeant), *havildar*-major, and quartermaster *havildars* of various levels. But above this there were *two* kinds of commissioned officers, the KCOs and the VCOs. The latter consisted of three grades: *jemadar* (who wore one star, as did the second-lieutenant KCO), *subedar* (two stars, equivalent to KCO lieutenant), and *subedar*-major (who wore a crown, as did the KCO major). These VCOs were not glorified warrant officers but officers in every sense of the word: they had power of command over Indian troops (KCOs could also command British troops) and they were greeted with respect and deference by Indian and Britisher alike. In fact, the power of the subedar-major (the "subedar-sahib" of innumerable works of popular British Indian fiction) was considerable, and many junior grade KCOs were terrified by him.

The VCOs filled the positions that the British could not fill with their own officers. The rank also provided an outlet for ambitious and able Indian sepoys, although they were not promoted beyond the regimental level. The subedar-major was often a man of great wisdom, experience, and power. Frequently he and the British commanding colonel had entered the unit together in their teens and had fought together on many battlefields. They often formed bonds of friendship and military brotherhood that were unbreakable under stress. These bonds partly explain the superb fighting record of many Indian units.

The friendship between subedar-major and commanding colonel contributed to the effectiveness of the Indian Army as a fighting machine in other ways. Just as the colonel served as a model for the young British officers, the "subedar-sahib" filled the role of patriarch, for the younger sepoys. He was at

the same time a village elder to obey and a professional standard to aspire to. The British officer, while impressive enough,
could not be imitated by Indian troops; the effect would have
been ludicrous. The experienced VCO was vitally needed in
the peasant army, and the combination of VCO, sepoy, and
KCO formed a stronger whole than the sum of the individual
components.

The Punjabization of the Indian Army occurred at the
same time as the adoption of the Bengali and Punjabi class
system of recruitment. From 1892 to 1914 Punjabi troops
increased rapidly:

NUMBER OF INFANTRY UNITS IN INDIAN ARMY
BY REGION, 1862–1914[30]

	1862	1885	1892	1914
Punjab	28	31	34	57
Gurkha (Nepal)	5	13	15	20
East of Yamuna	28	20	15	15
Bombay	30	26	26	18
Madras	40	32	25	11

The figures for Bombay are a little high because that presidency regularly poached recruits from the Punjab and Northwest India. In 1879, for example, 5,032 men of its total infantry
of 16,034 were recruited from outside the presidency.[31]

A necessary corollary to the Punjabization was the termination of recruitment of many classes. Between 1892 and 1914,
Mahars, Bengalis, many classes of Brahmins, Gujars, Ahirs,
and Hindustani Muslims were no longer recruited or were
drastically reduced in numbers. In Madras at the outbreak of
World War I recruitment had been so reduced that only eleven
infantry units remained, composed mostly of Tamils and
Madrassi Muslims. Telugus, who had once formed a quarter of the forty Madras battalions, no longer served at all.
Neither did Coorgs or Moplahs, who had been experimentally
recruited.

If recruiting had been carried on solely to support ethnic

30 *Indian Army, Recruiting in India Before and During the War of 1914–18,*
p. 7.
31 *Ibid.,* p. 6.

regiments it might have had a broader territorial base than it did, but many regiments were composed of different class companies (and still are) which meant that a very small area was combed for recruits. Recruitment on a class basis required recruiting officers to have an understanding of the classes (e.g., Gurkhas, Dogras, or Sikhs), and even more important, an understanding of the temperament and fighting characteristics of subclasses. Units not only recruited Punjabi Muslims or Rajputs, they recruited them from a particular clan, continually striving to make each battalion as homogeneous as possible. An enormous amount of time and effort was spent in procuring the right type of soldier from the right subclass for a particular unit.[32]

The shift in recruitment to the so-called martial, or warlike, races and classes continued. Placing the recruiting function in the hands of the regiment—itself not a fighting unit, but a recruitment and training organization—eventually created a unique military system. Considerable literature was created to explain, glorify, and justify this system. The focus of most of this literature was the idea of "martial races."

THE "MARTIAL" RACES

The idea of a "martial race" was and is less a theory than a catch-all phrase which has been used to justify a wide range of opinions on the inhabitants of India, and the best way to organize them into an army. Belief in the theory was not confined to the British: many Indians used the term during the days of the *Raj*[33] and it is in common use today among military and civilians, especially those from the Punjab.

Lord Roberts of Kandahar, who served as Commander-in-Chief of the Indian Army from 1885 to 1893, can be credited with (or blamed for) introducing the policy of fostering the

---

[32] Official literature on classes and recruitment of this period is reminiscent of Frederick the Great's obsession with oversized soldiers.

[33] See, for example, P. D. Bonarjee, *A Handbook of the Fighting Races of India* (Calcutta: Thacker, Spink & Co., 1899) and Saint Nihal Singh, *India's Fighters: Their Mettle, History and Services to Britain* (London: Sampson, Low, Marston & Co., 1914).

so-called martial races. Roberts was one of the great military heroes of India, a very powerful and popular man. The views of "Bobs Bahadur" became doctrine for a whole generation of Indian Army officers, and his monumental autobiography was cited as scriptural authority for many years.

Roberts' outlook was essentially that of an unsentimental professional, more interested in building up the Indian Army to meet the Russian threat than in keeping it fragmented in internal security duties. Roberts argued that the Russians, not the still docile Indians would have to be faced, and the former could not be met with an army of inferiors. In his view the best available material came from the northwest quarter of India, and that the army should be recruited from that area. He also felt that the class regiment fought better, and the classes that were recruited should be thus organized.

Roberts developed a theory of why and how some classes became better fighters than other classes, and used it to justify dropping several long-recruited classes from the army list:

Each cold season I made long tours in order to acquaint myself with the needs and capabilities of the men of the Madras Army. I tried hard to discover in them those fighting qualities which had distinguished their forefathers during the wars of the last and the beginning of the present century. But long years of peace, and the security and prosperity attending it, had evidently had upon them, as they always seem to have on Asiatics, a softening and deteriorating effect; and I was forced to the conclusion that the ancient military spirit had died in them, as it had died in the ordinary Hindustani of Bengal and the Mahratta of Bombay, and that they could no longer with safety be pitted against warlike races, or employed outside the limits of Southern India.[34]

Roberts tried, first when he was Commander-in-Chief of the Madras Army, and later when he was head of the entire Indian Army, to

substitute men of the more warlike and hardy races for the Hindustani sepoys of Bengal, the Tamils and Telugus of Madras, and the so-called Mahrattas of Bombay; but I found it difficult to get my

34 Lord Roberts of Kandahar, *Forty-One Years in India* (2 vols., London: Bentley, 1897), II, 383. Roberts served as Commander-In-Chief in India from 1885 to 1893.

view accepted, because of the theory which prevailed that it was necessary to maintain an equilibrium between the armies of the three Presidencies, and because of the ignorance . . . which encouraged the erroneous belief that one Native was as good as another for purposes of war.[35]

Roberts was no obscurantist or racist. He based his opinion on professional experience, and did not deny the possibility of martial races softening and becoming nonmartial, or *vice versa*, if conditions changed. After the development of the railways and the telegraph, theories of balance or of "divide and rule" no longer had to be met literally.

Deterioration of the quality of troops may have been due in large part to the deterioration of a good officer corps, and the development of the idea of martial races was perhaps designed as much to remove inefficient officers as inefficient soldiers. Madras had become an especially notorious backwater, and the terminal point of many military careers. The ambitious and the able posted there left as soon as they could, for that army engaged in very little fighting.[36]

Roberts' theory of military deterioration never waned, and is still widespread today in India. However, other more profound and romantic explanations were developed. Two of these deserve particular attention: the climatic theory of race, and the long-term historical theory of Aryan conquest.

The bulk of the fighting during the late nineteenth century was done in the Northwest, while the decline in the quality of the soldiers was most marked in the South. Some saw in this phenomenon the influence of India's dreaded climate. General Sir O'Moore Creagh[37] found a direct correlation between climate and martial character:

In the hot, flat regions, of which by far the greater part of India consists . . . are found races, timid both by religion and habit, servile to their superiors, but tyrannical to their inferiors, and quite un-

---

[35] *Ibid.*, p. 441.

[36] One British officer posted to an obscure and desolate post in South India made good use of his time by reading and studying before he wangled his way out. He was Winston Churchill, whose later disparaging opinion of the Indian Army may have been formed at that time.

[37] Commander-in-Chief, Indian Army, 1909–1914.

warlike. In other parts . . . where the winter is cold, the warlike minority is to be found, but its component peoples vary greatly in military virtue. Nowhere, however, are they equal in that respect to Europeans or Japanese.[38]

Creagh thought it an absurd idea that Indians could ever be expected to go to sea or to man a ship: they had no history of such an interest or capability.[39] Creagh's explanation was the simplest possible, and had an appeal to those who sought a simple justification for British recruitment practices and the continuation of the rule of an island people from a northern climate.[40]

A third explanation of the apparent differences in the Indian population concerned the long-term historical trends which antedated European contact. In one of the most popular and widely read accounts of the military in India—published just before World War I—the martial races were thus accounted for:

The people of Bengal, even those with the most cultivated brain, the trading classes, the artizan classes, and the outcaste tribes, are men to whom the threat of violence is the last word. . . . Presumably the great conquest of India away back in the mists of time, by the Aryan race, and the subjection of the original inhabitants, is at the bottom of this. Only certain races were permitted to bear arms, and in course of time only certain races remained fit to bear arms. Conquest, pure and simple, with cruel repression, is responsible for it in some places, such as in Bengal and Kashmir. It is extraordinary that the well-born race of the upper classes in Bengal should be hopeless poltroons, while it is absurd that the great, merry powerful Kashmiri should have not an ounce of physical courage in his constitution, but it is so.[41]

The races which remained "fit to bear arms" were those of the Kṣatriya (warrior) *varna* and their descendants. Rajputs thus

38 General Sir O'Moore Creagh, *Indian Studies* (London: Hutchinson, n.d.), p. 233.

39 *Ibid.*, p. 234.

40 A similar theory was propounded by President Ayub Khan on the occasion of the signing of the new Pakistani constitution. He noted that for the successful operation of a parliamentary system "above all, you need a really cool and phlegmatic temperament, which only people living in cold climates seem to have." Radio broadcast, March 1, 1962. *New York Times*, March 2, 1962.

41 Major G. F. MacMunn and Major A. C. Lovett, *The Armies of India* (London: Adam and Charles Black, 1911), pp. 129–130.

qualified, but so did many warlike classes who had, or claimed to have, Kṣatriya ancestry. The fighting ability and loyalty of many classes was first determined, and later an ancestry was "discovered."

Although the British differed on the appropriate theory to explain the origins of the martial races, they found such classes easy to identify. The martial classes could best be distinguished by their occupation. The British liked the "yeoman peasant" who was independent, sturdy, upright, honest, and reliable. In some cases landowners were acceptable, and some units drew from remote or nomadic tribal groups, but the favorite was the moderately wealthy farmer who had the right "outlook." Outlook and attitude towards soldiering were as important criteria as occupation. On the whole, the British played down the religious aspects of caste but stressed occupational and class characteristics of the prospective sepoy.

Officers and Jawans

All colonial relationships have much in common, but perhaps the most fundamental feature they share is a dependent relationship between the foreign conqueror and the native. The greater the social and technical gap between the two, the more one-sided this relationship will be. In exchange for a secure place in the new system established by the foreigner the native will respond not with gratitude but with obedience.[42] He will come to depend upon the foreigner for his status, but if the native comes to view himself in terms of Western equality, the relationship may be threatened. O. Mannoni attributes a weak ego to the native personality: if the institutional shell which protects that ego is dented, or if the ego develops to the point where the status of a dependent is seen as the status of an inferior, tension results.[43]

---

[42] For more thorough definitions of these terms, and a remarkable exposition on the colonial situation see O. Mannoni, *Prospero and Caliban: The Psychology of Colonization*, trans. Pamela Powesland, (London: Methuen, 1956), esp. pp. 42 ff. For a more systematic examination of the psychology of the colonial tie, see E. E. Hagen, *On the Theory of Social Change* (Homewood: Dorsey Press, 1962).

[43] *Ibid.*, p. 41.

The martial-races theory, as well as the close connection
of the officer to his troops, enabled the British to strengthen
the dependent relationship by going *beyond* it, giving the
Indian Army a character which was unique among colonial
armies.[44] This character was succinctly summed up by a British
Indian Army brigadier describing the relationship of officer to
soldier as

a unique phenomenon. No other army was ever quite like it;
the Indian Army was a brotherhood in which we fitted very well;
on duty very close attention was paid to rank, but this was not the
case off duty. Then the Indian Army was a classless society, officers
and men swore at each other in close friendship. We played sports
with the men, in perfect equality. It was a society within a society.[45]

In short, strict obedience, devotion, and deference—the de-
pendence relationship—was combined with a rough public-
school variety of equalitarianism.

The strengthening of this relationship in the late nineteenth century was symbolized by the gradual introduction of
the term *jawan* to replace sepoy; the good British officer was
regarded the "father" of his jawans (which can be translated
as "youngster" or "youth"), yet he was a brother to him as well,
although perhaps an older brother.

This relationship, which had extraordinary results in terms
of discipline and loyalty, was reinforced by the process of selection, recruitment, and training.

The very fact that the army was drawn from particular
castes and classes set these classes well apart. This status
brought them into a close relationship to the British and the
government, and some groups were encouraged to regard themselves as above the rest. The classes which contributed to the
military gave a great deal in terms of lives and service; they
gave it freely and willingly, with exuberance, in the knowledge that their efforts were recognized and needed, as well as
liberally rewarded. Each class was encouraged to develop

---

44 This character has been described by John Masters in several novels and
two volumes of autobiography. Of these the autobiographies are the most
useful and accurate: see *Bugles and a Tiger* (London: Michael Joseph, 1956)
and *The Road Past Mandalay* (London: Michael Joseph, 1961).

45 Interview, 1963.

particular attributes which set it apart both from other recruited classes and from the mass of Indian peasantry. There have always been important cultural and psychological differences between castes and regions in India. These differences were exaggerated and systematized by the British. Some military classes were relatively independent and calculating (Pathans), others were shy and proud (Dogras), others playful and comical, yet crazed and bloodthirsty in battle (Gurkhas), others prone to scheming and plotting, yet tenacious in defense (Sikhs), and still others stolid and dense (Jats).[46] Most of these tendencies—whether imagined or real—were encouraged and developed, and when new classes were brought into the military their particular virtues were quickly identified and exploited to improve group cohesion.

In addition to these particular characteristics the British also relied upon the peasant virtues common to all classes they recruited. The prime virtue was a willingness to face an enemy without fear; a willingness which remained as long as the jawans felt they were being properly led, and their cause was just. Ideological considerations rarely interfered, as the groups recruited into the military were from the politically most backward regions of India—another reason why they were desirable to the British. Efficient service and bravery in battle were matters of personal and class pride—*izzat*. The trust of the jawan once gained, was unshakable. The "Oriental" view of the cheapness of life, stoic tolerance of pain and discomfort, knowledge that bravery and obedience in this life —even if resulting in death or maiming—would only improve one's lot in the next, could be neatly turned to further the ends of the British.

These psychological materials were the basis for the officer-jawan dependent relationship. Fierce clan or class pride was gradually transformed into identification with the unit, a transition which was made easier by the homogeneous composition of many battalions or the pure class or caste composition of others.

---

[46] "Three things are improved by beating: women, wheat, and a Jat." Punjabi proverb.

This pride could not be ignored, and it could not be destroyed. Many of the recruited classes came to the military already secure in their status as warriors and proudly pointed to their long, glorious martial traditions. These feelings had to be handled with great care; but once the British had turned them in the proper direction, a class's fighting ability and loyalty was assured. The extreme example was the Gurkha, but the same situation existed in varying degrees among the other classes. The loyalty of these classes had to be won, and it was the British who were on probation:

The Gurkha does not love his officer because he is a Sahib, but because he is his Sahib, and the officer has to prove that he is his Sahib first . . . A strange officer . . . is not adopted into the Pantheon at once. He has to qualify . . . but once accepted, he is served with a fidelity and devotion that are human and dog-like at the same time.[47]

The British threw themselves completely into the task of bending class traditions to the purposes of the army. They not only praised the virtues of their "own" Indian regiment, but many Britishers identified with them. It was a common belief among the British that the British officers themselves represented a martial race; the landed aristocratic military-oriented segment of that race in particular. There was no harm, therefore, in one martial race adopting in part the outlook of another. Candler, a shrewd observer, noted:

One has to mix with different regiments a long time before one can follow all the nuances, but it it does not take long to realize to what extent the British officer is a partisan. Insensibly he suffers a kind of conversion. He comes to see many things as his men see them, even to adopt their own estimates of themselves in relation to other sepoys. And one would not have it otherwise.[48]

This could be carried to extremes where British officers would not allow their high-caste troops to play hockey with troops of a lower caste.[49] Often, familiarity bred favoritism to the point where some officers made themselves unfit for higher

---

47 Edmund Candler, *The Sepoy* (London: John Murray, 1919) pp. 8–9.
48 *Ibid.*, p. 46.
49 *Ibid.*, p. 47.

command by too intense devotion to one particular class of troops.[50] Such cases were not the rule, but they were common enough to be a minor problem; it was as if Crusoe, upon finding his Friday, would settle for no other. The period between World War I and World War II saw the high-water mark of this devotion; it faded when both the officer corps and the jawans were diluted with individuals less indoctrinated with the "system." Officer-class devotion has been revived to some extent in both India and Pakistan, but not in its former glory.

Whether or not a particular officer became a devotee of his particular class, he was certain to participate deeply in the personal and social lives of his troops. As a result of the involvement of the army in class and caste traditions, the army had to subsidize and participate in these traditions. Religious holidays were frequently given a strong military twist, and unit *maulvis, pandits,* or *gurus* blessed the weapons and the regiment; some of these celebrations were (and still are) gory affairs, with extensive animal slaughter, but all were entered into enthusiastically by the British. Induction into the service was similarly given a holy sanction, and the recruit swore allegiance to the King and Emperor in a ceremony and sealed it by a religious oath. The British officer was further brought into close contact with his troops by his trips to the recruiting area, and his service as father-counselor.

Great care was taken to avoid violation of the troops' religious scruples, especially in matters of food. Separate kitchens, washing facilities, and messing arrangements were maintained, lest anything paralleling the greased cartridges and leather caps of past mutinies reoccur. Many Indian officers thought the British were overcautious in these matters.[51] The British, despite their close relationship to the fighting men, were not as intimate with the troops as the Indian officers, and in their desire to avoid mistakes tended to err on the side of caution.

The British were also cautious on one other point. Although

[50] Interview with Field-Marshal Sir Claude Auchinleck, London, 1963.
[51] Lieutenant-General D. R. Thapar, *The Morale Builders* (Bombay: Asia Publishing House, 1965), p. 7.

they encouraged ethnic and caste sentiment, they avoided competition which could lead to open communal conflict. The number of classes in the army made it convenient to pit one against the other, but the terms had to be so regulated that the competition would be above the caste level, not part of it. The level of competition was in part controlled by mixing Muslim and Hindu troops in the battalions (but not in the companies) and, in fact, many regiments bore regional, not class, names. All religious and political agitation was suppressed, and any soldier even suspected of such activity was expelled. The officers were very firm on this point, for it touched their own principles of secularism as well as their fear of the army tearing itself apart in communal conflict. The British thought that the class basis of recruitment and organization, and careful nurturing of class traditions, helped reinforce caste and class compartmentalization. Once the distinctiveness of the recruited classes was well established, the British sought political and social protection for them, both as a reward and to shield the recruiting grounds from outside political agitation.

In summary, by the beginning of the twentieth century the British dominated India and had created a military organization which was reliable, efficient, and relatively immune to external disturbances. The Indian Army was adequate for brief, probing expeditions beyond the northern borders, for limited use as an imperial expeditionary force, and, above all, as a final line of defense for internal security. Its organizational integrity was due to two major accomplishments: the development of a highly competent officer corps and the recruitment of suitable soldiers. The most loyal and trustworthy classes were heavily recruited, but were in turn dominated by the all-British officer corps. The Army was representative in terms of fighting ability in that classes with recent military experience were chosen. However, in terms of geographical distribution the army was grossly unrepresentative, and became increasingly so until World War I. The army rank structure reflected the hierarchical structure of the social status system of pre-British Indian armies, with Britishers replacing Indian aristocratic elites at the top. Most soldiers were middle-class peasants; the camp followers, menials, and porters, were composed entirely of the depressed classes and untouchable castes. Promotion was by ability, and the Indian Army developed a unique and powerful esprit de corps based on the brotherhood of arms. This rough equalitarianism helped bridge the gap between British officer and Indian sepoy, and stimulated interclass and intercaste competition.

The system was obviously vulnerable. Over the years it was subject to severe stress from various external sources. The first of these was the antagonism against the recruitment policies of the British by those hitherto loyal segments of Indian society which were excluded from military roles. Large numbers of classes found a highly desirable avenue of mobility and status shut off to them. The high command of the army was manned entirely by Britishers, yet often the troops under their command had traditional loyalties to various regional elites. These elites could not be fully integrated into the command structure of the army without great difficulty, and although they were generally loyal had to be placated in various ways.

The Indian Army was also increasingly vulnerable to attack on ideological grounds. It had early been accused by Britishers themselves as being a parasite on Indian society. As political awareness developed, the Indians took up this charge. The disinterest of the army in "civic action" programs increasingly became a subject of political concern, and ultimately blossomed into a major issue in the 1930s.

Finally, the system of recruitment and training which seemed so stable in 1900 shortly proved to be inadequate. In 1914 and 1939, the base of recruitment proved too narrow, and the army could not expand rapidly enough because of the restrictions on "eligible" classes. Further, the system was not geared to receiving and absorbing technological innovations. All armies of this period were faced with the task of learning how to use relatively sophisticated communications and engineering technologies as well as increasingly complex weaponry. The martial esprit of the Indian Army proved increasingly irrelevant, and even a hindrance.

3

THE MILITARY
ENTERS INDIAN THOUGHT

Three variables seem to account for Indian attitudes toward the British-Indian military structure. The first is the culture in which an individual or group seeks to define its status. Is the referent culture traditional or Western? Or, is it an amalgam of the two: a neotraditionalism looking forward for means but backward for ends? The second variable is the degree to which a group or individual values the military. Is the military a prime value (an end) or an instrumental value (a means) to the group?[1] The third variable is the degree of xenophobia or nationalism: in the Indian context, to what extent was the group anti-British?

The movement of these three parameters was profoundly affected both by British policy and by events outside India. B. B. Misra describes the progressive Westernization of India under British-inspired economic, social, and educational reforms.[2] These reforms created an Indian "middle class," tied intellectually, professionally, and economically to the West.

[1] See Alfred Vagts, *A History of Militarism*, (rev. ed.; New York: Meridian Books, 1959), and, especially, Hans Speier, *Social Order and the Risks of War* (New York: Stewart, 1952), pp. 230 ff.

[2] B. B. Misra, *The Indian Middle Classes* (New York: Oxford University Press, 1961).

At the same time Western attitudes toward the role of the military developed in India, especially after the Indians gained an understanding of their own army and the armies of Britain, Japan, and—after 1917—Russia. The need for understanding their army increased after the possibility of home rule, dominion status, or some other form of relative autonomy was raised. Indian leadership soon realized that control over the military was closely related to control over other important levers of the state. Finally, the modern, and to some extent the traditional, sectors of Indian society became progressively more radical toward the British.

Two major sets of attitudes developed toward the military: traditional militarism and gradualism. Both attitudes shared one assumption: that the British were in India to stay and that their presence was not inherently evil. This assumption was challenged during and after World War I by more radical perspectives.

TRADITIONAL MILITARISM

There are two fundamentally different sets of Indian attitudes toward the British-Indian military structure, both of which may legitimately be labeled Indian militarism: "modern militarism" and traditional militarism." "Modern militarism," which we shall examine in Chapter IV, emerged in Bengal and western India, and spread to other regions; especially to the intellectuals, bourgeosie, middle classes, and professional families.[3] Modern militarism stressed the value of the military as a national universal solvent; as an expression of the national will, and demanded equalitarian recruitment.

"Traditional militarism" resulted from regional traditions and the recruiting practices of the British. It was confined to those castes and military classes which exercised the use of arms as a matter of birth and right and was unevenly distributed throughout India, the Punjab being at one extreme, Madras and Bengal at the other. Traditional militarism is

3 See Speier, p. 231.

usually confined to specific castes, while other castes have no desire to abandon their traditional occupations for military life. In the Punjab, for example, Chuhras, or untouchable sweepers, traditionally have not joined either indigenous military organizations or the Indian Army except as sweepers, yet former Chuhras who have been converted to Sikhism (Mazbhi Sikhs) have a long—if tenuous—history of military activity as sepoys.[4]

At the turn of the nineteenth century traditional militarists fell into two categories. First, members of classes which were no longer recruited, or recruited only in very small numbers; and second, those classes which constituted the army, but which sought even greater status as commissioned officers.

After the British radically changed the base of recruitment late in the nineteenth century, many classes were no longer taken into the military. Over a period of years these classes remained a large, and at times pathetic, group. After the 1890s they were again recruited, only to be once again dropped from the army list.

A typical such group was the Mahars, an untouchable caste of present-day Maharashtra. They were a sizable portion of the armies of the Mahratta chieftain Shivaji, served as hereditary local policemen, and were thus a "natural" martial class. Heavily recruited in the premutiny years, the Mahars constituted a fifth to a quarter of the entire Bombay Army.[5] A number of distinguished leaders of the Mahar community in the nineteenth century had at one time served in the Army, many as noncommissioned officers. One of these was the father of modern India's leading untouchable politician, B. R. Ambedkar, who had, in fact, grown up in a military cantonment.[6] In the reorganization of the recruiting base of the Indian Army in the late nineteenth century, Mahar recruit-

4 See Stephen P. Cohen, "The Untouchable Soldier: Caste, Politics and the Indian Army," *Journal of Asian Studies*, XXVIII, 3 (May, 1969), for further data on this caste.

5 See Sir Patrick Cadell, *History of the Bombay Army* (London: Longmans, Green and Co., 1938) and Lt.-Col. W. B. P. Tugwell, *History of the Bombay Pioneers* (London: Sidney Press, 1938), Appendix Two.

6 Dhananjay Keer, *Dr. Ambedkar: Life and Mission* (2nd ed. rev.; Bombay: Popular Prakashan, 1962), pp. 11–12.

ment was rapidly terminated, until there were only a few serving by 1900, practically none by 1914.[7]

The Mahars—like many other classes in the same position— were anxious and resentful when they were dropped from the army list. They were resentful because they felt they were being insulted, and they were anxious lest they suffer setbacks in other areas of government recruitment. Their reaction to their plight was typical; protests were essentially supplicatory: petitions, negotiations, speeches, editorials in sympathetic newspapers, and delegations to the authorities. These tactics were to be expected from groups which sought to retain or recover a privileged place in the British Raj (or rule as the British Indian Government was called.)

Ambedkar's biographer describes the protests of his father in 1892; Ambedkar himself later took up the cause of Mahar recruitment when he entered Indian politics after World War I. In 1910 the Conference of the Deccan Mahars petitioned the Secretary of State for India; the document deserves to be quoted at length for its style as well as its content:

> We, the Mahar inhabitants of India, residing in the Bombay Presidency, have experienced the vitalizing influence of the general awakening of our Indian people, and long to participate in the new privileges which have been granted by our illustrious Emperor and King to the people of our country, in accordance with the declarations of our late Empress, Queen Victoria the Good, in the celebrated Proclamation of 1858. We do not aspire to high political privileges and positions, since we are not educationally qualified for them, but humbly seek employment in the lowest grades of the Public Service, in the ranks of Police Sepoys and of Soldiers in the Indian Army.
>
> We are making no new demands; we do not claim employment in services in which we have not been engaged before. Indeed, some few of our people do still hold positions in the Police Force. . . . So also have our people been employed in the Indian Army from the very commencement of the British Raj in our country, and they have risen to the highest positions by their valour and good conduct.
>
> But the present changes in the Indian Army have been most

7 Tugwell, *op. cit.*

prejudicial to the interests of our people. We have been excluded from the Military Service entirely, for reasons unknown to us.[8]

The Mahars continued their plea by offering to serve in segregated regiments or in Muslim regiments if high-caste Hindus objected to their presence; they anxiously stated that they were not "essentially inferior" to their fellow Indians, and that, in fact, many Mahars were now Christians. Rather optimistically they continued that "the kindly touch of the Christian religion elevates the Mahar at once and forever socially as well as politically, and shall not the magic power of British Law and British Justice produce the same effect upon us, even as followers of our own ancestral faith?" The petitioners offered to serve in any capacity in the military, even as menial servants or as mule drivers, if they could not again serve as sepoys.

The Mahars were also concerned with the effect that dropping them from the recruitment rolls would have on their status in Western India. An important theme of their petition was that the British not accede to caste prejudice and discriminate against the lower castes, such as the Mahar community.

The petition of the Mahars was paralleled by petitions of other classes and castes, many with a distinguished military past. Maharashtrian Brahmins, Tamils, Telugus, Coorgs, and numerous other groups were cut from the army list. At a session of the Indian National Congress in 1891 the great western Indian leader, Bal Gangadhar Tilak advocated "organizing throughout the more warlike races of the Empire a system of militia service."[9] At a later Congress session, at Bankipore in 1912, two Telugus spoke feelingly about the exclusion of their community from the Madras presidency army list; they were particularly shamed because Muslims and "Pariah-Christians"

---

[8] Reproduced in: H. N. Navalkar, *The Life of Shivaram Janba Kamble* (Poona: S. J. Kamble, 1930), pp. 142–157. I am grateful to Professor Eleanor Zelliot for this reference.

[9] *Proceedings of the Seventh Indian National Congress* (Nagpur: December, 1891).

were recruited ahead of their own people.[10] They cited Hindu scripture in support of their contention that the Brahmins were a warlike race and invoked the ancient Hindu lawgiver, Manu, to refute Lord Roberts' alleged slights against the Telugu people.

The castes and classes which the British did recognize as traditionally warlike had different concerns. The prime objective of Punjabis, Muslims, Sikhs, Dogras, Jats, and Rajputs —to mention only the most prominent groups in the reorganized Indian Army—was to place their sons in a position where they might rise to the rank of commissioned officer. Similarly many hundreds of aristocratic families had had martial traditions (especially in the Punjab), and contributed troops to the Indian Army (or maintained their own army under the control of the British). They also sought a position alongside the British officer commensurate with their status in Indian society.[11]

The British had long been aware that the structure of the Indian Army was liable to produce tensions unless great care was taken to appease the leadership of the recruited castes by providing avenues of advancement for able Indians within the military. Before the establishment of the sepoy system, petty Indian noblemen were allowed to raise and lead their own men in battle—a practice which the all-British King's commissioned officer corps eliminated. Under the sepoy system, Indians could become Viceroy's commissioned officers, but they could never be promoted to senior appointments (all held by the British KCOs). The VCOs generally could not speak English and were untutored in modern theories of warfare. Their entire military careers had been spent within one

10 See the speeches of the mover, C. V. S. Narasimha Raju of Vizagapatnam, and of Prakasa Rao.

11 This demand was pressed through the Indian Army itself (which had strong links to the Indian countryside because of its recruiting apparatus) and later through caste associations and "front" organizations such as the Anjuman-i-Islah-i-Rajputan-i-Hind (All-India Rajput Conference). The Anjuman enjoyed the official patronage of the Commander-in-Chief, Punjab officialdom, and other high British officials. See, *Papers Relating to Constitutional Reforms in India* (Calcutta: Government of India, 1908), III, 1465.

regiment, and their experience was limited. In addition, they were usually too old to begin a new military career as a King's commissioned officer, even if they had been permitted to do so.

The problem of accommodating Indian opinion remained, however, and several alternatives were proposed over the years. In 1836 Lieutenant-Colonel John Briggs of the Madras Army argued for increased association of Indians with the military at the higher levels, and the Indianization, in part, of the officer corps. Briggs suggested that military colleges be established for the sons of native officers, and that professional and loyal Indians gradually replace the British officers, freeing the latter for more sensitive political jobs.[12] A few years later Henry Lawrence took up the argument:

There is always danger in handling edged tools, but justice and liberality forge a stronger chain than suspicious and niggardly policy. We hold that no place or office should be absolutely barred to the Native soldier . . . Legitimate outlets for military energy and ability in all ranks, and among all classes *must* be given. . . . The question is only whether justice is to be gracefully conceded or violently seized. Ten or twenty years *must* settle the point.[13]

Lawrence saw many able Indians leaving British service and hiring themselves out to Indian rulers; it was these men who had to be retained and controlled.

The Mutiny of 1857 put an end to such speculation for several years. The British were worried about the quality of their own officers, and few who had served during the mutiny were eager to place Indians in positions of command.

Yet the problem persisted, and pressure for change came from both the Indians and the British.[14] The first step toward the Indianization of the King's officer corps came in 1901 with the establishment of the Imperial Cadet Corps. In 1905, a special form of King's Commission "in His Majesty's Native

[12] Lieut.-Col. John Briggs (Madras Army), *Letter to the Rt. Hon. Sir John Hobhouse, Bart., President of the India Board* (Privately printed: n.p., 1836), p. 38. Copy in India Office Library.

[13] *Essays, Military and Political* (London: W. H. Allen, 1859), pp. 24, 276.

[14] Sir George Chesney, *Indian Polity* (2nd ed.; London: Longmans, Green and Co., 1870), p. 353.

Indian Land Forces" was instituted for Indians who had qualified through the corps.[15] It was different from the VCO primarily in method of entry. The VCO had to serve for several
years in the ranks as a sepoy before receiving his commission.
The new commission was somewhat more suitable for an Indian "gentleman," as he had only to attend an elite military
academy. The commission only carried the power of command over Indian troops, and those who held it could not rise
above the level of squadron or company officer. The main
instigator of the cadet corps was Lord Curzon, who saw in it
a means of providing a military career for those

whose pride of birth or surrounding prevents them from embrac-
ing a civil profession, whose interests lie naturally on the side of
the British Government, but whose sympathies are in danger of
being alienated, and their energies dulled by the absence of any
field for their natural ambitions.[16]

These individuals would come from the princely and noble
families of India; they would not be from "the newer aristoc-
racy, who, if the criterion were one of wealth or education, or
precocity in European manners, would flood us with a stream
of applications supported by every sort of examination test,
but resulting in the very last type of young officer that we
should desire to procure."[17]

The basic difficulty of Indianizing the officer corps was to
set up criteria for determining the qualifications of prospective
officers. This problem was not solved until World War II. The
martial classes argued on political grounds: they had been
loyal in the past, and must be kept loyal in the future. Yet,
what if loyalty was not accompanied by professional compe-

[15] The cadet corps was a military parallel to the Statutory Civil Service.
It was also designed for the younger sons of princes and nobles. But "no
one can make people give equal esteem to a service for where there are not
sufficient candidates and to another of men picked by keen examination."
Philip Woodruff, The Men Who Ruled India, Vol. II: The Guardians (reprint
ed. of 1954 publ.; London: Jonathan Cape, 1963), p. 167.

[16] Lord Curzon's Memorandum on Commissions for Indians, June 4, 1900.
Bengal Military Letters and Enclosures, vol. 639, Encl. to Letter No. 103 of
July 1900. India Office Library. Reprinted in C. H. Philips, ed., The Evolution
of India and Pakistan, 1858–1947 (London: Oxford University Press, 1962),
p. 518.

[17] Ibid., p. 521.

tence—which was to come first? Indianization posed a challenge to the standards of the British officer corps, and to their feeling of superiority over the Indians.

Despite the urging of civilian officials, the British military was reluctant to acknowledge the value of the small cadet corps and regarded it as a major encroachment upon their exclusive world. But just as important, it was not entirely satisfactory to the Indian officers. If they could only command Indian troops, their status was clearly inferior to that of the British officers who, as King's Commissioned Officers, could command British as well as Indian troops. Even if they were to be trained in India, at an Indian Sandhurst, many thought they could never be fully equal to their British colleagues. But to the Indians from traditional martial classes the challenge was learning to adapt their martial background to the technical and professional requirements of a modern military organization. As the Indian Army modernized the tension between the two sets of skills and values increased.

GRADUALISM

"Instrumental gradualism" was the second important strand of Indian thought on military matters to emerge before World War I. The gradualists were the forerunners of the Indian defense experts who came to prominence after 1920. They were "established" members of Edwardian India with close personal and intellectual ties to Britain and British thought, and constituted the loyal opposition to official British policy in India. They regarded military and defense matters as important but secondary to budget cutting, government jobs for Indians, and the removal of moral and social slights. The best expression of their views can be found in the records of the early sessions of the Indian National Congress—an organization founded in 1885 by a Britisher to enable loyal, educated Indians to ventilate their grievances even as they expressed their support for the Raj.

The first Congress, held in Bombay in 1885, set the tone for many years to follow:

That in the opinion of the Congress the proposed increase in the military expenditure of the empire is unnecessary, and regard being had to the revenue of the empire and the existing circumstances of the country, excessive.[18]

The mover of the resolution, P. Runiah Naidu (of Madras), stressed the loyalty of the natives of India to the Queen and their thanks for the "blessings conferred on us by British rule."[19] He and other delegates claimed that the Russian threat would be met by mass volunteering, because of this deep loyalty of the Indians to the British. Naidu argued that the poverty-stricken condition of the country required the government to rely upon such volunteers in a crisis, to cut the size of the Indian Army, and to significantly reduce the British element of the army in India.[20]

The high cost of the Indian Army was a recurrent theme (although dwindling in intensity) until the 1920s, but another problem concerned many delegates. At the second session of the Congress it was suggested that the government initiate a system of volunteering; but the speech by the mover of the resolution (Raja Rampal Singh) went beyond the content of the resolution itself. After timidly apologizing for being at variance with his government, and after stressing the Indians' gratefulness for British rule, he came to his main point:

. . . but we cannot be grateful to it for degrading our natures, for systematically crushing out of us all martial spirit, for converting a race of soldiers and heroes into a timid flock of quill-driving sheep (*prolonged shouts*). Thank God things have not yet gone quite so far as this. There are some of us yet, everywhere, who would be willing to draw sword, and if needful lay down our lives . . . for the support and maintenance of that Government to which we owe so much.[21]

The possibility of saving money by a voluntary system of recruitment was clearly a secondary motive for Rampal Singh

---

18 *Proceedings of the First Indian National Congress*, (Bombay: October, 1885), pp. 52 ff.

19 *Ibid.*

20 The concern over the defense budget was shared by the government of India. See B. B. Misra, *op. cit.*, p. 363.

21 *Proceedings of the Second Indian National Congress* (Calcutta: December, 1886), p. 93.

and many others. His main concern was that arms be given to the upper classes so that their self-reliance would not deteriorate further than it had since the mutiny. It was not a matter of tradition or of money alone, but of honor.

The same concern was behind the resolution urging repeal of the Arms Act in 1888. The majority of delegates, led by Sir Pherozeshah Mehta, succeeded in passing the resolution over the opposition of most British and a few Indian delegates. The real issue was the loss of self-respect.[22]

Another objective of many Indian moderates was to increase the number of government positions open to Indians. Their main interest was in the Indian Civil Service. Indians had theoretically been eligible for the Indian Civil Service since the Charter Act of 1853, but none were recruited until 1871, when four were taken into the elite corps. In 1879, as a result of agitation in both England and India, a statutory civil service was created and the number of Indians rapidly increased; by 1915 there were 63 Indian Indian Civil Service members, 5 percent of the total.[23] Although all lower ranks of the Indian Army were made up of Indians, they did not reach the 5 percent level in the officer corps until the 1930s, and even then were crammed into the lower levels of the hierarchy. Not until the twentieth century was there much pressure from urban India for increased places in the officer corps; but by that time Indianization was seen as something more important than prestige or jobs: Indianization had become linked to home rule and independence.

A leading spokesman for the moderate position was G. K. Gokhale. He dealt annually with military problems in his budget speeches before the Imperial Legislative Council.[24] His major concern was the reduction of the heavy defense expenditure—or at least a larger contribution by Britain, since the Indian Army was often used for imperial purposes. His most important contribution to the debate on defense, how-

22 *Proceedings of the Fourth Indian National Congress*, (Allahabad: December, 1888).
23 Sir Edward Blunt, *The I.C.S.: The Indian Civil Service* (London: Faber & Faber, 1937), pp. 53 ff.
24 Printed in G. K. Gokhale, *Speeches* (Madras: Natesan, 1909?).

ever, foreshadowed arguments which are still encountered in India today. Gokhale had some familiarity with foreign military systems; he argued that the mercenary Indian Army must be replaced by a cheaper, more effective citizens' army. Japan was an especially attractive model after that nation's triumph over Russia in 1905. If the British would establish a short-service citizens' army they would save a great deal of money, but more important, they would heal India's wounded self-respect.[25]

The British refused to reconsider the organizational premises of the Indian Army. Although some concessions were made to the martial classes in the form of token commissions in the officer corps, there was no attempt to resume recruitment of those classes which had been dropped, or to broaden the base of the army, let alone make it a "citizens' army." The army was especially reluctant to experiment with untried castes or with the new Indian middle classes, either as soldiers or as officers. They might well have, for World War I placed intolerable strains upon the capacity of the martial classes to produce recruits in adequate numbers, and this crisis led the British to make promises which they were reluctant to carry out after the war.

WORLD WAR I

Percival Spear remarked that "the First World War forms the portal through which India entered the stage of the modern world."[26] It was a bloody entry for the Indian Army which served in Europe, the Middle East, and Africa. More than 36,000 soldiers were killed and 70,000 wounded. Indian Army personnel won sixteen Victoria Crosses—the highest award bestowed by the British Empire—and ninety-nine Military Crosses for numerous deeds of heroism and gallantry.[27] The army suffered inordinate losses due to its obsolete equipment

25 Speech on the Budget, 1906. *Ibid.*, p. 174.
26 *The Oxford History of India* (Oxford: Oxford University Press, 1958), p. 779.
27 Brig. Rajendra Singh, *History of the Indian Army* (New Delhi: Army Educational Stores, 1963), pp. 121 ff.

and inadequate training against major military powers, but as an army and on an individual level the Indian expeditionary force performed magnificently.

Although the impact of World War I on Indian society was important and diverse, two developments particularly affected both the traditional military groups and the more Westernized gradualists. The first was the scope and intensity of recruitment. Classes which had been dropped from the recruitment lists were again recruited, as well as new classes which had never been recruited. Second, the British made promises to induce recruitment.

The Martial Races in World War I

One of the early casualties of World War I was the system of recruiting the martial races theory. Although the war verified the warlike characteristics of the classes designated as "martial," it also demonstrated that other classes—given adequate training and leadership—performed equally. It also revealed that the base of recruitment was far too narrow, and that threats, extortion, and a variety of promises were necessary to raise adequate numbers from the martial classes.

Between August, 1914, and November, 1918, the Indian Army more than tripled in size; from 155,000 to more than 573,000 men. Nearly 740,000 sepoys served at one time or another during the war. The bulk of the army was drawn from those classes which had traditionally been recruited, the largest being the Punjabi Muslims, who contributed more than 136,000 men. Sikhs (88,000), Rajputs (62,000), Gurkhas (55,000), and Jats (54,000) also provided significant numbers. Lesser contributions were made by Dogras (23,000), Pathans (28,000), Hindustani Muslims (36,000), and Ahirs (19,000).[28] Seventy-five "new" classes were "tried" during the course of the war, including many groups which in fact had had long and distinguished military histories.[29]

[28] These figures are from the official but unpublished history of recruitment during World War I: *Recruiting in India Before and During the War of 1914–1918* (Army H.Q., India, October, 1919), Appendix 9. The volume used is in the Archives of the Ministry of Defense, Government of India.

[29] *Ibid.*, Appendix 13.

There had been several warnings from within the military establishment in India (as well as from Indian civilians) that the base of recruitment was too narrow. In 1892 one officer of the adjutant-general's branch advised that "recruiting for the Native Army was practically breaking down toward the end of the Afghan War, and although at present a sufficient supply of men is forthcoming, I am of [the] opinion that it will again break down when stress is put on it."[30] Between 1892 and 1914 conditions of service had improved greatly, but even so, the last prewar inquiry into army affairs (the Nicholson Army Commission, 1912) found that in the event of a "serious war" recruitment might fall off, unless steps were taken to improve the attractiveness of the army to the sepoys. They suggested that Sikh recruitment be reduced, and that sparsely represented classes, such as Deccani Brahmins, and Nagas, be recruited, as long as the efficiency of the army was not diminished.[31] These suggestions, however, remained unimplemented.

The greatest problem was the recruitment of the Jat Sikhs. Although there were fewer Sikhs recruited from the Punjab than Muslims, the Sikhs had been contributing a higher percentage of their available manpower to the army. They were experiencing important social changes by way of the militant Akali reform movement in the early part of the twentieth century, and were regarded as one of the more recalcitrant and pugnacious classes.[32] In addition the Jat Sikhs had been the target of early nationalist propagandizing and many were impressed by the news before World War I that several retired Sikh sepoys had destroyed their medals and discharge certificates in a wave of anti-British sentiment in America and Canada. Restrictions on Indian immigration to Canada and the *Kotaga Maru* incident fed conspiratorial sentiment, and copies of revolutionary newspapers filtered back to the villages

---

[30] *Ibid.*, p. 16.
[31] *Ibid.*, p. 16.
[32] For the government view of Sikh unrest, see Major A. E. Barstow, *Sikhs* (Calcutta: Government of India, Central Publications Branch, 1928). This volume is one in a series of Handbooks on the Indian Army prepared for all classes.

of the Punjab.[33] These papers were followed by the revolutionaries themselves; acts of violence were committed during the first years of the war, but they were effectively dealt with by the British with the assistance of Punjabi—especially Sikh—gentry. Returning sepoys who had had an opportunity to compare British and French treatment of their colonials created additional unrest.

The final two years of the war brought enormous pressure upon civilian and military officials to speed the flow of recruitment from the Punjab. Sir Michael O'Dwyer, Lieutenant-Governor of Punjab, toured the countryside from division to division, district to district, exhorting the youth of the martial classes—especially the Sikhs—to come forward. In numerous speeches he argued that India's cause was that of Britain: therefore India should contribute a proportionate number of soldiers which he calculated to be three million.[34] He threatened that conscription would be necessary if Indians would not volunteer. A quota system was informally introduced and the threat of conscription was used as an incentive. O'Dwyer praised the districts which had contributed large numbers of troops and shamed those that did poorly, especially with the taunt that Bengal had provided a "keen and capable" unit. He attempted to stir Jat Sikhs by pointing to the rise in Mazbhi (untouchable) Sikh recruitment: "if regard be had to available numbers the Mazbhi Sikhs have far surpassed the Jats . . . do the Jats view the Cavalry of Mazbhis with equanimity?"[35] If the Punjabis—especially the Sikhs—really wanted

---

[33] The *Kotaga Maru* was a Japanese steamer chartered by 376 immigrants for a voyage to Canada. All but thirty were Sikhs. Upon arrival they were refused permission to land, although they fulfilled the extraordinarily rigorous requirements set by the Canadian government. After considerable hardship and two months in Canadian waters they returned to India. Upon arrival (in late September, 1914) they were forced to proceed back to the Punjab. Some Sikhs refused, and in a police firing twenty-one were killed. The rest were handcuffed and shipped to the Punjab by rail. This incident presaged a considerable flow of returning immigrants. Khushwant Singh, *The Sikhs* (London: George Allen and Unwin, 1953), pp. 124 ff.

[34] Sir Michael O'Dwyer, *War Speeches* (Lahore: Supt. of Government Printing, Punjab, 1919), speech of May 4, 1918.

[35] *Ibid.*, speech of April 17, 1918.

true *izzat,* they must obtain it through service to a noble and just cause *(khidmat).* The promise of further commissions as officers, however, may have been more effective in recruiting Sikhs than all the threats of the British.

As regards the further grant of King's Commissions the Government of India have already laid their proposals before the Home Government and we may be sure that they will receive early and sympathetic consideration. Meantime, eleven representatives of leading martial tribes have received commissions in the King's Indian forces within the last few months, but the number to be granted will naturally depend in a great measure on the response to the call for recruits. We have often been told by those who claim to understand the Indian mind [a reference to Indian politicians?] that the one thing wanted to open the flood-gates of recruiting is the grant of King's Commissions. The next few months should show whether that view is correct.[36]

There were, of course, other material incentives for joining the army or for assisting the British in the recruitment effort. Former soldiers received relatively liberal pensions, and those who served the British with distinction, or who were officers, were given grants of land, jagirs, and were further rewarded by having their relatives favorably considered for recruitment.[37]

Although the Punjab had performed magnificently, the manpower needs of the war were staggering, and the British turned to many "nonmartial" classes. Of the seventy-five new classes which the army recruited, many were either closely related to classes already on the army list (Dogra Jats, Mahtam Sikhs, Punjabi Brahmins, Punjabi Hindus, Punjabi Chris-

---

[36] *Ibid.,* speech of May 4, 1918.

[37] At the end of World War I, 420,000 acres of land were distributed among 5,902 VCOs and other ranking Indian officers. Over 14,000 persons received *jangi inams*—special pensions—for two "lives," i.e. the amount (ten rupees per month for a VCO) was passed on to the next generation. Specially selected VCOs received 200 *jagirs.* These *jagirs* included: a) grants of land with full proprietary rights, yielding a net annual income of 400 rupees, and assignment of land revenue for three lives; b) pensions amounting to 150 rupees the third generation, and c) 200 VCOs were granted honorary KCOs. The KCO received double the ordinary VCO pension upon retirement. One wonders about the economic and social impact of these awards in the Punjab, where most of them were granted. Data from the monograph, Bisheswar Prasad, ed., "Honours and Awards," Adjutant General's Branch, (India and Pakistan: Combined Inter-Services Historical Section, 1947?), on file in the Ministry of Defense, Historical Section Archives, New Delhi.

tians, South Punjabi Muslims, West Punjabi Muslims, and Oudh Rajputs) and many were formerly recruited classes (Mahars, Telugus, Bhils, Bengalis, Moplahs). Although some results were not satisfactory (the Bengal regiment mentioned by O'Dwyer was so unsuitable and unreliable that it was not put into action in Europe), by and large they performed as well as the older classes:

The war has proved that all men are brave, that the humblest follower is capable of sacrifice and devotion; that the Afridi, who is outwardly the nearest thing to an impersonation of Mars, yields nothing in courage to the Madrasi Christian. . . . These revelations have meant a general levelling and the uplift of classes hitherto undeservedly obscure.[38]

For any who cared to examine the performance record—still available in the unit histories of nonmartial classes which participated in the war—it was clear that with adequate leadership and training virtually any group could be successfully employed somewhere in the military. Nevertheless, the system of recruiting the martial races persisted up until World War II. It was invoked in the developing debate over *swaraj* (home rule for India) and the retention of defense matters in the hands of the British, long after other political functions were turned over to Indians or shared with them.

Raising of Hope

The most significant by-product of India's great material and manpower contribution to the Allies in World War I was the pledges and promises offered by the British to the Indians. In retrospect it is clear that there were mixed motives behind these promises: they were a reward for past effort but were also inducement for further endeavor. As the need for Indian assistance declined with the termination of hostilities, elements in both the British and Indian governments procrastinated in fulfilling these pledges. Nowhere was this postponement more obvious and blatant than in the Indianization of the officer corps. At the height of the war Indians who held the Viceroy's

---

[38] Edmund Candler, *The Sepoy* (London: John Murray, 1919), pp. 1–2.

commission were made eligible for the King's commission. This eligibility for advancement was a direct inducement to the recruited classes to increase their effort in the war, although it meant little in practical terms. By the time an Indian was made a VCO he was already advanced in age: he could never hope to rise far as KCO, and would have been ill trained for a major promotion. Another significant step was taken in 1917, when ten vacancies at the Royal Military College, Sandhurst, were ordered reserved each year for suitable Indians. The British did not attempt to chart out the effect of these programs on the Indianization of the army as a whole. The King's commissions were reserved for "selected representatives of families of fighting classes which have rendered valuable services to the State during the War," that is, the martial races. Indianization was seen as a reward for services rendered, not as a process in the evolution of India toward self-government.[39]

These limited rewards for faithful service were announced the same year as another important policy was set down. The Secretary of State for India, Edwin Montagu, announced in the House of Commons:

The policy of His Majesty's government, with which the Government of India are in complete accord, is that of the increasing association of Indians in every branch of the administration, and the gradual development of self-governing institutions, with a view to the progressive realization of responsible government in India as an integral part of the British Empire.[40]

Shortly after the announcement Montagu visited India, and with the Viceroy, Lord Chelmsford, attempted to give effect to the statement:

[39] The quote and evaluation are from the Preliminary Draft Report of the Indianization Committee of 1938/39. The report, in manuscript form, is in File 601/12810/H of the Archives of the Ministry of Defense, Historical Section, Government of India. The Indianization Committee was appointed subsequent to a resolution adopted by the Legislative Assembly on September 2, 1938, calling for a reexamination of the process of Indianization. Although the committee sat, heard testimony, and did preliminary work on its report, its efforts were interrupted and then terminated by the outbreak of war.

[40] Reprinted in Philips, pp. 264–265. For a study of the background and implications of the declaration, see S. R. Mehrotra, "The Politics Behind the Montagu Declaration of 1917," in C. H. Philips, ed., Politics and Society in India (London: George Allen and Unwin, 1963), pp. 71–96.

It is not enough merely to assert a principle. We must act on it. The services of the Indian army in the war and the great increase in its numbers make it necessary that a considerable number of commissions should be given. . . . Race should no more debar him from promotion in the army than it does in the civil services. . . . We feel sure that no measures would do so much to stimulate Indian enthusiasm for the war.[41]

While in India, Montagu found Commander-in-Chief Sir C. C. Munro interested in the cause of Indianization but not enthusiastic over it. Munro had attempted to get Indian officers into service clubs (most of which resented their presence), but had his own ideas about recruitment. Montagu wanted to open up an Indian Sandhurst and enable any qualified Indian to obtain a commission. However, Munro stipulated that first priority should go to the sons of servicemen. According to Montagu, Munro and the military regarded the demand for commissions as "political."[42]

A start had been made. In addition to the quota of ten vacancies per year at Sandhurst some King's commissions were given to specially selected noncoms, officers, and graduates of the Cadet College, Indore. Major-General Iskander Mirza, who became president of Pakistan, was among those in the first category. The first Indian Commander-in-Chief of the Indian Army, General K. M. Cariappa, was in the latter group.[43]

Both methods of obtaining the King's commission were temporarily disastrous for the cause of Indianization: selection was not careful enough, and many of the first Sandhurst cadets were unprepared for life abroad. A series of accidents had the

[41] Great Britain, *Report on Indian Constitutional Reforms*, Cd. 9109 (1918), pp. 209–210.

[42] Edwin S. Montagu, *An Indian Diary*, Venetia Montagu ed., (London: Heinemann, 1930), pp. 201, 352 ff.

[43] Cariappa graduated from Daly College, Indore. He was one of thirty-nine cadets given the King's Commission in December, 1919. Cariappa was from a "martial class," (a Kodava from Coorg) which had supplied a few troops to the army. He was the first Indian graduate of Staff College (Quetta), the first to hold a Grade II appointment, and the first Indian battalion commander. A later Commander-in-Chief, General K. S. Thimmaya was a cousin of Cariappa. Another Coorgi, Cheppudira Ponnappa, retired as a brigadier in 1951. For details about Cariappa's life see I. M. Muthanna, *General Cariappa* (Mysore: Usha Press, 1964).

result that few cadets graduated successfully.[44] Above all there was no set policy for the pace and objective of Indianization. Only in 1928 was Indianization linked to the progress of India toward self-government and dominion status.[45]

POSTWAR RETRENCHMENT

After the termination of hostilities, the Indian Army reverted to its peacetime manpower level and there were second thoughts about some of the promises made concerning Indianization.

A decision had to be made which classes and castes would remain on the recruitment list, and which would be dropped. Apparently no serious thought was given to an army with a relatively wide base of recruitment. The number of sepoys in the Indian Army dropped from 500,000 in 1918 to 120,000 in 1923.[46] The cut was made almost entirely in the classes recruited for the first time during the war or among those who had formerly been recruited and dropped and newly recruited for the war. The Mahars had been recruited in 1914–1918, and after a brief period under two Madras battalions, were given their own unit, the 111th Mahars. To the consternation of the Mahar community, this unit was disbanded. Another untouchable class, the Mazbhi Sikhs, was similarly again recruited during the war and then gradually "retrenched" although the last Mazbhi unit was not disbanded until 1932. Bengalis, Madrassis, and non-Punjabis were most vulnerable to these cuts. Undoubtedly the increasing political awareness in Bengal and Madras influenced the termination of recruitment from these regions, although the Punjab was also no

---

44 During 1918–1926 only 243 Indians competed for 83 positions at Sandhurst. The Skeen Committee calculated that the dropout rate of Indians was 30 percent compared with only 3 percent for Britishers. Indian Sandhurst Committee, *Report*, Nov. 14, 1926. (Calcutta: Government of India, Central Publication Branch, 1927).

45 Speech of Lord Birdwood. India Legislative Assembly, *Debates* Vol. II (1928), March 8, 1928.

46 For specific figures by year and class see *Recruiting in India op. cit.*, and *The Army in India and its Evolution* (Calcutta: Supt. Government Printing, India, 1924), various appendices.

longer politically quiet. The increase in recruitment from the lower castes, and nonmartial regions which was repeated during World War II, seems to bear out the hypothesis of several scholars that participation in military affairs is closely related to the intensity of warfare and the rate of social change.[47] High intensity demanded greater numbers, and lower castes eventually get an opportunity to serve in the military, an opportunity which is denied to them during peacetime.

The major political issue which faced the British, however, stemmed not from the administrative decisions which rather automatically dropped nonmartial races, but from the political promises of intensified Indianization. After the termination of hostilities the British hedged on the promises made under the pressure of war. This retreat was the subject of a political dialogue between the British and those Indians still regarded as loyal to the British Raj.

The report of the Esher Committee (1920) indicated the wide disagreement between these groups.[48] The committee which had been appointed to examine the future of the military in India was composed of high-level British civilian and military officials and had two Indian members. It rejected increased democratic control over the military, proposed strengthening the Commander-in-Chief's position, rejected a broadly based recruitment pattern, and only cautiously encouraged an educational buildup which would qualify Indians for Sandhurst. While paying lip service to the 1917 declarations on the future status of India, the committee proposed little which would have actually led to an Indian officer corps. The question of Indianization was, in fact, evaded, except in the minutes by the two Indian members.

The minutes indicated the split in approaches to military matters between Indian moderates and the spokesmen for the martial classes. Sir Krishna Gupta criticized the committee

---

[47] For a discussion of this question see Stanislaw Andrzejewski, *Military Organization and Society* (London: Routledge and Kegan Paul, 1954). Also, Marion J. Levy, Jr., *Modernization and the Structure of Societies* (Princeton: Princeton University Press, 1966), II, 600–601.

[48] *Report of the Committee to inquire into the Administration and Organization of the Army in India*, Cmd. 943 (1920), [The Esher Committee].

for ignoring Indianization. He urged the opening up of all branches of the army to all Indians on the basis of ability alone. A short-service, self-reliant military organization, backed by an extensive territorial force, with a broad system of preservice military education was required to help "achieve this goal of national unity and full responsible government."[49]

On the other hand, Sir Umar Hayat Khan, a Punjabi landowner and a leader of Muslim conservatives, went even further than the British and urged extreme caution in any innovations in the military. His minute contained both direct and implied criticisms of Sir Krishna's argument; a long-service army, recruited exclusively from the martial races was best officered by Indian officers drawn from the same "reliable" martial races. Sir Umar Hayat, hardly an advocate of Indian self-reliance or independence, argued that maintaining and intensifying the present system was necessary for the political safety of the British, and for military efficiency.[50]

THE SIVASWAMY AIYER RESOLUTIONS

Fortunately for the growing number of progressive moderates interested in military affairs, the first Legislative Assembly under the new constitution sat after the Esher Committee's report had been released. Sir P. S. Sivaswamy Aiyer[51] took advantage of the opportunity and introduced fifteen resolutions on the Esher Committee's report at the end of the first Assembly. The resolutions present a clear picture of what sophisticated Indian moderates and liberals wanted in defense matters. The resulting debates on the resolutions give some indication of different attitudes.[52] Most members were absent from Calcutta at the end of the session, and the government lost its majority. After attempting to modify the resolutions

49 *Ibid.*, p. 103.
50 *Ibid.*, p. 101.
51 A leading moderate from Madras who maintained a consistent interest in military affairs for many years.
52 India, Legislative Assembly, *Debates*, Vol. I, Part 2 (1921). The debate was held on March 28, 1921.

by amendment, it gave up and accepted them almost *in toto*. The British later felt it was a "tactical" mistake.

One of Aiyer's resolutions called for restrictions on the uses of the Indian Army; that it be used for Indian defense, internal or external, but not as a British imperial police force. Another called for the substitution of a civilian Member in the Viceroy's Executive Council for the Commander-in-Chief, paralleling British practice. Other resolutions called for a cut in defense expenditures and covered minor matters which had been or were going to be adopted by the government in any case.

Two crucial resolutions led to extensive debate, and were to have serious political repercussions. The first, resolution no. 7, called for admission of Indians into all branches of the Indian military and suggested that "every encouragement should be given to Indians—including the educated middle classes—subject to the prescribed standards of fitness, to enter the commissioned ranks of the Army."[53] It also suggested that a quota of 25% of new King's commissions be reserved for Indians.[54] The second proposed the establishment of preliminary military training to prepare Indians for Sandhurst, and the establishment of an Indian Sandhurst.[55]

The latter resolution was accepted by the government. In an unusual intervention the Commander-in-Chief, General Henry S. Rawlinson, gave his support to the part of the resolution calling for Indian facilities for pre-Sandhurst training. Rawlinson also stated that he was eager to see facilities for higher military training established, especially for the sons of Indian officers. He inadvertently referred to the proposed institution as a "college," and his statement that at no distant date "we shall be able to establish a College on these lines as suggested in the Resolution" made it appear as though he expressly hoped that an Indian Sandhurst would be established.[56]

[53] *Ibid.*, p. 1739.
[54] *Ibid.*
[55] *Ibid.*, p. 1753.
[56] *Ibid.*, p. 1754.

This was not in fact his view, for he later explained that he had in mind an expanded version of the old Imperial Cadet College, which was not able to produce KCOs.

The resolution calling for increased commissions for Indians was amended by the government, with the strong support of the many Punjabi representatives, Sikhs and Muslims alike:

and in granting King's Commissions, after giving full regard to the claims to promotion of officers of the Indian Army who already hold the commission of His Excellency the Viceroy, the rest of the commissions granted should be given to cadets trained at Sandhurst. The general rule in selecting candidates for this training should be that the large majority of the selections should be from the communities which furnish recruits to the army and, as far as possible, in proportion to the numbers in which they furnish such recruits.[57]

The amendment carried by one vote. The alignment of debaters was not unexpected: on one side was a former British Indian Army officer who had served with Punjabi units, three Sikhs, and a Punjabi Muslim. Opposing the amendment was a former British Indian Army officer who had served in the technical services and sappers (Madras), a Bengali Muslim, and a Punjabi Hindu of a nonmartial caste.

The advocates of the amendment presented several reasons for drawing officers exclusively from the martial races. First, men of the martial races could only be handled by officers of the same race; they cited disastrous incidents in which VCOs of one race tried to command troops of another. Second, the martial races were entitled to the lion's share of the officer commissions, because they had made the greatest sacrifices in the war. Third, for financial reasons, it would be easier to recruit from the races presently serving than to attempt to search all of India for the right type of officer. Fourth, for disciplinary purposes it was necessary to assure recruits from the martial classes the possibility of promotion to officer status; sepoys were already grumbling that not enough King's commissions were going to Punjabis. Finally, they argued that the

[57] *Ibid.*

amendment did not rule out the possibility of a military career for sons of nonmilitary families, but only established a priority which was just and necessary.

The amendment aroused the representatives of the martial classes. Khan Sahib Mirza Mohammad Ikramulla Khan, for example, related how his father, his uncle, his brother, and his son had served the British loyally for years in the Indian Army. He explained that the army needed men from families such as his, for they possessed "the great military qualities of courage, perseverance and endurance which are the product of social heredity, of moral traditions: they are not to be learned in any school or from books."[58] How could the army be officered by "the sons of lawyers and shopkeepers and others who, whatever may be their virtues, those virtues are not the iron virtues of our old martial classes."[59]

The Sikhs were equally adamant. They felt strongly that when the time came for distributing commissions, those classes who had shed their blood were going to be shortchanged. Where were the nonmartial classes when the blood was flowing? One Sardar (Bhai Man Singh) ridiculed the "airy idealism" which held that India consisted of one nationality. He argued that India was made up of many classes and races, and not even among the martial races could men of one race officer troops of another.[60]

The opponents of the amendment and of selective recruiting pointed out many of the obvious flaws in these arguments. It was ludicrous to claim that martial classes could only be officered by members of the same class, for the British had been commanding all of the various classes for years, and no one seriously thought they could be dispensed with overnight. The Bengalis and nonmartial Hindus argued that their communities should get an opportunity for military service, as long as the selection was based on fair criteria. Equal competition should be allowed, regardless of community. They and others argued that men of merit should be made officers, whether

---

[58] *Ibid.*, p. 1742.
[59] *Ibid.*, p. 1743.
[60] *Ibid.*, p. 1746.

they were British or Indian, martial or nonmartial. Selection on this basis would be the best guarantee of maintaining discipline, even among martial troops. Proponents of equal opportunity in recruitment did not raise the question of rewarding the martial races for the extra loss of life and blood in World War I. This moral obligation on the part of the government was the weakest point in the progressives' argument. In their demand for commissions the representatives of the nonmartial races stressed the unity of the Indian nation, and denied the strictness of the division between classes. They argued that the nonmartial classes had as much suitable officer material as the martial classes, untapped and waiting to be used, and that officer commissions required skills for which birth was irrelevant. Both the traditionalists and gradualists could base their arguments on army efficiency.

When the government of India and the Commander-in-Chief accepted the Sivaswamy Aiyer resolutions, they committed themselves to their implementation. Severe obstacles to this implementation developed on both political and administrative levels: neither the British government nor the British officers in the Indian Army were happy with it. We shall examine the administrative problems raised by Indianization in Chapter VI, but we will discuss the political objections now.

Commander-in-Chief Rawlinson formed a military committee to implement the Indianization resolutions passed by the Legislative Assembly.[61] The committee proposed an immediate statement of intention to Indianize and a policy of progressive Indian self-reliance in defense matters, including the eventual replacement of British by Indian officers. In addition, it recommended that recruitment be broadened to include youths from the "new" India: professional and middle-class families were to be eligible, and were to be inducted into all branches of the army.

[61] The activities of Rawlinson's Military Requirements Committee are recorded in: Government of India, Army Dept., Proceedings, December, 1923, Nos. 85–112, subject: Indianization of the Indian Army. Ministry of Defense, Historical Section, Archives, File 601/10798/H.

These proposals—which merely detailed a resolution already accepted by the Government of India—were not satisfactory to the Home government. An alternative to the Rawlinson proposals was suggested by the Secretary in the Military Department of the India Office (Lieutenant-General Alexander Cobbe), and later supported by the Secretary of State for India, Viscount Peel.[62]

Cobbe revived all the stock arguments for restricting commissions: a large influx of Indians into the officer corps would have a "detrimental" effect on the "efficiency of the military machine." As proof, he cited incidents during World War I when Indian troops, deprived of their British leadership, showed a "tendency to deteriorate seriously and quickly . . . few, if any, Indians apparently having the natural aptitude for leadership possessed by the average Englishman." He neglected to point out that various Western armies had fared equally poorly after losing their officers, and that much of the French Army had, in fact, at one point, mutinied. Cobbe believed that the social structure of India would never permit a suitable combination of indigenous troops and officers:

It is an unfortunate fact that the fighting races of India, from which the Indian Army is recruited, are the very classes who are most backward as regards education, and on the other hand those classes whose educational qualifications are the highest are generally regarded as lacking in martial qualities.[63]

Cobbe argued that Indianization must proceed with great caution, and that Indians should not be given the King's commission. Instead, Indian officers might be limited to a few units or, better still, confined to a dominion force, composed of retired troops, with a British commander. British officers would be allowed to volunteer for this force, which would gradually replace the regular Indian Army. This plan would permit Indians to serve as officers and would avoid the embarrassment of Indians serving alongside British officers or,

---

[62] *Ibid.*, Cobbe Memorandum, September 14, 1921, and telegram November 29, 1921, Secretary of State to Viceroy.
[63] *Ibid.*, Cobbe Memorandum.

even worse, Indians commanding the few British ranks found in some units of the Indian Army.

The Cobbe scheme was received with dismay by the government of India. The Viceroy, Lord Reading, replied by telegraph that the Rawlinson plan had in effect been accepted publicly by the government of India. Indian opinion would not tolerate any backsliding on the Indianization issue, which the Viceroy called "the crucial test of our sincerity in the policy of fitting India to advance towards the goal of self-Government."[64]

This exchange—marked by the difference in perspective and priorities which so often characterized Home and Indian correspondence—was resolved in favor of the Viceroy. The idea of a dominion force was abandoned, and eight units were earmarked for the Indianization "experiment." The government had earlier partly fulfilled one resolution and established the Prince of Wales Royal Indian Military College in 1922. This was not, in fact, a college, but a pre-Sandhurst institution run along the lines of an English public school.[65]

The Indians were temporarily satisfied with these schemes. Preference was clearly to be given to youths from the martial classes, but nonmartial groups were eligible for commissions as well. However, Indians who were attentive to defense policy matters soon realized that there were serious flaws in Rawlinson's "eight-unit scheme."

To the members of the martial classes military service was more than a prestigious occupation—it bordered on a moral

---

[64] Ibid., Viceroy to Secretary of State, India, February 18, 1922.

[65] The British believed that a public school education in India was an absolute requirement for becoming an army officer if an education in Britain was impossible. This belief was paralleled by similar beliefs in regard to the I.C.S. and the Colonial Service. The British believed a public-school education particularly necessary for Indian boys whose upbringing had made them unsuitable for the rigors and self-discipline of army life. This belief was shared by Indians, and has been put into practice both in India and Pakistan; the R.I.M.C. (Royal Indian Military College) has been renamed Rashtriya (National) Indian Military College, and is the military-oriented public-school equivalent of the nearby Doon School. For a study of the public school in the Colonial Service see Robert Heussler, Yesterday's Rulers (Syracuse: Syracuse University Press, 1963).

obligation, and might also have been a path for religious fulfillment. Furthermore, the attitudes that we have characterized
as traditional militarism permeated several levels of the martial regions: lower castes tended to emulate the martial posture
of higher castes. As these castes became socially mobile they
sought places within the military on the basis of real or con-
trived martial traditions.

Under the Raj the spokesmen for the martial classes had a
powerful instrument of leverage: their loyalty and cooperation was vital if recruitment were to proceed smoothly and if
the sepoys were to remain loyal. The spokesmen did not need
to threaten noncooperation to obtain concessions from the
government. The government willingly reserved places in the
officer corps for their sons. The implied threat of noncooperation still exists to a lesser degree today—the bulk of India's
and Pakistan's armies are still recruited from the martial
classes. Electoral politics has enabled representatives of regional martial classes—whatever political party they belong to
—to press their demands and resist broadened recruitment on
the highest levels of government.

The other set of attitudes discussed in this chapter—the
instrumental gradualism—also persisted to the last decades of
the British Raj, and in a modified form still exists today.
Three men whose careers overlapped formed the core of this
attitude: P. S. Sivaswamy Aiyer, Motilal Nehru, and Pandit
H. N. Kunzru; Kunzru is still active, productive, and interested in military matters, despite his advanced age. Others
were almost as active: Mohammed Ali Jinnah (in the earlier
years of his career), Nirad C. Chaudhuri, Sir Umar Hayat
Khan, Dr. M. S. Moonje, Dr. Amarnatha Jha of Allahabad
University, and a handful more. Some of these men were occasionally taken into the confidence of the government, allowed to examine classified documents, and generally treated
with great respect, for they were in most cases highly regarded
by the British for their knowledge. Some of them, particularly
Motilal Nehru, were politically influential. Over the years a
small pool of expertise was built up outside of the official
circles of government and yet not closely linked with the vig-

orous elements of the nationalist movement. These men were on occasion able to mount knowledgeable attacks upon government policy, and because these attacks were well informed they were particularly embarrassing for the government. This group further provided an important link between the British-dominated government of India and the nationalist movement. The relatively loyal opposition of these gradualists to the British may have been scorned by the more militant nationalists, but their presence continually reminded the British that there were indeed "reasonable" Indians, and that compromise was necessary to maintain the fading power of the gradualists. Compromises in the area of military affairs—especially Indianization—may have appeared insignificant, but they did result in the creation of a small but well-trained contingent of Indian officers. Although few in number, they were able to replace the British with little loss of administrative efficiency.

Two institutions established by the British enabled the two sets of attitudes to the military to survive. The Legislative Assembly provided a haven for the loyal moderates. There they were treated with deference and respect, and their suggestions on military matters were politely received—if not always acted upon. As the nationalist movement grew, however, power of the moderates rapidly dwindled, and they spoke with growing bitterness as the years passed. Kunzru was clearly frustrated and even angered in his role in the ill-fated Indianization Commission of 1939.

The Indian Army itself was the second institution and the stronghold of the traditional militarists. With its links to the Indian countryside and its own fertile recruiting grounds it was a vehicle for the expression of grievances and the instrument for the fulfillment of growing aspirations among the recruited classes. The army protected the interests of these classes who reciprocated with an almost unbroken record of loyal, competent service. When this link was partly broken in World War II the effect was shattering to both parties.

A strong tie had been forged. The army in India was permanently linked to the state. The state protected and provided for the military sectors of Indian society, and the army was left free to perform its prime functions of defense and internal security. Allegiance to the army meant permanent allegiance to the state and the idea of a state. Ironically, the British grossly underestimated the desire on the part of Indians from nonmartial as well as martial classes to commit themselves to this relationship.

4

DEFENSE PROBLEMS AND THE NATIONALIST MOVEMENT

The link between traditional Indian militarism and moderate gradualism was the belief in the desirability and permanence of British rule. As the twentieth century progressed, both attitudes weakened. A series of developments—some external, some emerging from British policy, and some emerging from Indian political currents—combined to produce new perspectives. The result was the radicalization of Indian attitudes toward the British in India, and a reevaluation of the military.

By the beginning of the twentieth century British rule in India had caused numerous changes in Indian society, particularly in urban areas. Yet, political mechanisms for accommodating these changes were rudimentary, and the British did not understand the impact they were causing. A sector of India was becoming a "disequilibrated" social system (to use the terminology of Chalmers Johnson), and values and institutions were no longer in conjunction.[1] We have seen in Chapter III how the British accommodated some Indians, particularly the martial classes. The moderate, Westernized Indian also found a place within the Raj, although he was in an increas-

[1] Chalmers Johnson, *Revolutionary Change* (Boston: Little, Brown and Co., 1966), pp. 59 ff.

ingly uncomfortable position. The significant political and social development of the first two decades of the twentieth century in India, however, lay not in the political integration of these groups into the Raj, but the rise of new, unassimilable viewpoints.

Several events in a short time made many politically conscious Indians aware that the authority of the British was immoral. Some of these same events also revealed the vulnerability of the British.

The year 1905 symbolizes the watershed of British rule in India. During that year two important events occurred: Curzon's resignation and Japan's victory over Russia. In 1905 the Viceroy, Lord Curzon, was finally forced to resign and leave India as a result of the bitter personal and political feud with his Commander-in-Chief, Kitchener.[2] With Curzon the notion of benevolent imperialism died; his partitioning of Bengal, reorganization of the university system, and deliberate slighting of educated Indian opinion precipitated a bitter reaction to him and to British rule among the most modern regions and classes of Indian society. The Indians were particularly attentive to the struggle for power between Kitchener and Curzon, and clearly understood that the outcome of that struggle would affect the future of all Indians.

In Bengal, *pujas* (prayer ceremonies) of thanks were offered to the Goddess Kali. *The Daily Hitavadi* of Calcutta gloated over Curzon's humiliation:

Alas, brilliant Lord Curzon! When you first came to Bengal, the people of that province, with hearts laden under the spell of hope, expected only happiness at your hands, we could not imagine that such a sharp butcher's knife was hidden under the flow of honeyed words which fell from your lips.[3]

The *Amrita Bazar Patrika*, another important Bengali newspaper, gave Curzon some sympathy, but saw in the resignation

---

[2] For a study of the origins of this dispute in the context of British Indian civilian-military relations see Stephen P. Cohen, "Issue, Role and Personality: The Kitchener-Curzon Dispute," *Comparative Studies in Society and History*, (April 1968), 337–355.

[3] July 22, 1905, Native Newspaper Reports, Bengal, 1905, India Office Library.

the hand of justice; the English-language *Bengalee* weighed the prospects of military dictatorship and Curzon's "autocratic rule," and found the former more inviting.[4]

The rest of India was not so convinced of Curzon's evil character. Outside of Bengal the dispute was considered more on its merits, although Curzon had few friends in Bombay and Madras. Most moderate or liberal journals viewed the Kitchener-Curzon affair as harmful because of economic or political reasons. *Rast Goftar* (a Bombay Gujerati weekly with a Parsi editor) expressed a typical viewpoint:

> Once the Commander-in-Chief is free from all control, the military expenditure will expand, with the result that numerous measures of development and progress will have to be starved, and the country will, instead of advancing in prosperity and civilization, fall behind by fully half a century.[5]

The increased role of the military in administration and politics, and the increase in India's financial burden, were perceived as the replacement of an already uncomfortable paternalism. In the eyes of many Indians, the British had betrayed their responsibilities to India, as well as their own values and beliefs. The Kitchener-Curzon dispute demonstrated to observant Indians that the British were apt to quarrel among themselves, and that military power counted for a great deal in such a dispute. They saw that India's progress might not advance in a straight line as predicted by liberal British civilians, and even by Curzon. If Curzon was forced out by the military, how could Indians ever hope to control the military by peaceful means?

The second important event of 1905 occurred outside of India, but had a considerable impact on incipient revolutionary movements throughout Asia. In the spring and summer of 1905 the Japanese decisively defeated Russia, in a struggle for control over Korea. An Indian historian records: "In India, particular interest was shown over the outcome of the War,

---

4 August 22, 1905, Native Newspaper Reports, Bengal, 1905, India Office Library.

5 July 2, 1905, Native Newspaper Reports, Bombay, 1905, India Office Library.

not so much because of [the] fight over Korea, but because it was a victory of the so-called barbarians and uncivilized Asians over a major European power."[6] The speeches and writings of Indian politicians and publicists from 1905 onward repeated the theme that Japan was as appropriate a model for India as was Britain. Indians increasingly felt that they did not need slavishly to model their institutions after those of Britain, but that they now had an Asian example. That many character-istics of the Japanese system were not appropriate for Indian conditions was less important than the fact that Indians could now point to other "Asian" ways of modernization, and argue that the British path was not the only route to development. Psychologically, the defeat of the Russians served as an im-portant accelerator, offering hope where the Kitchener-Curzon dispute had offered despair. Japan had demonstrated that the technical and organizational prerequisites of nationhood were not confined to Caucasians. Indians might also move toward greater independence; they could be confident that they pos-sessed—or would soon possess—the necessary skills. This new exuberance and confidence, which had been slowly building, affected Indians of all political persuasions, but was particular-ly evident in the activities of Indian terrorists,[7] and Bal Gan-gadhar Tilak.

TILAK AND THE
INTENSIFICATION OF ATTITUDES

Tilak's role in the Indian revolutionary movement has been skillfully analyzed elsewhere.[8] We shall only point out the important role the military played in his political outlook. Tilak's approach to politics was more prophetic than that of any other Indian political figure of his generation. His public career represented a bridge between regional (Maharashtra)

---

[6] R. P. Dua, *The Impact of the Russo-Japanese (1905) War on Indian Politics* (Delhi: S. Chand, 1966), p. 1.

[7] For a survey of terrorist activities in India, see Gobinda Lall Bannerjee, *Dynamics of Revolutionary Movement in India* (Calcutta: Oxford Book Store, n.d. [c.1967]).

[8] See especially Stanley Wolpert, *Tilak and Gokhale* (Berkeley and Los Angeles: University of California Press, 1962).

traditional Hinduism, British and Western thought, and an all-India perspective. He systematically applied values and concepts derived from his traditional background to contemporary issues, including the role of the military in Indian society.

Tilak had a shrewd appreciation of the importance of power in politics:

There is only one medicine for all people. That medicine is power, take it into your possession; when it comes into your possession, if there be any disputes between you and us, we should be able to settle them. . . . We want power for settling disputes. It is not wanted for increasing them.[9]

Such power was properly the attribute of a special and important class, the Kṣatriyas, according to the *Manusmriti* (ancient laws of Manu).[10]

The Kṣatriyas defended the dominion and defended the people against internal interruptions. Where are those? The whole of that caste is gone off and their duties devolve upon the British.[11]

Not only the Kṣatriyas, but the Brahmins and the Vaishyas had been disfranchised by the British. A return to a traditional polity, according to Tilak, was vital for home rule.[12] Tilak's support of the British during the war was not, then, surprising. It offered the Indian people an opportunity to rebuild at least part of the traditional system (and, in terms of power, one of the most important parts) by offering them an opportunity to enlist. It was not only an opportunity but a duty. In a recruiting speech in Poona he pointed out:

If you want Home Rule be prepared to defend your Home. Had it not been for my age I would have been the first to volunteer. You cannot reasonably say that the ruling will be done by you and the *fighting for you*—by Europeans or Japanese, in the matter of Home Defense. Show . . . that you are willing to take advantage of the opportunity offered to you by the Viceroy to enlist in an Indian Citizens Army. When you do this, your claim for having

9 Speech at Ahmednagar, May 31, 1916, in Bal Gangadhar Tilak, *His Writings and Speeches* (Madras: Ganesh, 1918), pp. 169–170.
10 Speech at Cawnpore, Jan. 1, 1917. *Ibid.*, p. 242.
11 *Ibid.*, p. 243.
12 *Ibid.*

the commissioned ranks opened to you will acquire double weight.[13]

Tilak was not alone in regarding World War I as an opportunity for something more than an expression of loyalty to the British. At a wartime (1917) session of the Congress in Calcutta this mood was given blunt expression. In a resolution on military training a new theme in the young history of Indian interest in defense policy was developed. The mover of the resolution, J. N. Roy of Bengal, stated:

I happen to be one of those, who believe that we could do little with responsible government in this country if we have not military training at the same time (Hear, Hear). In fact, speaking for myself, had I a choice between responsible government and military training, I would unhesitatingly choose military training.[14]

Freedom and arms were India's birthright; self-government without self-defense was not enough. Congress, under the influence of the Bengali renaissance and Tilak's leadership had radically transformed its earlier supplicant attitude towards military service.

Indian nationalists belabored the military as "mercenary," and the charge is still often heard. The term was primarily used in attacking the foreign control of the military, and the division of control between the British-dominated government of India and the India Office in London. Despite several organizational subterfuges, Indian influence in defense matters remained minimal until the end of British rule.

But on another level, the charge that the military was mercenary was more personal and bitter. No one better realized that the military is the ultimate sanction available to a government than the nationalist leaders who witnessed the military in "aid to the civil" operations and in the suppression of legitimate protests and meetings.

The Amritsar massacre was not the first or last such operation, only the most notorious.[15] The event did, however, draw

[13] Speech at Poona, n.d., *ibid.*, p. 365.
[14] *Proceedings of the Thirty-Second Indian National Congress*, (Calcutta: December, 1917), speech moving Resolution Six.
[15] Much has been written on the cause and political effects of the Amritsar Massacre. Virtually every Indian and British figure of note has at some time

attention to the Gurkhas, who in the eyes of the nationalists were the ultimate in mercenaries as they were not even Indians. Indians of all political hues—except those representing a particular caste or class—called for representative military service; if necessary, through universal conscription. Japan and Russia were early models:

What is the Army in Russia? It is a national army. It is the army of Russian peasants officered by Russians. Any amount of expenditure in the face of a common danger will not be grudged. What is our army? I have not the slightest hesitation in saying that our army is a mercenary army employed by foreigners to put down their own countrymen, and to keep them under foreign heels. Surely no self-respecting nation will without compulsion contemplate such a contingency as having to pay for a mercenary army in order to remain under control by an alien Government.[16]

In considering the relationship between the army and an independent India, Indians inevitably came to think of the army as a means for independence. What amazed (and discouraged) many was the effectiveness of the army in maintaining British power and its imperviousness to political influence. An underground war was waged between the British and Indians who tried to infiltrate the services for revolutionary or subversive purposes. All evidence indicates success for the British. Disruptions and problems occurred, but only illustrate the ineffectiveness of the infiltration and its dependency on nonpolitical factors.

Failures in Control

Most breakdowns in control of the military followed a pattern.[17] Local social or political issues, or some purely military grievance, created discontent in one area, and this discontent was sometimes exploited by agitators in the unit or with access to it. We have noted the British difficulties in recruiting

---

commented upon the incident. For an introduction, see Rupert Furneaux, *The Amritsar Massacre* (London: George, Allen and Unwin, 1963).

[16] Speech in 1928, reprinted in Motilal Nehru, *The Voice of Freedom* (Bombay: Asia Publishing House, 1961), pp. 349–350.

[17] For a discussion of the importance of military revolts in political revolutions see Chalmers Johnson, *op. cit.*

Sikhs during World War I: this community had been un-settled by the budding Akali reform movement and by the growing political activity in the Punjab. Returning Sikh sol-diers brought with them new ideas and a new understanding of the role of the Punjab in maintaining British power. Many were also impressed by the liberal treatment given French colonial troops, particularly the greater opportunities of these troops to rise to officer and command positions.[18] It was a startling discovery for men who had been repeatedly told that they were still years away from controlling their own army.

Upon their return to the Punjab many Sikh soldiers found a place in the growing Akali movement, and swelled its ranks with disciplined, trained fighters. The Akalis took special care to press their propaganda on Sikh soldiers on active duty. According to several British officers, there was much trouble with infiltrators and sympathizers. After the Nankana massacre in February 1921, black Akali *safas* (headbands) appeared in Sikh units. The massacre was followed later in the same year by the affair of the "Keys of the Golden Temple," and "for the first time in the history of this agitation recruiting officers reported difficulty in obtaining Jat Sikhs for the Army."[19]

Ultimately, whole villages which were known to be sym-pathetic with the Akali movement had to be blacklisted for several years for recruiting purposes, and every effort was made (most unsuccessfully) to keep Akalis out of the army. The Kirti movement and the Nau Jawan Bharat Sabha also emerged, and both eventually became linked to other revolu-tionary movements.

Apart from the Akalis, apparently no other nationalist group made a sustained effort to infiltrate or subvert the army. Occasional efforts were made by the Communist party of India in later years, but these were quickly detected by the British. The Akalis may have had an effect on the recruitment of Jat

[18] Interviews with several retired British Indian Army officers. See also Lieutenant-General D. R. Thapar, *The Morale Builders* (Bombay: Asia Pub-lishing House, 1965), p. 44.

[19] Maj. A. E. Barstow, *Sikhs* (Calcutta: Government of India Central Pub-lishing Branch, 1928), p. 44.

Sikhs in World War II, although the growing prosperity of the Punjab due to rapidly rising agricultural prices played a greater role.

The most notorious loss of control occurred at Peshawar on April 23 and 24, 1930, when two platoons of the Royal Garhwal Rifles "mutinied."[20] The so-called mutiny consisted of two separate but related incidents. On April 23, a company of Garhwalis was used in an "aid to the civil" venture in Peshawar. The Garhwalis were called on to face a large mob for several hours, during which time they were taunted and pelted with missiles. Several suffered injuries (their British captain was wounded and removed to a hospital), and they were required to remove the incinerated body of a British soldier attacked by the crowd. Under strict orders not to open fire without permission they were left in an untenable position. They had not been ordered to fire even in self-defense, and could not have been given such an order in any case because no responsible British officer or civilian magistrate was present. They were eventually relieved by a British unit.

On the next day, according to the Court of Enquiry, the company was insulted in a classic example of mishandling by their new British commander, and ordered in and out of waiting trucks. Some Garhwali NCOs were reprimanded and punished by the commanding officer of the battalion. One platoon submitted a petition asking for their immediate discharge, and later in the day two other platoons refused to board their busses for further duty in Peshawar. The platoons were peacefully disarmed, and no further incident occurred.

The Court of Enquiry found seventeen Garhwalis guilty in varying degrees and sentenced them to imprisonment or transportation. It severely reprimanded the company's havildar major for failing to report that two of his NCOs were members of a suspicious "religious sect," the Arya Samaj, and censured several British officers for permitting the Garhwali

---

[20] Most of the following is from: India Office Library, Military Collection, file No. 159/17, "Insubordination, Mutiny; Mutiny of the 2/18th Garhwal Rifles," and especially the Court of Enquiry held at Abbotobad and Peshawar between April 28 and May 7, 1930.

unit to deteriorate. The court determined that using the troops improperly as police units was the primary cause of the mutiny, but also noted the impact of "seditious propaganda" and the close contact the troops had allegedly had with disaffected or "actively seditious elements in cantonment areas." The court recommended a careful review of "aid to the civil" operations and greater care in isolating the soldier from political activity. Further, the court commented on the "psychology of the Garhwali soldier": a staunch, brave, and uncomplaining man, "blindly obedient to all orders and easily led. Slow in the uptake and in realizing exactly what is required of him when suddenly faced with an entirely novel situation." These attributes made him especially dependent upon his British officers, who in this case had failed him.[21]

The findings of the court were not made public, and Indians and Britishers alike who were not closely connected with the affair at Peshawar regarded the Garhwali Mutiny as highly important. They believed that the Garhwalis had been infected with political ideas. If other units could be similarly motivated, they might also revolt. If the army could not be trusted to control politically inspired crowds the entire fabric of army discipline and ultimately British rule might be unraveled with relative ease. These expectations were short-lived. Although many rumors circulated, no other military unit suffered a serious breach of discipline until the Indian National Army (I.N.A.), was created in World War II. In fact, the Garhwali Regiment's own official version of the mutiny—based upon intelligence police, and army records, as well as those of the Court of Enquiry—concludes that there was no evidence of outside influence in the battalion.[22] It noted that the two platoons which had been misused in Peshawar were number two and number three, but the platoons which had

[21] Court of Enquiry, "Findings," p. vi. One British officer who commanded a Garhwali battalion claims that "Garhwalis are dice" and must be led skillfully. He shared the Court's view of the cause of the mutiny. Interview, London, 1963.

[22] Lieutenant-General Sir Ralph B. Deedes, ed., *Historical Record of the Royal Garhwal Rifles*, Vol. II, 1923–1947 (Dehra Dun: The Army Press, 1962), pp. 20 ff. This history implies that the Court of Enquiry deliberately overlooked evidence incriminating some senior Garhwali VCOs.

actually refused to obey orders on the following day were number one and number four; it also claimed that the Arya Samaj link was nonexistent, and that the real instigator of the mutiny may have been an Indian VCO—the subedar of platoon number four—who was never punished. His grudge was personal, not political.

During World War II several unsuccessful attempts were made to infiltrate the ranks of the military. Occasional rumors of court martials and secret trials reached the public, but unrest was minimal, and loyalty persistent, especially after the war had taken a favorable turn. Exceptions occurred in Bengal and Bihar where revolutionary activity was intense; however, it tended to be blunted on the unsophisticated jawan:

There was no sedition in my unit, and the only case I heard about was phoney; a group of sepoys in Bengal were being paid one rupee per day to attend political meetings, but they could not even understand the language! They were sacked anyway.[23]

The one major scare in the postwar period occurred when units of the Royal Indian Navy revolted in 1946, and held control of Bombay harbor for several days.[24] The origins of this mutiny were not ideological, but rested in a clumsy and heavy-handed effort to deal with complaints about food and service conditions. After the mutiny began, members of the Communist party of India joined the mutineers and attempted to steer them onto a political course. Sardar Patel, fearing a Communist uprising, urged the British to crush the mutiny with force, but contact was established between Aruna Asaf Ali, who had joined the mutineers, and Jawaharlal Nehru, who was shortly to become de facto prime minister. After having some of their demands met, and after a promise of a fair hearing, the mutineers peacefully turned over their arms.

Terrorism, infiltration, and subversion were never effective political instruments in India. They alerted the British without materially damaging the administration. The failure of the military to participate in the nationalist revolution was

23 Interview with a retired British Indian Army brigadier, 1963.
24 One account, vigorously anti-British, is in Kusum Nair, *The Army of Occupation* (Bombay: Padma Publications, 1946), pp. 40 ff.

particularly important, but it was not surprising. While marginal sectors of the Indian nationalist movement attempted to infiltrate the military, the most powerful nationalist leaders rejected this path to power. Even the one great leader who did find the military attractive—Subhas Chandra Bose—had to wait until fortuitous circumstances placed him at the head of a nationalist army in 1942.

SUBHAS CHANDRA BOSE AND THE LEGITIMATION OF MILITARISM

Tilak's political philosophy and background were strongly traditional; Subhas Bose represents the transition to a "modern" political style, encompassing modern militarism as well. Historically, traditional militaristic beliefs were not strong in Bengal, although Nirad Chaudhuri traces "vicarious militarism" to the nineteenth-century Hindu renaissance, which began in Bengal, and finds evidence of Western militaristic themes in the renaissance Bengali novels.[25]

Subhas Bose did not revive this military tradition—that was the accomplishment of the terrorists—he altered it, and led those who believed in the value and usefulness of violence until his death in 1945. Remarkably, he stayed within the context of the Indian National Congress until his open break with Gandhi in 1938. Before World War II, he was undoubtedly as prominent a leader as Nehru, and had he survived, he would have become a serious threat to Nehru's leadership in free India.

Bose's career was prototypical of the development of a militaristic approach to political activity. He was raised in a Bengali family (in Orissa) at a time when the cult of the pistol was at its height. As a Bengali, he felt the British ridicule of the Bengalis for their alleged nonmartial, unmanly traits. This ridicule was expressed in many ways, but particularly by the lack of opportunities for Bengali youths to receive military training or participate in the defense of India. Bose's

---

[25] Nirad C. Chaudhuri, *The Continent of Circe* (New York: Oxford University Press, 1966), p. 103.

autobiography is peppered with examples of this nature: Anglo-Indian boys in Bengal could join the Volunteer Corps, but Bengali boys were excluded, even if they stood at the top of their class.[26] British soldiers were even worse than British civilians in insulting Indians on tramcars and railways.[27] Later, when Bose went to school at Cambridge, he led an unsuccessful campaign to get Indian undergraduates admitted to the University Officers' Training Corps.[28]

Two experiences forced Bose to "develop politically and to strike out an independent line for myself." The first was a series of unpleasant encounters in public places between Indians and Britishers—in tramcars, railways, and public streets. Bose records that since the law did not protect the Indians in interracial disputes, Indians began literally to hit back.

> The effect was instantaneous. Everywhere the Indian began to be treated with consideration. Then the word went round that the Englishman understands and respects physical force and nothing else. This phenomenon was the psychological basis of the terrorist-revolutionary movement—at least in Bengal.[29]

The second experience that shook Bose's political consciousness also concerned the use of force. He reconsidered his moral philosophy, just before World War I, and the war provided the final catalyst. He had earlier accepted the notion that the defense of India might be left to the British while internal politics could increasingly come under the control of Indians: this assumption was now challenged.

> Was it possible to divide a nation's life into two compartments and hand over one of them to the foreigner, reserving the other to ourselves? . . . The answer that I gave myself was a perfectly clear one. If India was to be a modern civilized nation, she would have to pay the price and she would not by any means shirk the physical, the military, problem. Those who worked for the country's emancipation would have to be prepared to take charge of both the civil and military administration. Political freedom was

[26] Subhas Chandra Bose, *An Indian Pilgrim* (reprint ed.; Bombay: Asia Publishing House, 1965), p. 23.
[27] *Ibid.*, p. 65.
[28] *Ibid.*, p. 91.
[29] *Ibid.*, pp. 65–66.

indivisible and meant complete independence of foreign control and tutelage. The war had shown that a nation that did not possess military strength could not hope to preserve its independence.[30]

Bose was expelled from Calcutta University for a year. While he was waiting to resume his studies, he tried to obtain military training. As a concession to vocal Bengali sentiment to allow Bengalis to participate in the war (and remove the nonmartial label) the military had instituted a Bengali regiment. Bose attempted to join but was rejected because of poor eyesight, first by an Indian doctor and then by a British military doctor. He returned to his studies in 1917, but "soon found something to add some spice" to his daily life. He joined the Calcutta University branch of the newly formed India Defense Force (equivalent to the British Territorial Army). He thoroughly enjoyed the experience: "What a change it was from sitting at the feet of anchorites to obtain knowledge about God, to standing with a rifle on my shoulder taking orders from a British army officer!"[31] Bose found that the training gave him something which he needed or lacked: a "feeling of strength and of self-confidence" which steadily grew; as a soldier he had access to Fort William, and was treated with respect by government officials.

Bose's interest in the military and militarylike behavior did not wane as he became a powerful political figure, first in Bengal and then in all India. Perhaps the most notorious incident was his organization of a volunteer corps during the Congress session in Calcutta in 1928. The corps was outfitted with military uniforms, and Bose designated himself commanding officer, replete in a uniform made by one of Calcutta's leading military tailors. The gesture was hardly appreciated by Gandhi.

Bose's interest in militarylike organizations and dress reflected his deep political differences with other Congress leaders, especially Gandhi and Nehru. He differed fundamentally with Congress leadership on the nature of British opposition to Indian independence. Gandhi and Nehru were imbued with

30 *Ibid.*
31 *Ibid.*, p. 80.

British liberalism and understood it thoroughly. They sought to direct their appeal for independence to this liberalism. Bose stressed the obverse side of the British Raj. He argued that the political development of Bengal revealed the true nature of British rule, as well as the proper Indian response. The Bengalis were the first to taste British rule, and they were the first to develop a revolutionary movement to break that rule. The revolutionary movement was "born out of a conviction that to a Western people physical force alone makes an appeal," and therefore Indians must learn how to use force to break British rule.[32] Through skilled employment of violence India could be freed, and through the unity forged in a violent revolution the Indian people themselves would be purged and elevated. As we shall see in Chapter VI, circumstances actually put Bose in command of an army—the Indian National Army—which was dedicated to freeing India by force of arms. Bose and the I.N.A. failed, but he remains the prime example of one who saw organized violence as a desirable end in itself, as well as a means of freeing India.

MAHATMA GANDHI

Gandhi's political success was in large part due to his ability to offer a promising path between the futile violence and extremism of Tilak, and the ineffective constitutionalism of the so-called moderates. The philosophy of nonviolent resistance to evil promised action and occasionally brought success; very few of Gandhi's colleagues actually shared his philosophical convictions, but many were willing to suspend criticism and follow his political leadership.

Although Gandhi believed in nonviolence, he was not an absolute pacifist. In a famous and seminal article, "The Doctrine of the Sword" (1920), Gandhi made his position clear: if pacifism meant cowardice, then he was for violence, although he preferred nonviolent resistance to violence. Fur-

32 *The Indian Struggle* (reprint ed.; Bombay: Asia Publishing House, 1964), p. 300.

ther, he argued, to forgive one's opponent is "infinitely superior" and more manly than to punish him, and soldiers might well be admired when they conducted themselves in the spirit of forgiveness.[33] This spirit of charity toward those who bear arms was not a temporary sentiment, but was held by Gandhi until his death. In 1925 Gandhi had no objection to those serving in the military if they "believe in the necessity of the use of arms."[34] He was, however, vigorously opposed to compulsory military training under any circumstances, regardless whether it was a nonnational government such as the British, or a national government.[35] The discipline and organization of the military greatly attracted Gandhi; he disliked the "brutalizing" features of the military but felt that its better qualities could be adopted profitably by peaceful organizations.[36] One of the worst features of the army was that those who served in it (under the British) had no choice whom they would fight. When *swaraj* came, he hoped the soldiers would not be "hirelings" but would "form the national militia for defensive and protective purposes alone. They will have a voice in the moulding of the affairs of the nation."[37]

But Gandhi saw a use for the military on a more important battlefield than that of war. In 1946 he wrote:

If *Swaraj* is round the bend, we can now look upon the military as ours and need have no hesitation in taking all the constructive work we can from them. Up till now they have only been employed in indiscriminate firing on us. Today they must plough the land, dig wells, clean latrines and do every other constructive work that they can, and thus turn the people's hatred of them into love.[38]

Like Punjab officers almost a hundred years earlier Gandhi saw a means by which nation and army might be brought closer together. And, as in Hodgson's time, a great calamity in-

[33] Gandhi, *My Non-Violence* (Ahmedabad: Navajivan Publishing House, 1960), p. 3.
[34] *Young India*, September 24, 1925.
[35] *Ibid.*
[36] *Harijan*, June 9, 1946.
[37] *Young India*, October 27, 1921.
[38] *Harijan*, April 21, 1946.

terrupted any step toward positive nonmilitary employment of the army.

Gandhi had some support for his proposals among civilians, but none in the military. In a widely read study of the military in India it was suggested that the military be stripped of all police duties and given nation-building tasks to make it popular throughout the country.[39] Among Indian officers, however, such a proposal was anathema. They were willing to drop the police functions although many believed the police themselves were not strong enough to bear the burden, but no military men thought that dam-building (let alone latrine-cleaning), would be feasible or desirable.[40] The issue arose again in India and Pakistan in recent years. We shall examine the political and military problems associated with public service and civic action programs in Chapter VII.

JAWAHARLAL NEHRU AND THE REJECTION OF THE MILITARY

Tilak, Bose, and Gandhi in varying ways admired the military. Jawaharlal Nehru rejected the military: although not a pacifist, he found too much in the military mind which appalled him; he saw too much horror in war for it to appeal to him. Nehru simply rejected the military and militarism as viable instruments or targets for the nationalist movement. His ambition was political control, which he assumed would bring control of the military; until Indian independence came it would not be necessary to deal extensively with military problems.

[39] Brij. Narain, *Post-War Planning of the Indian Defense Services* (New Delhi: Indian Institute of International Affairs, 1946), pp. 5 ff.

[40] General K. M. Cariappa's biographer records Cariappa's respectful dismay with the Mahatma and his ideas. See I. M. Muthanna, *General Cariappa* (Mysore: Usha Press, 1964), pp. 2–7. This view parallels the attitude of many professional soldiers in other nations towards "civic action" work. For a discussion of the theoretical bases for resistance to such a role see Samuel P. Huntington, *The Soldier and the State* (Cambridge: The Belknap Press, 1957), and for an examination of some of the institutional and practical bases for resistance see Willard F. Barber and C. Neale Ronning, *Internal Security and Military Power* (Columbus: Ohio State University Press, 1966), pp. 77–83.

Nehru believed in nonviolence as a tactic, not as an end in itself. In commenting upon Gandhi's article, "The Doctrine of the Sword," Nehru was careful to clarify his own position:

We were all moved by these arguments, but for us and for the National Congress as a whole the nonviolent method was not, and could not be, a religion or an unchallengeable creed or dogma. It could only be a policy and a method promising certain results, and by those results it would have to be finally judged. Individuals might make of it a religion or incontrovertible creed. But no political organization, so long as it remained political, could do so.[41]

Nehru was even more vehement in his rejection of the military as an organization and of war as an endeavor. Both of them brutalized and dehumanized mankind:

How different was the behavior of a person acting as an individual and obeying his own impulses from his behavior as an official or a unit in any army! The soldier, stiffening to attention, drops his humanity and, acting as an automaton, shoots and kills inoffensive and harmless persons who have done him no ill.[42]

And again,

The soldier is bred in a different atmosphere, where authority reigns and criticism is not tolerated. So he resents the advice of others, and, when he errs, he errs thoroughly and persists in error. For him the chin is more important than the mind or brain.[43]

Nehru argued that the social utility of war reflected and produced the crippled minds of those who engaged in it:

When there is conflict between races and countries even an attempt at impartiality is considered a betrayal of one's own people. . . . The mind coarsens and becomes closed to almost all avenues of approach except one. . . . Truth hides somewhere at the bottom of the deepest well and falsehood, naked and unashamed, reigns almost supreme.[44]

Nehru took little interest in the Indianization of the army,

---

41 *Toward Freedom* [Nehru's autobiography] (reprint ed. of 1941 publ.; Boston: Beacon Paperback, 1958), p. 82.

42 *Ibid.*, pp. 3–4.

43 *Ibid.*, p. 284.

44 *The Discovery of India* (reprint of 1947 publ.; London: Meridian Books, 1960), p. 287.

defense organization, or recruitment problems before he became Prime Minister. He scorned those who were interested
in Indianization as being motivated by "jobbery" rather than
real concern for the vital political, social, and economic problems facing the Indian people.[45] He disagreed with those—
including his own father—who felt that a major effort had to
be made to fill key civilian and military administrative positions in preparation for independence. To Jawaharlal Nehru
the complete withdrawal of British military control was a
prerequisite for India's freedom, partial steps avoided the real
issue.[46] Similarly, he had little interest in the attempts to infiltrate the Indian Army and weaken it with nationalist
propaganda. Nehru correctly interpreted the Garhwali Mutiny as an isolated incident, unlikely to be repeated elsewhere
in the Indian Army, although he incorrectly saw political
motives behind the Garhwalis' behavior. He thought that the
Garhwalis held the mistaken notion that the British power
was collapsing, but as we have already noted, the Garhwalis
were apolitically motivated. Nehru was even critical of Bose's
I.N.A., although he defended some I.N.A. officers against
brutality charges.[47]

Jawaharlal Nehru's disinterest in military affairs was historically important, because he was representative of liberal,
intellectual Indian thought, and because he played a key role
in shaping that thought. It was a rare Indian intellectual who
could find anything to admire in the British Indian Army or
its theories of the martial races. Nirad C. Chaudhuri was an
exception, and in the midst of arguing for a patriotic national
army he conceded the effectiveness of martial-race recruitment.[48] His position was atypical. In the fastidious minds of
most intellectuals the notion that men fought for the love of
fighting was an evil proposition, but systematically to exploit
such bloodthirstiness was doubly wrong. Only a very few
intellectuals and politicians ever came to an adequate under-

45 *Toward Freedom*, p. 208.
46 *Ibid.*, p. 271.
47 *Ibid.*, p. 161.
48 Nirad C. Chaudhuri, "The 'Martial Races' of India," *The Modern Review*
(Calcutta), Part III [of four], XLIX, (January, 1931), 67–79.

standing of the military organization and of the peculiar problems of recruitment in India. For most of them—including Nehru—the military remained barbaric and mercenary.

THE DEVELOPMENT OF
DEFENSE EXPERTISE

Moderate and traditionalist interest in defense matters did not wane as tension grew in Indian politics. It became clear that independence would not be won through the political or intellectual conversion of the tiny Indian segment of the commissioned-officer corps. It was also clear that should independence ever come, India would need a cadre of indigenous, competent officers. A handful of defense "experts" emerged in the interwar period, and with fitful support from the Congress and the major political parties, kept up the pressure on the British to fulfill the pledges of Indianization.

The pressure was justified, for the British were systematically trying to delay the Indianization process. The "eight-unit scheme" announced by Rawlinson in 1923 would have required twenty-two or twenty-three years to Indianize those few experimental units. Even then Indians would be competing against each other for many years. The units could not absorb all the junior Indian officers being made available, for the output of Sandhurst was much greater than the eight-units' wastage and promotion schedules. Despite this procrastination, the policy of segregating Indians into separate units was maintained.

An official committee appointed in 1925, composed of Motilal Nehru, Jinnah, and other leading Indians as well as a British contingent at first appeared to be a device for convincing the Indians of the correctness of the British view. Instead, the committee proposed a drastic increase in the number of Indian officers, the establishment of an Indian Sandhurst, and the abolition of the eight-unit scheme.[49] The government, taken aback by the liberality of its own officers, waited almost two years and then declined to accept the unanimous recom-

[49] Indian Sandhurst Committee, *Report*, pp. 23–28.

mendations. Instead, it doubled the number of places reserved for Indians at Sandhurst from ten to twenty. However, the eight units being Indianized were already packed with Indian officers on the lower levels. This problem was met by eliminating the intermediate VCOs in these units and appointing new KCOs to their jobs. In this way, the three-to-one odds of an Indian reaching the rank of lieutenant-colonel were reduced to eight-to-one, confirming in the minds of Indian officers their inferior and segregated status.

The next wave of political pressure came in the Defense Subcommittee on the Indian Round Table Conference, and again the government of India yielded. It increased the intake of Indian officers to sixty per year. The "experiment" of Indianization was widened to cover an eighth of the Indian Army, but this increase was still far from adequate to absorb the increased number of officer candidates without pushing officers down to the platoon level of command in the early stages of their career.

As part of the Defense Subcommittee's recommendations, an Indian military college committee had been appointed to work out the details of establishing an Indian Sandhurst. This institution, the Indian Military Academy (IMA), opened at Dehra Dun in the autumn of 1932. From this date Indians were no longer eligible for Sandhurst. The IMA's capacity was sixty regular Indian Army cadets and twenty for the Indian State Forces. The length of training was fixed at two-and-a-half years, somewhat longer than that at Sandhurst. A Dehra Dun graduate was called Indian Commissioned Officer (ICO). This commission was only valid in India, and carried lower rates of pay and allowances than those received by the Sandhurst Indians with the King's Commission.

A comprehensive statement of moderate nationalist thought on Indian military problems was contained in the Nehru report, prepared in 1928.[50] This report was conceived as an

---

[50] Official title: All Parties Conference, *Report on the Committee appointed by the Conference to determine the principles of the Constitution of India* (Allahabad: All-India Congress Committee, 1928). See also, All Parties Conference, 1928, *Supplementary Report of the Committee* (Allahabad: A.I.C.C., 1928).

Indian answer to the Simon Commission, an all-British committee of enquiry examining India's political progress. Although the report took the name of Motilal Nehru, many sections dealing with defense and military affairs were written by Sir Tej Bahadur Sapru, a noted liberal leader. The report makes a firm commitment to liberalism, democracy, and responsible government, and many of its recommendations were adopted as soon as Indians took power almost twenty years later.

The fundamental quarrel of the report with British rule in India was stated in forthright terms:

The real conflict lies between two sets of ideas—the democratic and the autocratic. We seek to establish a democratic form of government. Our English critics, long used to unfettered autocracy in India, cannot swallow this democratic pill, in spite of their loudly expressed enthusiasm for democracy nearer home.[51]

In the opinion of the moderate nationalists the "Oriental" constitution desired by Whitehall was synonymous with continuation of British autocracy. They reaffirmed their belief that democracy was the only form of government desirable for India, rejecting both "Oriental" and Western autocratic forms.[52]

In keeping with their desire for democracy, the authors of the Nehru report paid considerable attention to the role of the military in India. Motilal Nehru and others had waged an unsuccessful running battle in the Legislative Assembly trying to get information and concessions from the Commander-in-Chief. Consequently, one of their prime recommendations was

the transfer of the control over the Indian army with the necessary guarantees for the pay, emoluments, allowances and pensions of the officers. We believe that the representation of the army in the legislature by a responsible minister, who will, in actual administration, no doubt be guided by expert advice, is bound to lead to the establishment of more intimate relations between the army and the legislature.[53]

51 *Supplementary Report*, pp. 7–8.
52 *Ibid.*, p. 8.
53 *Report*, pp. 13–14.

They hoped that a civilian minister could make more progress in Indianizing the army, for they (correctly) perceived that the greatest resistance on this issue was concentrated in the military.[54]

The Nehru report also made suggestions concerning the formulation of defense policy, the most original of these being the idea of a high-level combined civilian-military Committee of Defense. "The functions of this committee shall be to advise the government and the various departments concerned with questions of defense and upon general questions of policy." The Nehru report added that special attention might be given by the committee to the problem of reducing defense expenditures, "retrenchment," in the then current terminology.[55] The committee was to be composed of nine persons: the Prime Minister, the civilian Minister of Defense, the Minister of Foreign Affairs, the Commander-in-Chief, the commanders of the air force and navy, the Chief of the General Staff, and two other experts, presumably civilian secretaries in key ministries, or additional military personnel. Although this "strategic legislature" was made up of high-level personnel, it was an advisory body, but presumably its deliberations would be acted upon. Apparently those who drafted the report wanted to avoid the imposition of a body containing nonelected military members on the government. The present defense advisory body in India, the Defense Committee of the Cabinet, has no outsiders on it, although the more recently established National Defense Council—a sounding board—does.[56]

---

[54] The Sapru Committee of 1944 also proposed a civilian defense minister, see Standing Committee of the Non-Party Conference of 18th and 19th November 18 and 19, 1944, *Constitutional Proposals of the Sapru Committee* (Bombay: Padma Publications, 1945).

[55] *Report*, para. 75 (a), (c), (d), p. 120.

[56] Fears of a military takeover were never justified. No Commander-in-Chief after Kitchener had his power and charisma. The military was increasingly tied down by the tight budgetary controls of the civil service. According to Philip Mason (Interview, 1963), the civil service was bound to the military in a relationship similar to that of Rajput warriors and their Brahmin advisors, or Mughal administrators and soldiers. Field-Marshal Auchinleck characterized the post-Kitchener years in this way: "The Kitchener tradition did not remain: it was not an autocracy. The Commander-in-Chief was tied

Motilal Nehru, Jinnah, Sivaswamy Aiyer, Amarnath Jha, and later H. N. Kunzru, were not only interested in Indianizing the officer corps and promoting equalitarian recruitment to the ranks, they were also concerned with the nationalization of the Indian military. After the British demonstrated how selective they would be in choosing candidates for Sandhurst, these men became aware of the intimate connection between the character of the officer corps—even if Indian—and the achievement of independence or some form of dominion status. For Indian political control to be effective, Indians would have to constitute a large percentage of the officer corps as well as be sympathetic and willing to work with Congress. The pressing demand for an Indian military college was motivated not only by a desire to increase the numbers of Indian officers—important as this was—but to change their training grounds and perhaps their political outlook. A professional military education was costly, and few scholarships were available. Only the wealthiest families could afford to send their sons to Sandhurst for several years. An Indian academy promised to be cheaper, and Indian leaders hoped that the candidates would be more representative of India than the Sandhurst candidates, making the Indian Army more of a national army.

The Indian nationalist movement differed from other such movements in that it was diverted by Gandhi from a direct, violent confrontation with British power.[57] With great skill and political astuteness he was able to make nonviolence serve many of the integrative and creative ends usually associated with violence as a political instrument. He had shared the plight of many educated, Westernized Indians: an advanced education which encouraged high expectations, and personal

---

down by the budget very closely; I couldn't increase or decrease my forces without permission. As for operational control I had less than your Pentagon perhaps! In the Middle East, even when there was direct contact with the Chief of the Imperial General Staff, orders had to be approved by Linlithgow."

[57] For an interesting discussion of the implications of the lack of a violent disruptive revolution in recent Indian history see Barrington Moore, Jr., *Social Origins of Dictatorship and Democracy* (reprint of 1966 ed.; Boston: Beacon Press, 1967), pp. 314 ff.

and social affronts by the British. In his hands nonviolence became a philosophy of action which was accepted by fellow Indians who might otherwise have resorted to violence. Both Gandhi and Bose channeled individual aggression into militarylike organizations which provided safe and predictable outlets for these emotions. The relative effectiveness of nonviolence on the British, and upon independent India will be discussed in later chapters.

Gandhi's lack of interest in infiltrating the military only partly accounts for the general disinterest in military affairs among Indian nationalists. Many castes and regional groups which had once supplied soldiers (especially Bengal and Madras), grudgingly came to accept their exclusion from military service. This acceptance was due in large part to the leadership of these groups which became exposed (after 1860–1880) to newer and equally attractive opportunities under the British Raj. Business and administrative careers for the regional elites quickly followed increasing Westernization in the new universities. Cut off from the peasant masses which supplied large numbers of troops, elite interest in the military turned to a more prestigious level, the officer corps. Many Bengalis were vociferous in demanding places as officers but provided only small numbers of troops when given an opportunity to join. Subhas Bose had been an enthusiast, but Bengalis were never forthcoming in large numbers.

The diverse interests and motives of Indian political elites made a united approach to military problems difficult, except perhaps in the case of the officer corps. Even here some of those interests clashed. This disparity of interests had some important implications: large numbers of politicians emerged who had little or no contact with military matters except as they were concerned with the army as an instrument of British and governmental oppression. The alienation of the leaders from the system encouraged a rejection of the military *per se*, and discouraged the systematic and disinterested examination of Indian military organization which was necessary for effective criticism. For most it gave rise to the charge that "we were kept from the military by the British," although, in fact, a few Indian politicians *were* able to develop considerable expertise in military matters. The British were not eager to encourage this expertise, but many recognized that sympathetic criticism could be beneficial to India as well as British rule. To take a moderate position on such a key problem as military policy was understandably hard for men who took extreme positions on other issues. Even if they had adopted the moderate position their intentions might have been suspect. The British were willing to listen to Indians who were harmless, and those who were dangerous were rarely willing to moderate one segment of their views lest moderation be mistaken for compromise.

5

THE PROFESSIONAL OFFICER IN INDIA

A trite but true conception of military theory sees the officer corps as the brain of the army, just as the noncoms are its heart and the ranking soldiers its muscle. Although this physiological analogy is relevant on the level of gross anatomy it does not account for all the important relationships of the officer corps to the army. Unlike a brain, an officer corps can *create* the other parts of the army, and can replace or replenish broken, defective, or weakened components. Although quality is important for the bulk of the soldiery, the quality of the officer corps will determine the quality and success of the army. A striking example of the importance of the officer corps can be found in South Asia when one compares the Royal Nepalese Army with the Indian Army. Both use Gurkha troops of the same ethnic background, yet the relative effectiveness of the two armies differs greatly. (Through the cooperation of the Indian Army, which supplied training facilities and a military aid mission, Nepali citizens have been given modern officer's training.)

The development of a corps of professional Indian officers is a matter of more than historical interest. Unlike the officer corps of most other former colonies, those of India and Pakistan have maintained or even surpassed colonial levels of professionalism.[1] The achievements of the Indian officers in World War II, in the postwar period, and in current conflicts are impressive when one considers the small number of officers taken into the army before 1940. While Indian politicians and publicists were struggling with the government to increase the rate of Indianization, these young Indians were being selected, trained, and indoctrinated. How the British felt about their presence, how the Indians reacted, and what they learned may prove to be one of the most significant episodes in the history of British India and in the development of the modern Indian and Pakistani political systems.

THE MILITARY SETTING

The Indian and Pakistani officers who took command of their respective armies after the withdrawal of the British received their professional training in the interwar period. The Indian army (and most other armies of that time) was the scene of a struggle between the younger professional officers and "old guard" of senior officers with ideas.

The Indian Army had always attracted economically poor but definitely upper-class and upper-middle-class British soldiers. Many officers used the Indian Army as a means of enjoying a standard of living and a status which they could not have aspired to socially, or afforded financially, at home.[2] The conservative elements of the officer corps tended to influence the army out of proportion to their numbers because of their senior rank:

There was an element among the senior British officers of the British and Indian Armies that what was good enough for us in pre-1914 was good enough for us post-1914. I myself had very little confidence in most of the senior officers of the Indian Army

---

[1] This was the judgment of several retired senior British officers interviewed in late 1963.

[2] For something of the style of life in the army in the interwar period John Masters' autobiographies are very descriptive. In a similar vein see also Capt. Freddie Guest, *Indian Cavalryman* (London: Jarrolds, 1959), by a superior polo playing officer, and John Morris, *Hired to Kill* (London: Rupert-Hart Davis, 1960), by the former director of the BBC's Third Programme.

in World War I and between the wars. "Yes men" were less nuisance than the "no men" and, though I may be biased in saying this, a succession of cavalry C.-in-C.s over a long period resulted in a horse soldier with a high handicap at polo and a good racing record being preferred to others who were generally much better officers. However, in all fairness, that was a situation which was prevalent in other armies before the World War II.[3]

The interwar period was the heyday of the "Poona Colonel" (since replaced in independent India by the "Agra Brigadier") and of polo playing, to the disgust of many young officers. The period saw the development to a high pitch of a unique, paternalistic, sports-orientated ethos, a politically quiet backwater around which nationalist and communal politics raged.

When Indians entered this hitherto all-white preserve, some British officers inevitably reacted strongly. These reactions influenced the relationship of British and Indian officers for years. For some Britishers, the entering of Indian officers into the army was a challenge. The newcomers had to be helped and guided in order to maintain the standards of the fighting units and to continue to keep the military out of nationalist or communal struggles. Many senior Indian officers today can recall individual British officers who encouraged and helped them.

But many British officers viewed the newcomers with hostility. In some instances undisguised racism was expressed:

I did not serve in an Indianizing unit, but served near them. They were not lower in status than regular units, but the good British officers did not care to join them. If the U.S. army decided to Negroize some units, would white officers rush to join them? Would you?[4]

A senior officer expressed the viewpoint of the older generation:

Before World War I the Indian Army was extremely popular, it had everything to offer: masses of sport, it was cheap, and there was a tremendous competition to get in. But after the First World War competition went down considerably with the *talk* of In-

3 Personal communication to the author from a retired British Indian Army general, 1963.
4 Interview with a retired British Indian Army brigadier, 1963.

dianization; the old blimps, such as myself, perhaps, did not want to send their sons to the Indian Army with its uncertain future. Chetwode's solution was to get around this by getting the very *best* British officers into the non-Indianizing units, segregating the Indians. At that time there was not the same feeling of equality as there was later, if you want to call it that, there was a definite color bar, it was in people's blood.[5]

Other Britishers were critical of the Indians from a social viewpoint. One English general claimed that many Indian wives spoke only Hindustani, and that meant that this "native" language had to be spoken within the precincts of the officers' mess. Later, problems with moneylenders and inadequate salaries were also held against Indian officers.[6]

Another difficulty with Indianization was the feeling on the part of the British that the Indian officers might come between the British and the troops, or mishandle the troops through communal prejudice or a lack of fairness and understanding. According to some, the intimate relationship between officer and class unit was threatened by the presence of Indians of other classes; many Britishers could not shake themselves of the notion that all Indians were inevitably committed first to their caste and only then to their duty. One retired British officer expressed his doubts (in 1963!) whether a "Bengali Brahmin babu intelligentsia would be able to take over my job after 40 years in the Indian Army; a Martial Sikh or a Garhwali wouldn't obey a Bengali, they just wouldn't."[7] Others interviewed in 1963 admitted that they had shared this viewpoint in the interwar period, but changed their opinion when the war and independence proved otherwise. In some ways (for example linguistically) Indians proved more competent in commanding Indian troops and understanding their needs than the British.

Much of the suspicion against Indians was based on genuine doubts; questions were being asked such as which type of

[5] Interview with a retired British Indian Army general, 1963.
[6] B. M. Kaul (a KCO) was in serious financial trouble early in his career and, to his ultimate embarrassment, was forced to resort to a money lender. ICOs were paid less than KCOs and had an even harder time meeting personal and professional expenses. After 1947, some of the latter costs were reduced.
[7] Interview with a retired British Indian Army brigadier, 1963.

Indian could become an effective soldier, what made a good officer, and whether "unsatisfactory material" could be trained up to the level required. As Morris Janowitz has pointed out, every officer must at one time or another perform tasks that demand heroic and personal leadership, and tasks that demand organizational and manipulative skills.[8] The two different sets of skills are required of every officer unless he remains a low-level field officer or serves in technical or noncombatant units. The British argued that "the right type" of officer followed the heroic pattern; he had to possess moral character, leadership ability, and personal courage to lead his troops into the teeth of a battle.

At first the British took the position that only selected representatives of the martial classes trained alongside their British peers at Sandhurst were acceptable. As we have seen, pressure from Indians and British civilians brought an acceptance of carefully selected nonmartial men. However, the same criteria were applied to them: they must be trained to perform "heroic" tasks adequately. The martial classes were not dropped from the recruitment rolls, but greater attention was given to educating them in English-style state-supported schools. They had proved too poorly educated, and lacked the facility and flexibility of mind to master the many service schools and stiff examinations which commissioned officers periodically encounter.

The sons of the new urban elite, including many Bengalis, Madrassis, and non-Kṣatriya castes did significantly better in examinations, and would have crowded out the martial classes from the Indian sector of the officer corps had it not been for the many (50 percent) appointed positions. The new urban elite were no less heroic in the field than officers from martial or Punjabi backgrounds.

After the Indian Military Academy opened at Dehra Dun, all Indian officers were trained in India. The Indian training was better than the Sandhurst training, although the Anglicizing process was not as complete. According to the British offi-

[8] Morris Janowitz, *The Professional Soldier* (New York: The Free Press, 1960), pp. 21 ff.

cers who served through the period, the quality of I.M.A. officers was uneven, but the best of them was as good or better than anything Sandhurst produced, British or Indian.[9]

OPPORTUNITIES AND OBSTACLES

Although the young Indians who entered the army in the interwar years were trail blazers, few wanted the role and many recoiled from it. This reluctance was particularly true of the first "generation" of Indian officers; those who went to Sandhurst before 1932, and received the King's Commission, which entitled them to command British as well as Indian troops. They were almost all sons of Indian princes, wealthy zamindars, planters, or they came from military families. Of the eighty-three boys that passed the Sandhurst entrance examination from 1918 to 1926, thirty-five were Punjabis, twelve from Bombay, nine each were from the United Provinces and Bengal, five from North West Frontier Provinces, six each from Rajputana and Hyderabad, two each from Burma and Coorg, and one each from Bihar, Assam, and the Central India Agency.[10] Collectively, they were the most reliable, politically inert, aristocratic, and conservative group the British could select. Most had an aptitude for sports, and few were strong academically. The story of one retired KCO is exceptional only in the source of the suggestion that the army was an appropriate career:

My father was a doctor, a famous doctor in Bombay. Mahatma Gandhi was a patient of his. Once, after finishing an examination my father asked, "Mahatmaji, what will my boy become?" I was only 15 at the time, I thought I might become a lawyer, but I liked sports, very much, and I was very chubby. Gandhi suggested I join the army. "But Mahatmaji," my father replied, "what kind of life is that for an Indian?" Gandhi answered, "every tree starts with only one branch: it will grow in time, there will come a time when many Indians will be officers. Besides, the army is just the

[9] At Sandhurst, Dehra Dun, and in the units themselves, no concessions were made to the Indians. They were made to meet the same exacting standards required of British cadets and officers. The military would not have yielded this point, even if the civilians had considered asking them.
[10] Indian Sandhurst Committee, *Report*, p. 11.

place for games, that's all they do; it's a good, outdoors, healthy life."[11]

Once past the various stages of screening in India (which often included an interview with the Viceroy or the Commander-in-Chief of the Indian Army) the potential KCO spent up to two years at Sandhurst. There he received a brief but intensive social as well as military indoctrination. One of the best descriptions of the impact of Sandhurst has been written by B. M. Kaul:

I learnt a code of conduct, a sense of discipline and the significance of honor (honor is something within one, synonymous to one's conscience and with which one has to live). I was taught a set of principles true to spiritual values by which can be judged what is right. I acquired the rudiments of military knowledge, the basic techniques of my profession and to appreciate the importance of turnout and skill at professional work and games [and] also to face agreeable and unpleasant situations alike. I was taught how to play the game, to know what the qualities of leadership were, the sense of many values and the honour of serving one's country selflessly and with devotion.[12]

After the new KCO was commissioned as a second lieutenant, he was seconded to a British unit in India and given the opportunity of commanding white troops for a year. He was then sent to an Indian Army unit which would become his "home" for the rest of his professional career.

The army thus offered not only an opportunity for sports, hunting, and fun, but a unique status for an Indian KCO. Pay and service conditions were identical to those of their British colleagues and the Indians were in every way their professional equals. For a certain kind of family a son in the Indian Army officer corps was as prestigious, if not more so, than a son in the Indian Civil Service.

The young Indian KCOs tried to live up to the status of

11 Interview with a retired Indian lieutenant-general, 1963.
12 Lieut.-Gen. B. M. Kaul, *The Untold Story* (Bombay: Allied Publishers, 1967), pp. 30–31. Field-Marshal Mohammad Ayub Khan described another facet of the Sandhurst environment in the early years of Indianization when he wrote of the "tragedy of belonging to a subject race" in free England, and of the color consciousness of the British. *Friends Not Masters* (New York: Oxford University Press, 1967), p. 10.

their rank. With few exceptions they were utterly disinterested in politics. Until they were forced to think through their position, they spent most of their energy in modeling themselves after their British superiors. General K. S. Thimayya has recounted his admiration of the British and all things British in his early teens, an admiration which still persists, and is typical of the senior KCOs.[13] The years in Britain, the year of secondment to a British regiment, and the long contact with British officers in their units (especially before these units began to fill up with Indians) gave them a clear idea of the career pattern of the Indian Army officer. Most of them followed the pattern closely.

The next "generation" of Indian officers, the Indian commissioned officers, differed from their KCO elders in training and diversity. They had no British experience, and as military units became clogged with Indian officers, they had little contact with British officers of their own age. Many were relatively poor and joined the army not for prestige or honor but for career opportunities. Mohan Singh, founder of the I.N.A., joined the army despite his rebellious personality in order to capitalize on his skills as a field hockey player. The military was the center of organized sport in India.[14] The ICOs received a lower scale of pay than the KCOs, and held a less prestigious position. Their training was as good or better than that of the KCOs but their quality varied.[15] Politically they were also more diverse than the KCOs, and many came into the army under the influence of nationalist ideas.

The task of integrating the Indian Army fell upon the KCOs, for by the time the ICOs entered the military the

[13] Humphrey Evans, *Thimayya of India* (New York: Harcourt Brace, 1960), p. 40. Even Kaul, one of the most politically minded of all of the KCOs expressed his admiration for individual Englishmen, an admiration which developed simultaneously with a strong dislike for British rule. Interview, 1965.
[14] Information from interviews and unpublished manuscript of General Mohan Singh.
[15] In testimony given in 1939 the commandant of the Indian Military Academy indicated that the quality of I.M.A. cadets was not declining and that the quality of Army cadets (taken from the Indian Army) was improving slightly. The main problem, he asserted, was that suitable boys were not directed to the army by their colleges and homes. Witness No. 9, Indianization Committee, Government of India, Ministry of Defense, Archives, New Delhi.

eight-unit scheme had been operating for some time. These KCOs found themselves, especially in the early years, in the unwanted and unfamiliar role of social reformers. Frequently they were the first Indians to break the color bar in many contonment clubs. When their unit moved from cantonment to cantonment they found the same difficulties and embarrassments repeating themselves. It was somewhat ironic that the group which was most carefully selected for reliability and conservative attitudes should be the first to encounter British hostility.

The encounter between upper class, proud Indians and British officers who maintained a patronizing attitude toward Indians was not without problems. Unlike Indian officers who came from poorer military families, or were promoted from the ranks, the elite officers were accustomed to high status, and felt themselves closer to the British elite than to the Indian masses. They shared the colonial outlook and rebelled when denied the fruits of the colonial position; but they never rebelled for the sake of anything broader than what they felt their proprietary rights should be.

One Sandhurst man—conservative, able, distinguished, and highly Anglicized—related his experience:

There was some anti-British feeling among Indian officers but it was generated by the British themselves. Indians *felt* there was discrimination; the first groups were evenly distributed throughout the army, but when the Indianization scheme came they were made to feel they were second class citizens. There were one or two good British officers in the Indianizing units, but most were deadwood, the best ones avoided us. There were also a few who made life hell for us. Chaps 5 or 10 years older treated me as a pariah: I was called a wog in my own mess.[16]

Even the food in the officers' mess pushed this Indian officer to the edge of rebellion. He demanded Indian-style food not because he liked it, but because he wanted to assert his rights as an equal.[17]

16 Interview with a retired Indian lieutenant-general, 1963.
17 Ayub Khan mentions such incidents in his autobiography, but indicates that he felt less strongly about "little things" than his fellow Sikh and Hindu KCOs. *Friends Not Masters*, p. 13.

A few Indians fought back openly. Some who were too vocal were eased out of the army; others later took advantage of the opportunity to join the I.N.A. The latter groups' motives were as personal as they were political. Others yielded to British antagonism and accepted an inferior position. It was this type which let himself be "run" by a junior British officer when he held a command position, and who doubted the capabilities of Indians to take over senior posts at the end of the war (or, in a few instances, who wanted the British to stay on in India).

Racial discrimination had the side effect of provoking the few contacts that were made between Indian officers and nationalist politicians. K. S. Thimayya has recounted how he and several fellow officers sought out nationalist politicians for help after being criticized by the British.[18] Another officer, as professional and Anglicized as Thimayya had a similar experience:

We couldn't retaliate when we were insulted, we were not steeped in political ideology. But this did force us to look into politics and find out about the nationalist movement, the independence movement. Only when the British were antagonistic did the Indians think about Independence and getting rid of the British, especially the bad ones. I had no contact with Indian politicians, but there were times when I might have wished to tell someone of the things that were going on.[19]

These contacts were rare, but important, for they were the only link between the two groups other than an occasional personal connection.[20]

The net effect of racial discrimination was an intensification of the professional outlook of the Indian officers. Open clashes were usually fruitless because the Indians were in junior positions and their service security was in jeopardy. No

---

18 Evans, pp. 116 ff.

19 Interview with a retired Indian lieutenant-general, 1963.

20 B. M. Kaul was the most important exception to this pattern. Although he had only limited contact with Indian political leaders before World War II, he had been active in nationalist terrorist activities before entering the army. During World War II he developed or maintained ties with Ashok Mehta, Sardar Patel, Asaf Ali, J. P. Narayan, Ram Manohar Lohia, Sheikh Abdullah, and Jawaharlal Nehru, who was a family relation. Interview, 1965.

one profited from disputes, and the rules of the Indian Army messes helped: no discussions of women or politics. The environment of the young Indian officer encouraged intense professional development. When a Britisher ventured some gratuitous criticism of Indian politics or society within earshot, it usually went unanswered, although not unheard.

ATTITUDES AND OUTLOOK

Whatever their motivation, most Indians came to share a number of political, social, and professional attitudes with their British fellow officers. Some conformed because they had to, and some because they wanted to; on the whole, the latter pattern was the rule. This conformity was mainly due to their own social and political background. As we noted, many came from conservative, landed, and aristocratic families; they viewed India "from the top" down. Indians from landed rural or professional urban families tended to have an influence in the military disproportionate to their numbers. Frequently they had a broader background, greater intellectual flexibility, and better education than the officers who had come up from the ranks. As a result they were more likely (then and now) to reach high command positions.

Army and Nation

Is India a nation? When confronted with this question, the British gave many answers. The Orientalists, the higher civil servants, and many British rulers answered yes; the military usually answered no. The British Indian Army officer did not give his answer out of ignorance. The military were the least surprised when riots tore India apart after World War II, although it was the military which was also the most bitter and disappointed group when partition—and "vivisection" of the army came.

The Indian Army saw itself as a sword which held India together. Many officers learned the maxim that in India the sword is mightier than the pen, for it ultimately enforces the laws and rules which are enacted. The emphasis varied through the years, depending upon the degree of local unrest, but from the early years of chaos until partition most British officers believed that their own profession was more important in India than in England.

Part of this attitude was due to the self-elevation of a distinct, colorful, and tradition-minded elite. The need to overcome the feeling that the Indian Army was in some way inferior to the British Army reinforced this self-elevation.[21] Also, an emphasis on the need for meeting force with force is expected from a professional military man: he understands the mechanism of violence because he is experienced in its use. He sees the beginning symptoms of violence before others are aware of them, or where others do not see them at all. It is his job to prepare for violence when others are talking of peace.

Yet, beyond these predilictions, the experiences of the British officer in India reinforced his image of his role as vital and crucial, for he saw structural and cultural reasons for emphasizing force. The history of the Indian Army taught him that it was not until the 1890s that the armies of the three presidencies were effectively united. Until then, officially at least, the internal defense problem had not eased enough to permit centralized direction of military activity. Communications and logistics also had not developed enough to permit centralization.

Another reminder of the disunity of India was the existence of the Indian princely states, many of which had their own armies and were officered by Britishers seconded from the Indian Army. Some of these states were models of eighteenth-century autocracy. They made control of the entire subcontinent difficult, and compounded regional, cultural, economic, and social differences.[22]

The military required extensive schooling in weaponry, staff affairs, and troop movements as well as visits to regi-

21 Peter E. Razzell, "A Sociological History of Officers in the Indian and British Home Armies: 1785–1912," Paper No. 1, Center for Social Organization Studies, University of Chicago, May, 1962.
22 See Appendix: "A Note on the Indian State Forces."

mental recruiting areas. In his travels the officer saw for himself something of the staggering diversity that is India. Especially after railroads were pushed through, the officer gained a view of the linguistic, physical, and cultural differences which have impressed Westerners in India since their earliest contacts.

The Indian Army officer saw sharp distinctions between regions, especially the relative distribution of the martial races. Many saw in the Punjab a state which possessed all requirements for forceful domination over other regions. By the 1930s it was a standard argument that "the amount of natural military aptitude possessed by the country's different inhabitants, amongst them . . . races which are entitled to be considered among the most formidable fighting forces in the world, and others which alike by their physique and traditions are rendered practically incapable of resisting military aggression of any kind," might lead to conflict requiring the intervention of British troops.[23] After *swaraj*, the 30 percent of India which supplied 87 percent of the troops would naturally be expected to exploit the other 70 percent.[24] Some held that the obverse was true; that the British had to keep the military classes from being emasculated by the "babu" Congress nationalists.

This image of Indian society was generally shared by Indian officers of the prewar generation. If they agreed that Muslim-Hindu disunity was inevitable, they also went out of their way to see that it did not occur in the army. If they agreed that India's political unity was fragile, they doubled their efforts to improve one of the all-Indian services—the army—which maintained that unity. Throwing themselves into their jobs was a way of averting disunity and demonstrating that Indians could assist in the management of the subcontinent. They may have had more confidence in the capabilities of Indian

[23] Government of India, *India in 1929–30* (Calcutta: Government of India, 1931), pp. 61–62.
[24] Government of India, *India in 1930–31* (Calcutta: Government of India, 1932), p. 5.

politicians than did the British, and, looking toward the future, may have seen more clearly the triumph of the nationalist movement, but by and large they (along with the civil service) were the most Anglicized of elite groups. Until the formation of the I.N.A. they were under close scrutiny and in a relatively inferior position and had little opportunity openly to differ with their British fellow officers. In the meantime their major contact with Indian society—"aid to the civil"— reinforced their views.

"Aid to the Civil"

Hardly a few months pass in India without the military being called out to assist the civilian administration. Frequently they provide "positive" aid: road repair, flood control, disaster relief, or distribution of food and medicine in times of famine or epidemic. Frequently the military is used to help patrol large *melas* (religious fairs or gatherings). These tasks are welcomed by the military, and have been for many years: they provide an interesting break from the training cycle and improve the image of the military among civilians.[25]

But, almost as frequently, aid to the civil means exercising the police function in times of breakdown of law and order. Military police action remains today, as in the British days, the most unpopular and distasteful task a military man can undertake. It raises several delicate problems of civilian control, and illustrates some characteristics of the military mind in India and Pakistan which have been carried intact from the British days.

There are several good descriptions of a typical aid to the civil operation.[26] Invariably, almost every aspect was hated

[25] They could also have an impact upon the officer. When assigned to patrol duty at a *Kumbh Mela* Thimayya received a strong cultural shock when he viewed the kidnapping, prostitution, and crime which was carried out under the name of Hinduism on that particular occasion. "The hypocrisy, ignorance, and suffering he saw sickened him. For a while, at least, he was content to have little contact with both the religion and those who practiced it." Evans, pp. 112–113.

[26] For the military viewpoint see Field-Marshal Sir William Slim, "Aid to the Civil," in *Unofficial History* (London: Cassell, 1959). For the civilian

by the military. First, it was never free to deal with a riot situation as they saw fit. To avoid disaster and to apply force discretely the civilian magistrates often wanted the military to break up into small roving forces. Such tactics violated one of the principle tenets of military doctrine: not to disperse one's strength in small "penny-packets." The relationship with the magistrate himself could be a source of difficulty, particularly if he and the senior military authority were of different nationalities. A few British Commanders-in-Chief who were faced with the problem wanted the military to decide when to fire, not an Indian magistrate.[27] The military was also limited in the kind of weapons it could use. Both Birdwood and Chetwode, who together were Commanders-in-Chief from 1925 to 1935, pressed for the use of tear gas to disperse crowds. The government of India rejected this demand, for tear gas had not been used against dacoits (gangs of bandits) up to that time, let alone civilian crowds.

The aid-to-the-civil operation required careful application of violence guided by an official with intimate knowledge of the particular crowd and their particular grievance. Preferably, the civilian magistrate (or collector) remained in the area to reestablish a relationship with the local leadership, while the military departed after its job was over, perhaps never to return again. The military often suspected the civilian magistrate of being unduly timid in dealing with a raging mob, and the civilians were no less wary of a repetition of the Amritsar massacre.[28]

viewpoint see Philip Woodruff, *The Guardians*, Vol. II of *The Men Who Ruled India* (reprint of 1954 ed.; London: Jonathan Cape, 1963), pp. 257–266. Perhaps the most insightful of all accounts is contained in several chapters of Robert Scott's novel, *The Jewel in the Crown* (New York: Dutton, 1966).

27 Field-Marshal Lord Birdwood, *Khaki and Gown* (London: Ward, Lock and Co., 1941), p. 378.

28 Dyer's actions at Amritsar were an indication of what could happen if the military were given a free hand. He envisioned his actions as having a salutory effect on the nationalist movement. In his subsequent difficulties he received his strongest support from fellow officers, who agreed with him that to prevent nationalist violence it was necessary to use severe force early and crush all immediate resistance. See Rupert Furneaux, *The Amritsar Massacre* (London: George, Allen and Unwin, 1963) for a critical study of Dyer's actions, and the Hunter Commission for extensive documentation: India, Committee

A second major objection to aid to the civil was the danger that the Indian troops would react sympathetically to the rioters, and the British would lose control. At best the task was one which both officer and soldier tried to carry out with a minimum of critical examination:

No one liked quelling riots, but it was a continuous task. The military were not allowed to take action until the civilians gave permission, and even then we had to use the minimum force under strict control. We officers accepted this control, we did not think about it; the Indian troops also did not think about it, if Sahib says it must be done, then do it, that was their view. The trust of the officers by their troops, that was the key relationship.[29]

However, there were constant reminders of the narrow margin of control. It was always regarded as dangerous to use troops of one class or religion in quelling a riot by the same class. For this reason Gurkhas—with few ties in India except near Dehra Dun—were extensively used in civilian-riot control. The British also feared that if a particular effort of aid was carried on long enough, outside agitators would propagandize the troops. Such a disaster was thought to have occurred once, when the Royal Garhwal Rifles became disaffected in April 1930. Both Indians and Britishers regarded the incident as of great significance, the first crack in a hitherto impregnable wall.[30]

Not only did the military resent interference with their handling of riots, and fear the contamination of their troops, but few officers—British or Indian—had anything but scorn for

on Disturbances in Bombay, Delhi and the Punjab, *Report* (London: H.M.S.O., 1920).

29 Interview with a retired British Indian Army lieutenant-general, 1963.

30 The effect of propaganda was a major point in the official enquiry into the Garhwali Mutiny. One entire section was devoted to the problem of "seditious propaganda and the close contact in which troops are forced to live with disaffected or actively seditious elements in cantonment areas." The enquiry proposed complete abolition of political activity in cantonment areas: "It is felt that cantonments should be regarded once more as Military Encampments or Islands in which no public meeting or speeches should be tolerated. With the purging of cantonments, temptation will be removed from the Soldier, as City areas are placed out of bounds when it is deemed necessary to do so." India Office Library, Mil. Collection, file No. 159/17, "Insubordination, Mutiny: Mutiny of the 2/18th Garhwal Rifles."

both sides in civil disorders. The greatest contempt was reserved for leaders of communal or political agitations, who, as one officer pointed out, frequently removed themselves to the rear if there was a prospect of a shooting or lathi charge. (Lathis are brass-tipped truncheons used in crowd control by police.)

In addition to a disdain for the mob, many Indian officers felt a special sense of shame at the disorderliness and chaos which lay behind many disturbances. As a group, Indian officers were extremely conscious that the military was free of caste and communal discord, and could not help but compare the orderliness of military life—despite the diversity of classes—with the disorder of civil society. Their professional outlook reinforced their feeling of the superiority of the military way of life.

Professional Problems

In addition to their objections to performing police functions, the military felt frustrated in two other areas. One was a question of operations, the other of service conditions.

In the interwar period the Indian Army was engaged in extensive operations in the Northwest Frontier Province, quelling tribal insurrections and maintaining order. Many stories have been told of this peculiar half-war, half-police action. The British had great difficulty in conducting operations against a shifting enemy who was frequently advised and supported by Indian government political agents. The military was sent to punish and patrol, but was severely limited (by the local political agent who was usually negotiating with the rebel tribes) in the amount of force they could employ. They obeyed, because they were good soldiers, but all except the most politically perceptive were puzzled or angered by this twilight war; especially when heavy casualties were suffered or friends were killed.[31]

---

[31] Ayub Khan refers to the "sheer futility" and great waste of time and men on these frontier struggles. He took an active role in liquidating the forward positions immediately before the creation of Pakistan. *Friends Not Masters*, p. 18.

These operational restrictions were tolerable because the relatively low level of the conflicts made it possible for the military to cope with them. If worst came to worst the military could always overpower a technically inferior opposition. However, there was a nagging fear which grew to major proportions as World War II approached, that against a major army the Indian Army would be seriously—perhaps fatally—handicapped for lack of equipment.

Some of the major armies in the world, such as the American and most European forces, could rely upon civilian society for emergency support in time of crisis or rapid expansion. However, the Indian Army was, and is, largely dependent on its own equipment and could draw upon civilian society only for a small amount of war materials. Any new type of equipment, or any weapon of considerable sophistication had to be bought from abroad, or else a laborious effort had to be made to manufacture the item in India. Thus, the Indian Army relied heavily on scraps from the British Army and tried to make do with a small indigenous manufacturing capacity. Reoutfitting was seriously begun only in 1938 when Auchinleck undertook to find out what would be necessary to equip the Indian Army for a major war. His findings were incorporated into the Chatfield Committee's report the following year.[32]

For most units it was too late, and it was not until the flow of American supplies began that the military caught up with its material requirements. The experience of being caught unprepared was bitter for many officers. One Indian, who was captured by the Japanese, recounted his personal experience:

I was in an old cavalry unit. We were made into mechanized cavalry and sent to Malaya. We were mechanized to the extent that we had had our horses taken away from us. The Japanese had tanks

---

[32] Prasad, pp. 19 ff. summarizes the findings. The entire *Report of the Expert Committee on the Defense of India, 1938–39* (Chatfield Committee) is on file in the Ministry of Defense Archives, File No. 601/12808/H. The report documents the gross unpreparedness of the Indian Army. In view of this unpreparedness, the commission's gratuitous criticisms of the "striking ignorance" of Indian politicians seems in retrospect to be misplaced.

and armor, they surrounded us three times, and we were caught the last time.[33]

The bitterness about being ill-equipped was compounded by a unanimous feeling that the soldiers of the Indian Army were the most loyal, dedicated, and effective in the world: to give them less than they deserved was not only militarily unwise but it was morally wrong, a betrayal of their trust.

A final point of dissatisfaction of some Indian Army officers —and almost all ICOs—was the question of pay and service conditions. Most young British officers did not marry until they had reached the rank of major, and were able to live rather comfortably in the officers' mess. The pattern for Indians, however, was radically different. Many were married early in their careers as a result of a planned arrangement or family pressure and had families to support, as well as a mess bill to pay. In addition, some were deeply in debt as a result of earlier borrowing from a moneylender to pay for their Sandhurst or Dehra Dun military educations. They were unable to make ends meet on a salary schedule which had been cut, not increased, through the years. It was becoming increasingly difficult for officers to maintain servants, polo ponies, and other luxuries deemed necessary in a number of regiments, unless they came from wealthy families.

Politics in the prewar Army

One facet of military professionalism, was the resistance of the officers of the Indian Army to any notion of politics.[34] With the exception of the program of Indianization—which would never have come about had it not been for the efforts of Indian politicians—army officers agreed that they were remarkably successful in this effort. In the prewar years, politics meant

[33] Interview with a retired Indian lieutenant-general, 1963. This officer resisted the appeal of the I.N.A., but his attitude explains why many fellow officers did not.

[34] In this notion there is a touch of scorn for the practitioners as well as the art: "The early Indian officers were just like the British were, they had the same views and attitudes. A soldier has the vote, but in our army, the British and the Indian, there is no politics—this is left alone—the Indians were more critical of Indian politicians than were the British officers." Interview with a retired British-Indian Army brigadier, 1963.

one of two things, or both: allowing communal or caste sentiment to develop within the army which might be linked to
outside political parties or movements, or openly taking a position on, or working for, independence.

Every Indian Army officer was and is intensely proud of
what he calls the army's lack of communalism in general, and
Hindu-Muslim conflict in particular. The creation and maintenance of an equilibrium between communities based upon
a competition in excellence and not a spiral of hate was perhaps the greatest military achievement of the British. With
the exception of a few sectionalists, the Indians—Muslim
and Hindu—were no less occupied by this task than the British. Constructive competition required an enormous amount
of energy, patience and "man-management," as the Indian
Army called it.

Most prewar Indian officers agreed with the official doctrine that the military was best organized along caste lines,
and that martial classes were to be favored above the non-
recruited classes. Thimayya and B. M. Kaul, who represent the
two political extremes of the old Indian KCOs, agree that pure
battalions are the most effective.[35] The rationalization of the
theory of martial races is no longer racial, but based on the
long tradition of military service of some classes. These classes are most easily recruited, and therefore make the best
fighters. All prewar infantry officers served with class units
and became attached emotionally in varying degrees to their
particular class; they strongly defended the system as a rough
form of democracy in which each caste or class is separated
from, but competitive with, every other class. This attitude
reflects a trace of class pride (or more particularly, Punjabi
pride) as most prewar officers were from martial classes. Assignment to units was random, and Hindu, Sikh, and Muslim
officers wound up commanding troops of different faiths when
they were subalterns or junior officers. When they took up
higher command positions they usually commanded units
made up of diverse communities. Each class unit had its own

[35] Evans, p. 285 and Welles Hangen, *After Nehru Who?* (New York: Harcourt, Brace and World, 1963), p. 269.

good features, and these were sharpened in interunit competition. The military felt strongly that if the political parties gained any foothold within the army the delicate balance could be upset, and the army might destroy itself like some complicated machine gone berserk.

The massive upheavals at the time of partition confirmed the dangers of sectionalism. Parts of the army became seriously infected and useless as a police instrument.[36] But the amount of provocation, and the relative success of the military in holding together as long as it did seems to confirm the good intentions of most of the officers. Hindus and Muslims in the officer corps remained remarkably free of pro- or anti-Pakistani sentiment until partition, when the likelihood of Pakistan became a certainty.[37] At this time most Muslims broke away —hardly surprising when one considers the enormous opportunities opened up by the creation of a new army. However, the break was made in good faith and with little, if any, bitterness—least of all because of communal hatred.[38]

Another aspect of the ban against politics in the army concerned the nationalist movement. The junior Indian officers were more restricted than their senior British officers, who at times felt free to deride the nationalists. Nehru ("a Communist") and Gandhi ("Gandy's legs are bandy") were special

[36] The difficulties of the Indian Army in this period are described in John Connell, *Auchinleck* (London: Cassell, 1959), and Lieut.-Gen. Sir Francis Tuker, *While Memory Serves* (London: Cassell, 1950).

[37] Ayub Khan relates that the Muslim officers had "an instinctive sympathy for the great struggle in which . . . Jinnah . . . was engaged to ensure the creation of the state of Pakistan. But we had no real knowledge of the personalities involved in this political struggle; and by training we had been taught that as army officers we should stay out of the political arena. So the politicians were largely an unknown quantity to us, as we were to them." *Friends Not Masters*, p. 19.

[38] For a bitter (and semi-official) account of what little antagonism there was between Muslim and non-Muslim officers during the days of partition see Maj.-Gen. Fazal Muqeem Khan, *The Story of the Pakistan Army* (Karachi: Oxford University Press, 1963). Interviews with several Indian Army officers (British, Muslim, and Hindu) confirm the existence of some hostility based on religion at the time of partition, but all point out the unusual amount of provocation and personal stress the officers were under at the time. Some (the exact figure is unknown) Muslim officers chose the Indian Army, and have risen to relatively high positions since the war. To my knowledge no Hindu officer chose the Pakistan Army.

targets. The effect of these jibes was mixed: some Indians agreed with the British, some did not but kept quiet, and some fought back. A few officers established covert contacts with the nationalist movement, and some engaged in open argument. Most kept quiet. The most troublesome Indian officers were eased out of the army or given undesirable assignments. However, such measures were rare. An uneasy silence typically surrounded nationalist politics. The subject was avoided rather than worked out. As units became increasingly Indianized, however, and especially after the beginning of the war, political discussions became more frequent.[39]

The progress of Indianization in the interwar period was characterized by slow, hesitant concessions on the part of the British and an increasing resentment and sense of isolation on the part of the Indian officers. The eight-unit scheme had the effect of segregating Indians; they not only resented the mark of inferiority but sincerely felt that they were being cheated out of the best available education. To borrow a phrase from a similar controversy, separate but equal was not really equal.

Indian politicians who had been following the progress of Indianization were genuinely afraid that Indian officers would create an inferior army within the larger Indian Army; many British military men, especially those who were commanding Indian officers and had daily contact with them, also had misgivings about the eight-unit scheme and its effect on the morale and proficiency of their charges. The Indian officers were themselves hardly happy with a situation which markedly reduced their chances for promotion and status.

One outcome of this growing resentment was the 1939 Indianization Committee of the government of India, made up of high-ranking British officers and prominent Indian civilians. The committee had just completed the initial phase

[39] One British Indian Army brigadier noted that the older Indian officers were apolitical, but during the war the educational level and quality of officers decreased while interest in politics increased. He recalled a group of young Indian officers who had regularly been tuning in to Japanese English-language broadcasts. Interview, 1963.

of its work and begun to draw up a report when World War II broke out. The war forced the military members of the committee to return to their military positions, and eliminated the need for further examination of Indianization, for the segregated Indianizing units were broken up.

Of greater significance than the rate of Indianization was the quality of professional training received by Indian officers before World War II. When the war came, these men proved their competence and were promoted rapidly. In fact, the KCOs and ICOs were so valuable that when the Indianizing units were broken up, their Indian officers were used throughout the Indian Army (with the exception of Gurkha units).

The prewar Indian officers were subject to the same currents of professional change and development as were their British peers. The Indian Army was undergoing the same revolution in military thought and organization that had earlier swept other military establishments. After World War I the Indian Army remained an important example of what Maury Feld has termed a "primitive" military organization: a caste-like association isolated from a hostile outside world, which regarded itself as self-sufficient and unique.[40] The intrusion of Indian officers into this isolated world aggravated the conflict between the primitivists and those who saw the military as a "competitive," achievement and change-oriented organization.[41] Both images are "professional," but

[40] "Primitive military organizations characteristically consider themselves to be the embodiment of rational practices. They select as leaders only the genuinely rational and superior applicants; rejected candidates and non-applicants are thus inferior to members of the organization. . . . All members of the military, by the fact of their membership, possess these superior qualities. The total absorption of all its members in the institutional routine is, therefore, a rational objective. The round of drills, rituals, and disciplinary measures results in a range of refined characteristics according to which every member can identify himself with the organization and be recognized as such by every other member." Feld, "The Military Self-Image in a Technological Environment," in Morris Janowitz, ed., *The New Military* (New York: Russell Sage Foundation, 1964), p. 163.

[41] "The competitive approach . . . holds that no single profession or organization has a monopoly of effective and rational behavior. Society . . . develops distinctive bodies of operational criteria and systematic rules, and it is on the basis of skill and mastery in such areas, rather than on the simple fact of

very different. Indian officers resented the racial discrimination practiced by the British, but they often differed among themselves about the purpose of the military, and the role of the officer.

In retrospect, the development of an indigenous "brain" for the Indian Army—which was split into two separate officer corps in the postwar partition—will stand as a major accomplishment of colonial Britain. The performance of the indigenous military leadership in both successor states was almost as good as that of the civil service; it was even more remarkable when one considers the direct challenge to the concept of a professional, apolitical army which was mounted during World War II. The Indian Army under physical attack from the Axis powers, and its purpose was challenged by another army, led by the Indian political leader, Subhas Chandra Bose. The following chapter will evaluate both the technical accomplishments of the Indian Army as it underwent wartime expansion and its relative success in maintaining organizational integrity in the face of this unexpected threat.

---

membership in one social group or another, that the attribution of rationality is determined. . . . The term is descriptive of occupational proficiency rather than the primitive outlook of social affiliation." Feld, p. 164.

6

THE TEST OF WAR

After 1939 the Indian Army encountered three successive crises, resulting from India's enforced participation in World War II. The first crisis developed as the Indian Army attempted to expand its small prewar base. Many problems India had already encountered in the World War I expansion reappeared with greater severity. The second crisis was more dramatic: the Indian Army found itself facing not only Axis troops, but an Indian National Army led by Indians, and commanded by the most prominent and aggressive of all Indian politicians, Subhas Chandra Bose. The final crisis occurred when India became independent and the army was left without British direction. Independence required a reassessment of the fundamental relationship of army to state and society; the results of that reassessment have never been effectively challenged in free India.

THE EXPANSION OF THE
INDIAN ARMY: 1939–1945

In 1939 the British Indian Army was a small, tightly knit, politically reliable constabulary force, composed of members of martial races and suitable for border wars. To the extent that stability, reliability and continuity were important values the theory worked. As long as the Indian Army was a technical backwater and expansion was slow, the martial races were able to provide suitable numbers of dedicated and competent recruits. When both these factors changed in World War II, near-disaster occurred. The old principles of recruitment had to be abandoned before the Indian Army could again become an effective force.

Before World War II no plans had been made for the expansion of the Indian Army. The military had assumed that the old, trusted classes would yield adequate numbers. As in 1914–1918, this proved incorrect, and the army paid a heavy price in inefficiency, time, and money for maintaining the interwar balance of classes. Part of the trouble was financial. Not until 1939 was the policy firmly laid down that Indian and imperial interests were so interlinked that large-scale aid to India for modernization and expansion would be made available.[1] The Indian Army's commitment to internal and local defense before World War I was broadened to include extensive imperial responsibilities. However, the funds necessary to equip the army for such a role never actually arrived. The army's prime responsibility was internal security and border defense, and this required only a small professional army. The Indian Army budget was cut from 652.3 million rupees in 1922/23 to 474.7 million rupees in 1932/33, a remarkable reduction. In 1933, as a result of the recommendations of the Garren Tribunal, a slow reversal began, and the British began to supply an annual subsidy of £1,500,000, increased in 1939 to £2,000,000.

After the fall of France and the withdrawal of the British from Dunkirk the British decided to employ Indian troops extensively overseas, and immediately in the Middle East.

---

[1] For a summary of the vicissitudes of the military in Indian-Imperial relations see Sri Nandan Prasad, *Expansion of the Armed Forces and Defense Organization, 1939–45* (India: Orient Longmans, 1956), pp. 8–52, a volume in the series of the *Official History of the Indian Armed Forces in the Second World War*, Bisheshwar Prasad, general ed., sponsored by the Combined Inter-Services Historical Section, India and Pakistan. See also P. N. Khera, "Role of the Indian Army, 1900–1939," *Journal* of the United Service Institution of India, XCIV (July–September, 1964), 277–289.

Until this time "expansion had not been foreseen, rather the reverse, and up to the outbreak of war, and to the commencement of expansion no real survey of manpower had been attempted."[2]

Another reason why the Indian Army was unable to expand rapidly was the continued reliance on the martial races theory and the reluctance to experiment with new classes. The favoritism of many officers toward the martial races was actually intensified by the nationalist movement. As an often used metaphor would have it, the Punjab and other traditional recruiting grounds constituted the "sword arm of India." The rest of India had to be protected from this "sword arm" by the continued presence of the British in the subcontinent, and the sword arm itself had to be protected from politicians and nationalists who were eager to blunt its keen edge. British officers argued that it was easier to keep the military uncontaminated if its recruiting base was narrow and if only reliable and trustworthy classes were taken in. As a result, the recruiting system hardly changed between the wars, and, in fact, the government continually had to prod the military to broaden the scope of recruitment.[3] These efforts were unsuccessful, and only war brought about significant change.

The departure of the prime units of the Indian Army, sent intact to the Middle East, brought on an organizational crisis. When the call for recruits went out, the youth of the more prosperous ethnic groups (such as Jat Sikhs) barely trickled in; with food prices rocketing upward they preferred to remain on the land. As a result, the infantry was short of trained non-commissioned officers and VCOs. Those who were available for new units were largely surplus Sikhs, for whom sufficient numbers of troops were lacking. This difficulty

[2] War Department (Government of India), History Head 2—Expansion of the Armed Forces, Infantry Memorandum. See also Prasad, pp. 53 ff. This memorandum and those cited below are in the Ministry of Defense Archives, Historical Section. They constituted the official summaries of the problems encountered in the expansion of key branches of the Indian Army.

[3] Interview with Philip Mason who served in the Defense Department in the prewar years. London, 1963. Mr. Mason claims that Army Headquarters urged the units to draw from broader sources, but they resisted, arguing that they wanted only the best men available.

proved almost insurmountable for two to three years after the war began. The British first had to train a class and then select its superior talent for officer-training. In the meantime many newly recruited classes in all branches of the army had to get along with officers from another class. The new Madras infantry, Army Service Corps, and artillery and Armored Corps units were largely commanded by Jat Sikh VCOs and noncommissioned officers, and the clash of culture and language led to serious discontent in some units.[4] In a few instances "borrowed" officers fit in to the new unit: Mahrattas helped set up the Mahars and Jat Sikhs aided the Mazbhi and Ramdasias Sikhs. Such cooperation was exceptional. More commonly the troops greatly resented the imposition of "foreign" VCOs and noncommissioned officers.[5]

While cultural clashes hampered the war effort in some branches, lack of trained manpower were especially troublesome in others, particularly the technical branches. The cavalry, for instance, had been a real cavalry before the war, namely mounted soldiers. It was composed of the "elite" of the army: rugged Rajputs and Punjabi Muslims, superb horsemen by tradition and training. During World War I it was obvious even in India that there was no future for the cavalry. Therefore the military converted the cavalry into units of the newly formed Indian Armored Corps. The results were pitiful as the stalwart horsemen tried to learn how to operate and maintain complicated mechanical and electrical gear. They lacked both the technical knowledge and the facility of mind to learn their new trades, and large numbers of new classes with higher educational levels had to be recruited; classes such as Madrassis, and even Bengalis.[6]

By the end of the war large numbers of "new" classes had been heavily recruited to the military in numbers and percentages much greater than during World War I. An official summary of the manpower problem concluded that many

[4] Infantry and Artillery Memoranda.

[5] *Ibid.*, and Royal Indian Army Service Corps Memorandum, which points out the language difficulties. Artillery expansion fell "well behind" that of infantry in the first three years of the war.

[6] Indian Armoured Corps and Infantry Memorandum.

prewar notions had been "exploded," especially those regarding the usefulness of nonmartial groups and the degree to which Indians of different but related *jati* could be mixed.[7] For the first time Sikhs from various regions of the Punjab were mixed in the same units, as were Jats and non-Jats, Punjabi Muslims and northern Muslims. Some Dogras, Brahmins, and Garhwalis were found to be freely interchangeable as were all Madrassis, whether Hindu, Christian, or Muslim. Some interclass mixing was also found to be effective. Sikh units were "diluted" with Hindu Jats and Gujars, and Dogra units were mixed with Ahirs, Gujars, Kumaonis, and other Punjabi Hindus. Generally, untouchables did not mix successfully with high-caste soldiers, and separate untouchable units were revived (the Mahar Machine Gun Regiment, the Mazbhi and Ramdasias Sikhs, and the Chamar Regiment).[8]

The lesson of these departures from the prewar pattern of recruitment was not lost. Several different evaluations of recruitment policies arrived at the same general conclusions: if the peacetime Indian Army were to expand rapidly, an entirely new system of recruitment and training had to be instituted. The *Infantry Memorandum* argued that proportionate representation of all classes was necessary, and suggested that less reliance be placed upon the "fighting" classes if these classes were not large enough to contribute effectively during wartime. Another recruitment and manpower memorandum argued the same point:

It is most necessary that the pre-war conservative system of enlisting from only small subareas and favoured subclasses should not be allowed to creep in again. Every effort should be made to keep all areas and all classes and subclasses "ticking over" in peacetime in the recruiting field.[9]

This epitaph of the martial-races theory went on to criticize "vested class interest, bogus caste prejudice, and parochial

7 War Department History, Head 2—Expansion of the Armed Forces [Recruiting Officers, Non-technical, Technical, Publicity, Personnel Selection, School boys, Cadets, Indian Air Force Manpower] Recruitment and Manpower (1939044), file 601/9055/H.
8 *Ibid.*
9 *Ibid.* See also Prasad, Chapter XII.

minded B[ritish] O[fficers] and Viceroy Commissioned Officers for trying to maintain a narrow class composition."

The military further recognized that the Indian Army of the future would have to maintain a higher standard of education if it wished to develop a capability for rapid expansion. The average peacetime soldier would have to move up one or two ranks in time of expansion. For this promotion he would need intensive training. "Soldiers have to be trained in the shortest possible time, and the better educated a man is before he joins the army the quicker he learns to be a soldier."[10] Thus, the memorandum rejected the policy of recruiting the most backward, illiterate, and martial sectors of Indian society. It also emphasized the need for a common language, and suggested an "endeavour to persuade Government to introduce as compulsory a universal language for India." The memorandum also urged the introduction of modern psychological tests to enable the technical branches to recruit the ablest individuals.[11]

The Indianization of the Officer Corps

The British would never have been able to organize the two and one-half million Indians recruited during the war had not educated Indians come forth in sufficient numbers to serve in the officer corps. Despite the noncooperation of most nationalists, thousands of Indians were enrolled, primarily as emergency commissioned officers (ECOs). Although British officers

[10] Infantry Memorandum.

[11] Many of these steps had been taken earlier in the war by the Royal Indian Navy (R.I.N.) and the Royal Indian Air Force (R.I.A.F.). Under the pressure of a more sophisticated technology they readily resorted to psychological tests and a nondiscriminatory system of recruitment. One result was that the R.I.N. and R.I.A.F. contained smaller percentages of "martial" castes than the Indian Army. The following expresses the attitude of the more technically oriented services: "The pre-matriculation Madrassi, whose English is usually good and his general education standard high, enters as a seaman at Rs. 40, where he is certainly useful, but the matriculate from the N.W.F.P., who can hardly speak or understand spoken English, comes in as a writer on Rs. 60, to the despair of the wretched accountant officer whose office he encumbers." From: R.I.N. Monograph, General State of the R.I.N. on Outbreak of War in 1939 and R.I.N. Expansion, No. 601/7450/H (A). See also: Monograph, Manpower Review of the R.I.N., 1939–45 (1945), No. 601/7188/H. See also Prasad (various appendixes) for tables of caste and class composition of the services.

controlled the upper levels of the military during the war, the ratio of British to Indian officers changed dramatically. In combatant units the ratio of British to Indian officers changed from 10.1:1 to 4.1:1, and more than 8000 Indians were serving in almost every fighting unit. (They were excluded from a few elite regiments, such as the Gurkhas.) Collectively the increase was even more dramatic. The number of Indian officers increased from 1500 before the war to 15,000, and some branches, such as the medical, were almost entirely Indian.[12]

The increase in Indian officers took place despite, rather than because of, the troubled political environment.

At the time neither patriotism nor interest had appealed to the educated youth of India to give of their best to the defense services. The best did not always come forward and that may account for considerable rejections and some wastage in training.[13]

Because of the intense official interest in Indianization, the work of the 1939 Indianization Committee was revived by the Historical Section of the War Department, which had a unique opportunity to find out exactly how well Indian officers performed during the war. How well did the Indian officer of 1945 shoulder responsibility in comparison with the Indian officer of 1939? How did Indian officers compare with British officers, and with the Indian State Forces officers?

Many units were polled, and their answers were no less direct than the questions. The replies from a wide variety of military units (staff, line, technical services) were quite consistent. Most felt that the standards of the wartime Indian ECO compared unfavorably with the prewar ICO—and for good reasons. The ECOs received shorter training, many had nonmilitary backgrounds, their English was weaker, and many were motivated by a desire for a government job rather than military service. But, not a few British officers noted that the standards of recruitment had varied greatly during the war, and those officers who had been carefully selected to begin with were just as good, if not considerably better in

12 Prasad, p. xxvii.
13 *Ibid.*, pp. xxvii–xxviii.

many instances, than the prewar Indian officers, despite their handicaps.[14]

The poll also indicated that the Indian ECOs were considered by their superiors to be slightly, but not markedly, inferior to the British ECOs. Both British and Indian cadets were graded in officer training schools during the war, and the percentage figures from one school provide a comparison:[15]

	British Cadets	Indian Cadets
Well above average	2.07	1.36
Above average	16.60	7.60
Average	75.33	76.84
Slightly below average	5.60	13.10
Well below average	0.40	1.10

The evaluation of most unit commanders was in rough accordance with these figures. A few rated Indians higher than their British counterparts, and a few rated them much lower. In most units there was no difference.

When queried about the special merits and demerits of Indian officers British commanders agreed almost unanimously on the superior ability of the Indian to handle his troops. Superior knowledge of Indian habits, customs, likes and dislikes, and language enabled him to come closer to his troops than a young Britisher fresh from England, with only an elementary knowledge of Urdu. The defects of some Indian ECOs were also noted. The most common complaint was "lack of initiative and drive," and the related criticism of poor ability at improvisation, lack of original thinking, and a consequent tendency to "stick to the letter rather than the spirit of instructions." Another complaint was that some In-

[14] A 75 percent rejection rate still existed among Indians applying for commissions on the national level even after provincial boards rejected at the rate of 50–75 percent. This high rate was explained by the ingenuous remark in a recruitment and manpower memorandum that "it is believed better types are available but are reluctant to come forward and the general conclusions are that such personnel are too comfortable in their own homes [!] or insufficiently national-minded [!!] to want to come forward." War Department History—Head 2—Expansion of the Armed Forces/Recruiting officers . . . / Recruitment and Manpower (1939–44), Historical Section file 601/9055/H.

[15] See citation of footnote 7, reporting information from the Indian Army's Military Directorate. Figures cover 1940–1945.

dian officers were not conforming to the Indian Army's great
tradition of loyalty and self-sacrifice, or, as a high-ranking
officer in artillery put it: "personal comfort, welfare, and self
interests are put before loyalty to State, Army, and Regiment."

Yet, even though the British noted these defects among some
Indian officers, virtually all reports bore heavy qualifications,
and cautioned against generalized criticism. The same artillery officer quoted above noted that "those Indians who have
'made the grade' compare more than favourably with the
British Regular Officer, and the better of the ECOs are equal
to the British ECO."

The faults of the Indian ECO, whether compared with the
Indian VCO or to the British ECO, were nothing when compared with the slovenliness, unmilitary attitude, and incompetence of the Indian State Forces officers, who were universally
criticized.[16] The striking difference between the two clearly
indicated that professional training—no matter how short—
and an association with other professional officers produced
significant results. In fact, most unit reports speculated that
with adequate selection, training, and supervision a corps of
Indian officers could be created which would equal, or be
superior to the British officer corps. Some felt that this training would take much time, and all felt it meant that the educational background of Indian youths would have to be vastly
improved, either by upgrading the universities or by setting
up a chain of precadet schools which could feed the Indian
Military Academy. Many officers strongly recommended a new
service academy with an enriched academic program. These
proposals ultimately led to the creation of the National Defense Academy at Khadakvasla.

However, before the academy became politically and or-
ganizationally possible, and before the British Indian Army
could serve as the model for a free army of India, a different
kind of challenge had to be overcome.

---

[16] This was a good military reason for eliminating the State Armies after
independence, although there were compelling political reasons for this
action.

THE CHALLENGE OF THE
INDIAN NATIONAL ARMY

The Indian National Army (I.N.A.) was the Indian counter-part to several other national liberation armies organized by the Axis powers during World War II.[17] It differed from other such armies, however, in the relatively substantial political, economic, and social base on which it rested, and in its control at all times by Indians themselves. The twin objectives of the I.N.A. were Axis victory and Indian freedom; but from its inception I.N.A. leadership was aware of the possible conflicts between these goals.

Although the I.N.A. ultimately comprised several combat divisions, its main challenge was not its size but its purpose and ideology.[18] Its objective was psychologically to demoralize the regular Indian Army, for which large numbers were not necessary. The I.N.A. was largely composed of and primarily aimed at members of the Indian Army. It was a part of that army which had broken away and turned against its parent organization. The I.N.A. used persuasion tactics, and although its official slogans were *Chalo Delhi* [On to Delhi] and *Jai Hind* [Victory to India], its real message was: "Why fight for the foreigners? Join us and fight for freedom!" *This* battle cry raised hope in the Indians and fear in the British. Had it been answered by mass defection, the course of the war and South Asian history would have been radically altered.

The Attractions of the I.N.A.

India had several I.N.A.s. One was composed of Indian troops captured in the West and recruited from European

[17] The following pages draw in part from the author's "Subhas Chandra Bose and the Indian National Army," *Pacific Affairs* XXXVI (Winter, 1963/64), 411–429.

[18] British figures indicate that some 20,000 of the 60,000 captured Indians joined one of the Asian I.N.A.s. See Winston S. Churchill, *The Hinge of Fate*, Vol. 4 of *The Second World War* (Boston: Houghton Mifflin, 1950), p. 100; see also Lieut.-Gen. Sir Francis Tuker, *While Memory Serves* (London: Cassell, 1950), p. 69. Unofficial Indian accounts of the I.N.A. indicate a somewhat larger number.

and African prison camps.[19] This I.N.A. (originally the Indian Legion) numbered only 3500 men, and was briefly led by Subhas Chandra Bose after his dramatic escape from India. This force never saw serious action. It was too small and too far from India to be used effectively. In addition, it suffered serious leadership and organization problems. Bose left this I.N.A. to its own devices and sailed on an Axis submarine to Singapore where more important developments had taken place.

In the earliest stages of the war the Japanese had swept down the Malayan peninsula capturing thousands of dispirited Indian troops along with their Indian and British officers. The crowning humiliation for the British was the loss of Singapore. The Japanese persuaded several Indian officers to organize an Indian national army from captured Indian Army troops, and to work with the Independence League of India. This League was a spiritual remnant of one of the most important Indian revolutionary movements, the Ghadr conspiracy, and was inspired by Rash Behari Basu, a terrorist who had taken permanent refuge in Japan in 1916.[20]

The most important figure in the first Asian I.N.A. was Captain Mohan Singh, an Indian commissioned officer, who later styled himself general of the I.N.A.[21] There is considerable evidence to indicate that Mohan Singh's I.N.A. differed in many ways from its successor which was organized by another ICO, Shah Nawaz Khan, and ultimately led by Subhas Bose.

Mohan Singh claims that he was actively considering joining the Japanese before he was captured. He correctly guessed

---

[19] A full-length and sympathetic treatment of the European I.N.A. appears in N. G. Ganpuley, *Netaji in Germany* (Bombay: Bharatiya Vidya Bhavan, 1959). For a balanced history of the I.N.A. movement by a former British intelligence officer, see Hugh Toye, *The Springing Tiger* (London: Cassell, 1959) and Bombay: Jaico, 1962). Pages quoted below are from the Indian edition. A young Indian scholar, K. K. Ghosh, had written an authoritative account of the Asian I.N.A., using Japanese and Indian sources. See Ghosh, *The Indian National Army* (Meerut: Meenakshi Prakashan, 1969).

[20] Toye, pp. 5-6.

[21] I am grateful to General Singh for several interviews and for permission to consult his unpublished history of the I.N.A. I am also grateful to several former I.N.A. officers for additional interviews.

that the lack of loyalty of Indian officers who joined the I.N.A. would come as a shock to the British. In an unpublished history of the I.N.A. he relates that the anti-British sentiment of the Indian public had penetrated the army, and that the ICOs were secretly celebrating Axis victories. After Singh was captured in Malaya, he assisted the Japanese in subverting the Indian Army, and became the creator of a new model Indian army, the Indian National Army. His success demonstrated that under some circumstances the loyalty and organizational integrity of the Indian Army could be replaced by new loyalties and new principles of organization. These new values were not "foreign" (as was the organization of the European I.N.A., which closely followed German military practices). They developed out of the ideals and ambitions of Indian officers themselves.

Mohan Singh began the reorganization of the Indian Army into the Indian National Army with one important asset: both officers and soldiers were in a state of psychological shock. The Indian Army had been grossly underequipped and was tactically unprepared to fight the Japanese. The result was a defeat so resounding that the confidence of all Indians in their British leadership was badly shaken. The esprit of the army had revolved around a history of glorious victories. World War II was not even a glorious defeat.

While the officers and men of the Indian Army were in this unstable psychological condition, Mohan Singh moved quickly against the organizational barriers between the new revolutionary leadership and the masses of soldiers, whose *voluntary* cooperation was essential. British officers were removed from their troops, as were Indian commissioned officers who remained uncooperative. Two key layers remained: the Viceroy's commissioned officers, and, beneath them, the noncommissioned officers. Mohan Singh offered flattery and an inflated status. Because of the numerous kinds of officers (KCOs, ICOs, VCOs, ECOs, States Officers, and NCOs) there was "a sort of caste-system amongst the officers which was detrimental to the solidarity and the healthy growth of a brotherly feeling amongst officers so essential at the time of war. . . .

With one stroke of the pen, I abolished all those classes and introduced only one class of officer. . . . This step had its magic effect on the spirit and morale of N.C.O.s and men. They all started confiding in me to an extent never before experienced."[22] Singh also played upon "differences in rates of pay, rations and status of British soldiers *vis a vis* the Indian soldiers and the lower status of the VCOs who in fact were the real backbone of the Indian Army," and "Subedar Majors and Jemedars (VCO ranks) were made captains and lieutenants, respectively, and in some cases were older men than the ICOs who held those same ranks."[23] These attractions, as well as the unfavorable treatment given those who refused to collaborate (they were turned over to the Japanese) had a significant impact upon the VCOs. Although they were frequently unenthusiastic about the ideals and goals of the I.N.A., their cooperation was effectively secured.

After the I.N.A. had "neutralized" the intermediate layer of officers (the VCOs) it was able to begin the reconstruction of the Indian Army.

Mohan Singh and his supporters instituted many reforms in their attempt to construct the first Asian I.N.A. Politically, they adopted the Congress program—a move which ultimately led to conflict with the Japanese who demanded complete subservience, and who ridiculed all Indian political movements. Singh also attempted to break down many of the caste and class distinctions found in the Indian Army, and make the I.N.A. truly representative. Separate kitchens were abolished, common messing was instituted, and according to Mohan Singh, "Hindu-Muslim unity was no more a problem. . . . Men began to mix freely and started eating together. . . . It was perhaps for the first time in our known history of thousands of years that we became true Indians and rose over and above the fetters of castism and communalism."[24]

One of the most difficult obstacles to the growth of the

---

[22] Gen. Mohan Singh manuscript, p. 78.

[23] *Ibid.*, pp. 104, 106.

[24] *Ibid.*, p. 79. Other officers who were present verify these attempts, which were largely abandoned after Mohan Singh's arrest and Bose's accession to I.N.A. leadership.

I.N.A. was the oath of allegiance that the British had required of all officers and other ranks. Mohan Singh later wrote:

Like some politicians the soldier does not treat his oath of allegiance as a transferable commodity. It was a tough job for me to explain to the men that an oath taken from us to keep our country a slave of the British was one of the meanest actions of the British. To break that oath and take a fresh one for freeing our country was a true and real religious action. . . . A true religion should be of revolutionary nature and an enemy of social and political injustice.[25]

Clearly, Mohan Singh attempted to construct his army on the basis of nationalism, social idealism, and equalitarianism. The oath of allegiance was sworn to him personally, and he tried to act as a charismatic leader who would take responsibility for all his supporters, and guarantee their personal and moral security. When Subhas Bose arrived on the scene it was relatively easy for those who had broken their loyalty to the British to transfer their allegiance from Mohan Singh to the even more charismatic Bose. The importance of the oath reflected the very personal character of loyalty and commitment, especially in the lower ranks of the Indian Army. Once the troops were sufficiently psychologically dislocated they were eager to take an oath to Mohan Singh or Bose to replace their oath to the King-Emperor, who had "failed" them in their disastrous defeat. The I.N.A. members had greatly depended upon the character of the leader rather than on direct loyalty to abstract principles. We shall see, however, that this loyalty to abstract principles—particularly to military professionalism—was much stronger among Indians in the commissioned ranks of the army, and many of them never did join the I.N.A.

Mohan Singh's I.N.A. was disbanded and he himself was arrested after he resisted Japanese attempts to limit the size of his force and exercise greater control over it. As an authentic nationalist and patriot, he had no wish to replace British with Japanese imperialism.

The I.N.A. was reorganized by Shah Nawaz Khan, another

25 *Ibid.*, p. 124.

young ICO, before Bose's arrival in June, 1943. This force
was the third to bear the name Indian National Army. Unfortunately for Bose, neither the military situation nor his
Japanese allies were very helpful. By the time he arrived, the
most suitable moment for an I.N.A. attack on India had
passed, and the British had begun to take the offensive. The
Japanese wanted to keep the I.N.A. small, and use it as a
shield for the Japanese Army. They saw it as playing a minor
role in the invasion of India and expected that it could be
easily crushed, should it become too independent. Therefore
the I.N.A. was starved of equipment, logistics support, and
information, and although it did occupy Indian soil briefly,
its battle history was dismal. Above all, it failed to serve as the
catalyst which would trigger revolution within the Indian
Army.

The I.N.A. and the Indian Officer

What were the motives of the I.N.A. leadership, especially
of the commissioned Indian officers who comprised its leadership? Why did many join, and why did others refuse—at great
personal cost—to collaborate with the Japanese? At least three
factors influenced the decision to join the I.N.A.: personal
comfort, nationalist political beliefs, and the charismatic appeal of Subhas Bose.[26]

A few of the defecting officers anticipated personal rewards
for themselves when they transferred allegiance to the Japanese, and to this extent the British label of "treasonous
rabble" was accurate. No I.N.A. officer has ever admitted
such a motive, but interviews with former I.N.A. leaders and
British officers indicate that money and security were important considerations for a few Indians. However, a greater
attraction of the I.N.A. was the organizational format of the
British Indian Army, particularly in such matters of prime
concern to professional military men as promotion policy,
devolved authority, trust, and personal treatment by British
fellow officers.

[26] The following interpretation was developed independently from but
parallels that of Philip Mason in his foreword to Toye.

Several officers cited the difference in treatment in the Indian Army between its Indian and British officers as an important reason for joining the I.N.A. Shah Nawaz Khan, testifying at his trial, noted that in the Indian Army "not a single [Indian] officer was given the command of a Division and only one Indian was given command of a Brigade." He concluded that, since there were highly competent Indians, "it appeared to me that lack of talent could not have been the reason for more Indians not getting higher commands."[27] The British had been cautious in their Indianization program, and later, when the I.N.A. was formed, many felt that this caution had been justified. But it can also be argued that giving more authority to Indians would have made them more loyal, even when captured.

A second attraction of the I.N.A. was the opportunity it offered to act in the interests of India, or at least to attempt to protect those interests. Many Indian officers, particularly those newly commissioned, were strongly attracted by the nationalist movement and saw the I.N.A. as an opportunity to use their profession to eliminate the British from India forever. An extreme statement of this position was given by Colonel P. K. Sahgal in his autobiography: "My father had taken an active part in the 1920–21 non-cooperation movement and from him I inherited an intense dislike for the alien rule. Added to this my own study of History and Political Science taught me that complete freedom was the birth right of every human being and it was the sacred duty of every Indian to fight for the liberation of the motherland."[28] Other officers appear to have been influenced by a wish to protect India from the Japanese, as much as to liberate it from the British. Shah Nawaz Khan claims originally to have opposed the I.N.A. but joined it to protect his men better from Japanese cruelties. He adds that he made sure that everyone joining the I.N.A. realized they might eventually have to fight the Japanese after fighting the British.[29]

[27] Maj.-Gen. Shah Nawaz [Khan], Col. Prem K. Sahgal, Col. Gurbax Singh, *The I.N.A. Heroes* (Lahore: Hero Publications, 1946), pp. 80–81.
[28] *Ibid.*, p. 106.
[29] *Ibid.*, p. 7. Mohan Singh vigorously defends the patriotic intent of the

The third, and probably decisive, factor in the continued
adherence of large numbers of Indian Army personnel to the
I.N.A. (especially in Singapore), was Subhas Bose. He was one
of the few Indians of his time qualified to assume the role of
militant director of the I.N.A. The data on the third I.N.A.
show the importance of his singular role. Bose's charismatic
leadership alone was undoubtedly sufficient motivation for
many Indians to join the I.N.A. He actually managed to put
a force into the field and engage in several battles, even if the
results were dubious. Without him, it is doubtful whether a
force could have been deployed at all, and the I.N.A. personnel would probably have joined the many other Indian
prisoners of war on forced-labor projects.

Bose's "magnetic personality" and his "hypnosis" of the
I.N.A. have been described by his Propaganda Minister, S. A.
Ayer, in a panegyric to his *Netaji* (leader).[30] If we are to believe this and similar accounts, Bose's effect upon both the
officers and men of the I.N.A. was instantaneous and electric.
However, other factors reinforced Bose's appeal. The Indians
in the I.N.A. were cut off from their native land. Their British
leadership had surrendered them to a cruel and ruthless opponent. Bose was an individual with enough international
prestige to deal with the Japanese and regain some independent status for the I.N.A. officers and men. His leadership offered them some hope of obtaining lenient treatment for their
men and even a chance for military success, however slim.
Consequently, any charismatic or personal appeal he had was
reinforced by the desperate position of the captured Indian
troops. Bose's leadership was crucial in transforming the
I.N.A. from an historical footnote into enough of a threat to
create serious concern among the British.

Those Who Refused

Despite the dramatic appeal of the I.N.A., most Indian officers who were not captured remained loyal to their British

first Asian I.N.A., and claims that it was as genuinely nationalistic as Bose's
successor force. Interview, New Delhi, 1965.

30 S. A. Ayer, *Unto Him a Witness* (Bombay: Thacker, 1951).

commanders and performed their duties with distinction. (Several Indian officers captured by the Japanese refused to join the I.N.A.) Even in the Eastern Command, where the India Army fought the I.N.A., and members of the same family faced each other, the officers of the Indian Army showed no sign of disloyalty. Indian Army officers, however, were under severe psychological and political pressure. Their nationalist and patriotic feelings were challenged directly by the I.N.A.'s call to overthrow the British. Balancing this challenge, however, were two counterconsiderations held by many nationalist-oriented Indian officers. First, many doubted that the I.N.A. would be able to resist Japanese dominance, and that Japanese rule would be more tolerable than British (especially to those who had been fighting the Japanese). A second consideration was discussed by General K. S. Thimayya's biographer: Many Indians realized that their countrymen in the military could best serve India in the long run by learning as much as possible from the British in the arts of war. Humphrey Evans related a discussion between Motilal Nehru and several Indian officers (among them Thimayya) held around 1929. Nehru urged the officers to remain loyal to the British until the day of independence came. The same sentiment held during the war for it appeared more likely that the British would grant independence, than the Japanese.[31]

The professional soldier had another reason for being less than sympathetic to the I.N.A.; his oath of loyalty. All officers joining the I.N.A. had broken their oath of loyalty to the Crown and to the Viceroy. Many did not regard lightly the breaking of these oaths. One of the fifteen captured Indian officers who did not join the I.N.A., and who spent the war in a prison camp (and was at times tortured by his own troops) talked about the importance of the oath:

I disliked the British as much as anyone else; they had not equipped us properly and they botched the defense of Singapore and Malaya, they let us down. But I had taken an oath, and you just don't break your word once you have given it; Nehru and the

[31] Humphrey Evans, *Thimayya of India* (New York: Harcourt Brace, 1960), pp. 116, ff.

politicians realized this later, how important the oath is; what
if we had a war with Pakistan? Would these men who broke their
oath once go over to the enemy again?[32]

Another senior Indian officer (who was not captured) also
alluded to the same problem:

The I.N.A.! They should have all been court-martialed in the
field and shot. [Q: All of them?] Yes, all that were guilty, it was
stupid bringing them back. It should have been handled as a military matter; it was very bad to let them off with little or no punishment, they were soldiers and had taken an oath. I had Muslim
troops under my command after the war. What kind of precedent
was the I.N.A.? To let a group rebel and then not punish them?[33]

In 1943–1944 it became apparent that although the battles
might continue, Japan could not successfully invade India.
Joining Japan proved to be a strategic error for the I.N.A.,
even though her chances appeared good when Singapore fell.

Another consideration (which emerged during the I.N.A.
trials) was the problem of promotion policy. As long as the
British retained control over the Indian Army, there was
little doubt where loyalty should be directed, and what kinds
of loyalty were rewarded with promotion (along, of course,
with factors of skill and talent). But, when the nationalists
defended the I.N.A. as patriots and true loyalists, how did the
Indian members of the Indian Army react? There was great
anxiety that the I.N.A. officers would be let off lightly and
perhaps rejoin the ranks of the Indian Army. Indian Army
officers feared that former I.N.A. members would be favored
over those who remained loyal to the British, should a viru-
lently nationalist policy be followed in the promotion policy
of free India. These fears did not materialize. The problem
had been recognized by their British superiors, and no whole-
sale reinstatement of I.N.A. officers was carried out, either by
the British or the new Indian government.[34]

---

32 Interview with a retired Indian lieutenant-general, 1963.
33 Interview with a retired Indian lieutenant-general, 1963.
34 See note of Field-Marshal Sir Claude Auchinleck to Defense Member
Sardar Baldev Singh, Jan. 6, 1947: "The Indian officers of the Army, already
uneasy and apprehensive lest the officers of the 'I.N.A.' should be reinstated

The I.N.A. and the Nationalists

Despite their vigorous defense of the I.N.A. at the end of the war, an undercurrent of doubt existed among Indian nationalists, particularly in Congress, about the meaning of the I.N.A., both in Indian and international terms.

The Indian Communists were opposed to Bose and his army. Their policy was derived from their support for the British war effort when it became clear where the Soviet Union's interests lay. Despite the ideological similarities between the Communists and the I.N.A. (or perhaps because of it), the Communists called Bose a "lackey" and "a fascist tool." These attacks were later turned against them by their opponents such as the "Society for Defence of Freedom in Asia," which reprinted Communist wartime attacks on Bose.[35] The policy of the Communist Party of India (C.P.I.) toward Bose and the Forward Bloc took several twists and turns as the "line" changed through the years. The British Communist adviser to the Indian Communists, R. Palme Dutt, argued that against a free India Bose's "hypocritical pretense" would have no effect, but against a subject India, it did have some influence.[36] Dutt recognized that Bose and the I.N.A. had had an enormous impact upon the Indian people during and after the war (particularly during the I.N.A. officers' trial); yet he could still class Bose with the Axis powers. Although his treatment of Bose was undoubtedly convincing to most C.P.I. members, the vast number of Indians thought otherwise.

The Muslim League was at first reluctant to express support

would, I fear, regard this action [release of I.N.A. prisoners] as the thin edge of the wedge and would become increasingly nervous of their future prospects." Reprinted in John Connell, *Auchinleck* (London: Cassell, 1959), p. 857. The military finally decided that I.N.A. officers who had not committed atrocities would be offered reinstatement in the Indian Army, but that they would *not* be given credit toward seniority for the period they spent in the I.N.A. This policy was unacceptable to them, for they would then have to serve two to three ranks below those who had stayed in the Indian Army.

[35] Sita Ram Goel, *Netaji and the CPI* (Calcutta: Society for Defense of Freedom in Asia, 1955).

[36] R. Palme Dutt, *India Today* (Bombay: Peoples' Publishing House, 1947), p. 5.

for the I.N.A. Later, however, when it became apparent that
the I.N.A. trials were to become an important issue in the
jockeying between the British and the nationalists, the League
joined with Congress in a wholehearted defense of the I.N.A.
The League thus shared in the popular acclaim of I.N.A. de-
fenders, and obtained another lever of negotiation for use
against both Congress and the British.

Jayaprakash Narayan, a leading Socialist, held that Bose's
motives and those of the I.N.A. were the highest possible: they
wanted to free India of British control. Narayan himself was
working for independence underground during the war, as
were many Socialists, but he nevertheless expressed grave
doubts over some practical aspects of the I.N.A. movement.
He was not impressed by the size of the I.N.A. or by its efficiency as a fighting force. If India were to be invaded, Narayan
wrote, it would be by the Japanese, and he was not impressed
by their treatment of the Burmese.[37] Citing Machiavelli and
Kautilya, Narayan cautioned Bose against seeking help from
a stronger ally in his otherwise praiseworthy enterprise. He
concluded that India must be strong enough to free itself from
British control, and that external aid would only perpetuate
India's subjugation.[38]

Most Congress members of the Indian National Congress
agreed. They shared Nehru's 1946 evaluation that "the men
and women, who had enrolled themselves in this Army and
worked under Shri Subhas Chandra Bose's guidance, had done
so because of their passionate desire to serve the cause of Indian freedom" even though they may not have been sure "as
to how far the formation and activities of this Army had been
justified, keeping in view the wider scheme of things and the
implications of the World War."[39] Leaders of Congress argued
that worthwhile people should not be punished because of
their I.N.A. activities; their motives had been good, even if
their aims were misguided, and India, in any case, needed

[37] Jayaprakesh Narayan, *Toward Struggle* (Bombay: Padma Publications,
1946), pp. 44–46.
[38] *Ibid.*
[39] Maj.-Gen. Shahnawaz Khan, *My Memories of I.N.A. and It's Netaji*,
Foreword by Jawaharlal Nehru, (Delhi: Rajkamal Publications, 1946).

their help.[40] Nehru did yield to the British, particularly
Auchinleck, on the question of treatment of those accused of
specific brutalities and war crimes. This displeased many nationalists, particularly in Bengal where pro-I.N.A. sentiment
was strong.

The entire I.N.A. affair under Bose raised a direct challenge to Gandhi. The way Gandhi reacted to this challenge is
revealing. It was not a consistent reaction, particularly during
the early years of the war. Azad records that Gandhi became
increasingly doubtful of an Allied victory during the war and
that Bose's dramatic escape to Germany

had made a great impression on Gandhiji. He had not formerly
approved many of Bose's actions, but now I found a change in his
outlook. Many of his remarks convinced me that he admired the
courage and resourcefulness Subhas Bose had displayed in making
his escape from India. His admiration for Subhas Bose uncon-
sciously colored his view about the whole war situation.[41]

Azad claimed that this admiration affected Gandhi's position
during discussions with the Cripps Mission. At the time of
Cripps' arrival, a report of Bose's death in an air crash was
circulating. The message of condolence sent by Gandhi to
Bose's mother was in glowing terms. Cripps complained to
Azad that he had not expected a man like Gandhi to speak of
Bose in such a manner.[42]

When the war ended, and Bose's death was fairly certain
(rumors that he is alive still periodically circulate through
India), Gandhi summarized the lessons of the I.N.A. in articles
in Harijan and in interviews with former I.N.A. officers.

Gandhi (along with most of India) praised the I.N.A. and
Bose for their patriotism and for demonstrating "self-sacrifice,
unity irrespective of class and community, and discipline."[43]
Gandhi stressed that these virtues must be employed in the

---

[40] Ibid., Foreword. See also Bhulabhai J. Desai's address at the trials reprinted
in his I.N.A. Defense (Delhi: Rajkamal Publication, 1947).
[41] See Maulana Abul Kalam Azad, India Wins Freedom (Bombay: Longmans, 1959), p. 41.
[42] Ibid.
[43] Mohandas K. Gandhi, Non-Violence in Peace and War (Ahmedabad:
Navajivan Publishing House, 1942, 1949), II (1949), 30.

service of nonviolence, not the bearing of arms, and he praised
the declaration of Shah Nawaz to become a soldier of nonviolence in the Congress ranks.[44] Gandhi challenged the I.N.A.
to replace their martial attitude of violence with the more
difficult attitude of martial nonviolence and to take to *ahimsa*
as had the Pathan leader Badshah Khan. Gandhi did not pro-
pose yielding to the Japanese if they invaded India, but, in fact,
outlined his own plan for dealing with such an eventuality.[45]

Gandhi drafted the Congress Working Committee Resolution, issued to reaffirm the Congress's creed of nonviolence.
That part of the December 1945 resolution which deals with
the I.N.A. clearly indicates an attempt to capitalize upon the
I.N.A.'s popularity without associating Congress with its
actions:

Whilst the Congress must feel proud of the sacrifice and discipline,
patriotism, bravery and the spirit of unity displayed by the Azad
Hind Fouz, organized as an independent force in the foreign
countries under unprecedented conditions by Shri Subhas Chandra
Bose, and whilst it is right and proper for the Congress to defend the
members of that body, now undergoing trial, and also to aid its
sufferers, the Congressmen must not forget that this support and
sympathy do not mean that the Congress has in any way deviated
from its policy of attaining independence by peaceful and legitimate means.[46]

A sense of doubt about the possible results of allying with
the enemy of the enemy runs through almost all nationalist
reaction to the I.N.A.; yet when the trials began, Congress, the
League and many communal groups came to the I.N.A. officers' defense. Aside from the reasons for the popular support
of the officers on trial, which we have already mentioned,
another factor probably accounts more for the fervor of the
defense of the I.N.A. than any other: to almost all but the
Communists, the I.N.A. symbolized a united India struggling
against British colonialism. The I.N.A. was a truly non-
communal, united nationalist movement, even though it had

[44] *Ibid.*
[45] *Ibid.*, pp. 37–39.
[46] D. G. Tendulkar, *Mahatma* (Bombay: Times of India Press, 1953), VII, 23.

relied upon Axis aid. That this unity should have arisen from the Indian Army added to its interest, for the army had been the one group most sheltered by the British from nationalist sentiments. The I.N.A. seemed to prove the British wrong who maintained that India was not really a nation, and that Indians could not work together. The theme of unity in Subhas Bose's propaganda war against the British does not seem to have been recognized by the British themselves when they made the major blunder of putting a Muslim, a Sikh, and a Hindu on trial together in the Red Fort.[47] But to many Indians the Indian National Army, not the Indian Army, was an object of true devotion; as K. M. Panikkar notes, it was not until the Indian Army acted swiftly and decisively in Kashmir that it was generally venerated and vindicated of British leanings.[48]

THE SEARCH FOR A NEW ETHOS

Every military system has an ethos which embodies—especially for the officer corps—the principles on which that system is based. War, revolution, defeat, or political change may on occasion produce an historic reexamination of that ethos. Such reexaminations are rare, and they are rarer still if they are overt and deliberate. Military organizations thrive on permanence, and selfexamination is administratively difficult and emotionally painful.

At the end of World War II, the impending transfer of power, domestic, social, and political turmoil, and the impact of the I.N.A., brought about such a reassessment. At this time several different systems were competing for dominance. Because the individuals concerned were largely officers, the debate focused on the "proper" role of the officer in the army and in India.

[47] According to Philip Mason the first defendants' cases were incomplete and the next three accused I.N.A. officers took their place. By coincidence, the three represented the major Indian religious communities, and were not even guilty of any major crimes. No senior civil servant or military man bothered to substitute more guilty defendants for these three. Interview, London, 1963.
[48] K. M. Panikkar, *Problems of Indian Defense* (Bombay: Asia Publishing House, 1960), p. 27.

At least three different images of the proper role of the officer were projected for serious evaluation. The first was held
by die-hard British officers who had originally opposed Indianization, or who felt that at the end of the war, the military
still had too few Indians of sufficient quality to run the army.[49]
Many British officers interpreted the formation of the I.N.A.
as proof that Indians were still irresponsible and might ruin
the Indian Army. Examination of published memoirs, and
interviews with senior British Indian Army officers, indicate
that the number of Britishers opposed to rapid Indianization
may have been as high as two-thirds. Many were convinced
that the lightness of the punishment given to I.N.A. officers
was proof that Indian politicians were still irresponsible and
that British presence in India was politically desirable. They
viewed the I.N.A. trials as a severe blow to the morale of the
loyal officer cadre, British and Indian alike. However, those
who held this view were soon to depart from India, and what
was once a powerful body of opinion was subject to considerable discount.

The crucial struggle occurred between the two other images
of the proper role of the officer. The first was the moderate
image, shared by some British military men (Auchinleck being
the most notable), many British civilians, many Indian officers,
and Indian civilians. The second was the radical approach of
Bose.

Bose viewed the I.N.A. and its officers in highly political
terms. Like the military of totalitarian states, the I.N.A. was
regarded as a center (or one of the main centers) of politics
and national regeneration. It was the model of an Indian
"people's army," a military organization truly representative
of the nation, the focus of national attention, the servant of

[49] "In 1947 the question was whether there were enough Indians, sufficiently
trained and experienced, to fill posts as commanders and staff officers in the
new regimes. . . . In my opinion, at that time, I considered that the army
required a further period of at least 5 years of intensive tutelage before
it was ready to undertake its full duties. . . . " Lieut.-Gen. G. N. Molesworth,
Curfew on Olympus (Bombay: Asia Publishing House, 1965), p. 275. Molesworth had been Military Secretary and Adviser to the Secretary of State for
India from 1943–1946.

a neototalitarian ideology.[50] Bose's remarkable political philosophy and even more spectacular political activity made his image of the military popular among extremists of the left and right. The I.N.A. shared in this veneration. Bose constantly and consciously borrowed from both Nazi and Communist ideology, and brilliantly buttressed his own activist and authoritarian inclinations with military symbolism. Bose's sudden death left the I.N.A. leaderless, for he had permitted no alternative leadership to develop. For the moderates his death was a blessing, removing what might have been an insurmountable obstacle.[51]

The dominant concern of the moderates was to nurse the Indian Army through the difficult transitional years. They envisaged an independent stable, democratic, and civilian-oriented India. The slightly divergent motives of the British, the officers, and the leaders of Congress were complementary enough to permit a consistent policy toward the future role of the officer. The British were trying to transplant their own image of the officer, the Indian officers themselves were more concerned about their status and future, and the Congress party leadership was concerned about getting the most skilled and reliable military leadership available. It was an act of great political skill to smooth over the conflicts among these groups in relation to the I.N.A. viewpoint.[52]

[50] For a work typical of the period (anti-British and dedicated to Subhas Bose and the future of a "people's army") see Dr. Lanka Sundaram, *India's Armies and Their Costs* (Bombay: Avanti Prakashan, 1946).

[51] The I.N.A. disbanded after the war, for the officers had little desire to keep it together. In 1947, Sarat Chandra Bose made an attempt to revive the I.N.A. as a political force by way of the Forward Bloc, but this effort was not successful. Perhaps the I.N.A. faded away as an organized force because many of its important members were sent abroad as ambassadors or given civilian duties. For example, K. P. Menon became ambassador to China, A. M. Sahay to Thailand, N. S. Gill to Mexico, A. H. Safrani to Syria, A. D. Loganathan to Indonesia, and M. Thevy to Rome. Shah Nawaz Khan and Dr. D. S. Raju joined the Congress, and were both eventually given posts in various ministries as Deputy Ministers. Other I.N.A. officers also joined Congress, including General Mohan Singh who was an active supporter of the late Pratap Singh Kairon in the Punjab. In Pakistan M. Z. Kyani was active as an organizer among tribesmen in Kashmir, and once served in President Ayub's secretariat.

[52] When full documentation is available it may well be seen that Nehru and Auchinleck played key roles in the relevant decisions.

Bose's death opened the way to a temporary continuation of the British pattern of officer recruitment and training. With the I.N.A. model eliminated from consideration, the army returned to its recent past for guidance. Young Indian officers reexamined their own British-derived traditions, and gave those traditions an overwhelming vote of confidence.[53]

The participants in this debate had to deal with the implications of an independent India and the changes necessary in the British-derived system to make the Indian military compatible with the aspirations and goals of the new Indian nation. Should the Indians reject Western traditions and make the army uniquely "Indian"? Should the new army be a balance between Western and Indian tradition? Should military efficiency be sacrificed for the sake of tradition, and if so, which tradition, British or Indian? These questions could not easily be answered, but were raised and discussed for the first time since Indians served in the officer corps. The professional legacy of the British Indian Army was generally affirmed on a wide variety of subjects, ranging from the relevance of such purely British institutions as the officers' mess to the principles of scientific selection.

The debate concerning the officers' mess was particularly interesting, for it had important professional, political, and social overtones. The officers' mess had been instituted by the British long before any Indians were commissioned. The rules of the mess covered more than dining etiquette. They prescribed a system of social behavior in the precincts of the mess. Each unit had its own rituals, laws, and customs, which contributed to the effectiveness of the mess as a focal point for loyalty and as an instrument of group control. The values transmitted in the mess were not only personal, but often professional as well. After Indianization began, Indian officers were also subjected to the constraints of the regulations of the

[53] This self-examination was encouraged by the British, who themselves contributed to it by stepping up the number of "pep" talks and lectures dealing with the future role of the officer corps in a free India. Contributions by Indians on the subject were not only encouraged but were solicited by the English editor of the professional officers' quarterly, the *Journal* of the United Service Institution of India.

mess. They were socialized professionally through the mess, and their personal and political beliefs controlled. Many Indians argued that the mess was undesirable and unnecessary, because they resented prewar mistreatment and because the mess had fallen into disarray during wartime. Others recalled pre-British indigenous armies, which had no messes, and pointed out the alien character of messes in India.

Some of the ablest Indian officers defended British institutions such as the officers' mess not because they were British and were thus of sentimental value, but because they were efficient devices for maintaining professional standards. One officer, D. K. Palit,[54] argued that nationalist India need not abolish the mess merely because the ancient Indian armies did not have one; he was more concerned with the danger of slipping back into the feudal pattern than being accused of copying the British.[55]

The continuation of the principle of scientific officer selection was also strongly defended on professional and political grounds. Lieutenant-Colonel Rajendra Singh, a prolific writer and influential soldier analyzed the motives which should cause men to fight:

Some consider that the spirit of the Forces depends on the motives of the individual. This may be true to some extent, but the corporate spirit of the Army must be based on discipline, morale and efficiency. Some do not understand the functions of the Forces, and consider that as a political instrument they should be used in the attainment of freedom. It is only during a revolution, when the authority of the Government is broken, that the indisciplined army takes political sides.[56]

The quality of an army depends upon the "spirit to fight till the last" like the heroes of Saraghari. The inward spiritual

---

[54] "Monty" Palit retired as a major-general. He has had a reputation as one of the ablest and most intellectually inclined officers of his age group.

[55] Lieut.-Col. D. K. Palit, "Are Officers' Messes Suited to Indian Conditions?" *Journal* of the United Service Institution of India hereafter referred to as U.S.I. *Journal*, LXXVI (January, 1946), 10. Colonel Palit's article was the annual Gold Medal Prize Essay Winner in 1945.

[56] Lieut.-Col. Rajendra Singh, "Is Scientific Selection Successful?" U.S.I. *Journal*, LXXVI (October, 1946), 335.

urge to fight must not come from politics but must grow from
the faith of the soldier in himself and his leaders. If the will to
fight is linked to propaganda or "political dogma" it will waver
according to the fortunes of the political party.[57]

Another officer pointed out the difficult environment in
which the Indian Army had to operate and the need to
continue British patterns of recruitment to keep the army
uncontaminated:

To have a politically minded army is to head for a national disaster. Politics, unfortunately, colour the tenor of all life in India
to-day, but if our future Army is to carry out its normal military
functions efficiently, politics should be taboo. A cadet therefore
who comes from a politically active class is most undesirable in the
officer ranks of the Army. I am aware that soldiers have the right
to vote and are, of course, entitled to their individual political
opinions as long as they do not make a public exhibition of them.
A soldier's duty and loyalty is to his country and not to the party
government of the day.[58]

This was also the official view. K. M. Cariappa (then
lieutenant-general) lectured to a group of Indian officers
shortly after partition. He bluntly demanded that officers
simply minded their own business and let their seniors and
the politicians handle the problems.[59] Sir Roy Bucher, a British officer who stayed on as Commander-in-Chief, spoke to the
staff and cadets of the Indian Military Academy, Dehra Dun,
at great length and in great detail on the relationship of the
military and politics; it is worth quoting his authoritative
statement:

The interests of the Army must come first in your thoughts and in
your actions all the time. Remember that the Army, and indeed all
the Services, are the servants of the Government in power at the
time, and the political complexion of a particular Government
makes not the slightest difference to this fact. As soldiers you are
not concerned with politics. There is nothing wrong in your hav-

---

[57] *Ibid.*

[58] Maj. Burbachan Singh, "The Right Type and Some Thoughts on Indianization," U.S.I. *Journal*, LXXVI (July, 1946), 444. He added that the
"right" type was neither the British officer nor the I.N.A. type, but the prewar Indian officer.

[59] Speech to Indian officers, October 8, 1947. Reprinted in U.S.I. *Journal*,
LXXVIII (January, 1948), 4.

ing political opinions and in expressing them with moderation in private conversation, but that is a very different matter to express-ing political opinions in public or allowing such opinions to in-fluence your action in any way. No Army which concerns itself with politics is ever of any value. Its discipline is poor, its morale is rotten and its reliability and efficiency is bound to be of the lowest order. You only have to look at certain foreign armies which are constantly mixed up in politics to realize the truth of what I say. It follows, therefore, that the Army has never the slightest right to question the policy of Government. Implicit obedience to the orders issued by Government is essential, and only in this manner will the interests of the country be fully served. And so you see that devotion to the Service implies devotion to the Country as well.[60]

The Indian military reaffirmed the attitude of political aloofness that it had been taught by the British.[61] As long as the government did not break down, the military had no busi-ness in civilian matters; it had to have "one faith—loyalty to the Government, and one fanaticism—'Izzat'—of the country and the forces."[62] If the government was duly elected by the people it made no difference whether it was socialist or re-publican. Its character was no concern of the military as long as it was representative. The military owed its allegiance to any elected government, and through it to all the people.[63]

The Safety, Honour and Welfare of Your Country
Come First Always and Every Time.

The Honour, Welfare and Comfort of the Men You
Command Come Next.

Your Own Ease, Comfort and Safety Come Last,
Always and Every Time.

This oath was inscribed on the main building of the Indian Military Academy, Dehra Dun, by order of Sir Philip Chet-

[60] Speech to the Staff and Cadets, May 28, 1948, reprinted in U.S.I. *Journal*, LXXVIII (October, 1948), 331.

[61] The story of the British officers who stayed on in senior and technical posts has yet to be told. At least one of them saw his task as that of a teacher, explicitly guiding and instructing his future successors. From an interview with a British Indian Army general, London, 1963.

[62] Lieut.-Col. B. L. Raina, "Leadership," U.S.I. *Journal* LXXX (January, April, 1949), 18. This article won the Gold Medal Prize Essay Competition for 1949.

[63] *Ibid.*

wode, Commander-in-Chief of the Indian Army in 1932. It summarized the code of conduct which the British attempted to impart to their Indian "gentlemen cadets." Today, the officer candidates are still referred to as gentlemen cadets, the oath still remains on the wall (although joined by excerpts from the *Gita*), and the oath still embodies the character and ethos of the several officer-training establishments of the Indian armed services.

This continuity of almost forty years was in part due to the great sense of corporateness and professional identity of the officers of the Indian Army, both British and Indian. Officers have been able to hand down, from KCO to ICO to wartime and postwar generations, many of the moral values and high professional standards which distinguished the British Indian Army.

Other important factors contributed to the success of the Indian armed services in making the transition from an "army of occupation" to a national army. In both successor states the transfer of power to the new national regimes was legitimate, visible, and complete. Those in power prevented ambiguity or uncertainty about the location of authority, and the military had no opportunity to intervene or expand its influence. The military, in fact, was not disposed toward intervention, despite its increased activities in domestic civilian aid tasks and external defense. The Indian officers were relatively junior in rank and status, and had taken no part in the great national struggle for independence. Civilians were so preoccupied with the problems of partition, and with fitting themselves into their new roles of constitutionally bound statesmen that they left the military free to devote its energy to internal cohesion. In part this nonintervention was due to a preoccupation with one's own affairs, and in part it was due to apathy and a lack of sustained interest. Many politicians, especially, sought only loyalty from the officers, and put off major changes or pressures toward conformity. The military was content to be left alone and permitted to rebuild its precarious organizational integrity.

7

THE INDIAN ARMY
AFTER INDEPENDENCE

The partition of British India into the states of India and Pakistan after independence in 1947, was accompanied by the division (some have said vivisection) of the British Indian Army into two national armies. Each of these armies shares the legacy of the British Indian Army, although that legacy seems to have been differently interpreted in the two successor states. What follows is not a history of the military in India and Pakistan since 1947, but an examination of the legacy and an interpretation of the organizational and ideological imperatives which have shaped and will continue to shape the two successor armies.[1] Briefly, these imperatives were:

1) Under the British important decisions could be (and sometimes had to be) referred to London. Severe civilian-military disputes in India were decided by the Home government, which had the power to make its decision stick. In

---

[1] For recent histories of the two armies the following are useful: Lorne J. Kavic, *India's Quest for Security* (Berkeley and Los Angeles: University of California Press, 1967), S. S. Khera, *India's Defense Problem* (New Delhi: Orient Longmans, 1968), A. L. Venkateswaran, *Defense Organization in India* (New Delhi: Publications Division, 1969), and Maj-Gen. Fazal Muqeem Khan, *The Story of the Pakistan Army* (Karachi: Oxford University Press, 1963).

independent India and Pakistan new systems of decision-making had to be created, and the Indian elite had to learn how to operate in these systems.

2) The central position of the Indian Army in the British Raj was unacceptable in nationalist Pakistan, and especially India. The military was omnipresent in British India. It was particularly visible in its support of local police forces suppressing nationalist agitations. Presumably, independence meant a sharp reduction in the military's internal security role, and a parallel reduction in the hostility between the military and Indian politicians, many of whom had their own images of the armies of a free India or Pakistan.

3) The organization of the British Indian Army was particularly subject to criticism during the preindependence years, and was regarded by many political leaders as hopelessly feudal, inequalitarian, and caste-bound. In particular the "martial races theory" and the selection of commissioned officers by social status were regarded as anachronistic, if not dangerous to the fledgling Indian democracy. The limited contact of politicians with the military before 1947 reinforced their suspicion of the motives and loyalties of those who had voluntarily served under the British.

Had partition been followed by a long period of relative peace, the changes implicit in the nationalist criticism might have been speedily effected. However, partition also ushered in a period of permanent Indian-Pakistani hostility, complicated after 1959 by the presence of China as a major threat to Indian security. The effect of these hostilities was to postpone, rather than to precipitate, change, for the military resisted organizational changes in times when troops were needed for active defense. Civilians, overwhelmingly inexperienced in military affairs, were reluctant to press for change.

CIVILIAN-MILITARY RELATIONS AND
THE HIGHER DIRECTION OF WAR

During most of the British rule strategic decisions were jointly made by India and Whitehall. The Indian Army had considerable autonomy in minor matters, but important decisions were made with the concurrence of the Viceroy, and often referred to London for further consideration by the British government and senior military leadership. Independence meant that decisions would be made in India and Pakistan, and that new personnel would be making these decisions.

In India civilian-military affairs quickly resolved themselves into a three-cornered relationship between young Indian officers, none of whom had served in a rank higher than brigadier during World War II, members of the civil service (very few of whom had served in the Defense Ministry or had been connected with military matters under the British), and the political leaders, who had even less defense experience. The administrative and organizational changes introduced after independence indicate a fairly effective alliance between the civil service and the politicians, an alliance created for the purpose of reducing the role of the military in the decision-making process.

A major blow to the autonomy and influence of the military —especially to the only substantial service, the army—was struck on Independence Day, August 15, 1947, when the position of Commander-in-Chief in India was abolished. India had always had a Commander-in-Chief, and he had hitherto been the single source of military advice for the Indian government. (The navy and air chiefs were his subordinates.) After this date the three chiefs were responsible to the Defense Minister, and were collectively the professional military advisers to the government.[2] The ostensible reasons for this drastic reduction in the relative influence of the chief of the army were: to promote "balanced" growth among the three services, to provide better advice on technical navy and air force matters, and to follow all "modern" armed forces, which have each of the three services under an independent chief.[3] There were also good unofficial reasons for this step. The only challenge to civilian authority could come from the numerically dominant army; reducing the authority of its chief

---

2 Venkateswaran, p. 139.
3 *Ibid.*

to the point where he was not even first among equals made it easier to balance off the army with the other two services.

The strengthening of the civil-service dominated Ministry of Defense was a second critical organizational change. The military had always been under the close financial scrutiny of the Ministry of Finance. This scrutiny was not reduced, but it was complemented by the growth of the Defense Ministry's role in the decision-making process, quite often at a low level. Charged with the responsibility of providing expert advice to the minister or the Cabinet, the Defense Ministry expanded its capacity to control information and make decisions. It also assumed some of the former powers of the Commander-in-Chief, and it "became the responsibility of the Ministry to ensure that a uniform policy to the greatest extent possible was evolved and that decisions taken in respect of one Service did not produce repercussions on the other two Services."[4] Information policy and—critically—responsibility for defense production were placed under the control of the Ministry of Defense.

These and other bureaucratic changes were accompanied by many adjustments in the status of the military in India. Some of these adjustments were symbolic, others were substantive. The adjustments made in the Warrant of Precedence during the postindependence years were of particular interest. A secretary in the government of India ranked lower than a lieutenant-general until 1947; afterwards he was made to rank with a full general. The Chief Secretary of a State formerly ranked with brigadiers; after independence he was made to rank with a major-general. In 1948, the Chief of the Army Staff ranked with judges of the Supreme Court of India, but was senior to chief ministers outside their states or the Secretary General of the External Affairs Ministry. In 1951, Chief of the Army Staff became junior to the Supreme Court justices, and in 1963 he became junior to chief ministers outside their states, to the Cabinet Secretary, and to the Secretary General. Disparities in pay also developed. A deputy secretary in the

4 *Ibid.*, p. 123, and interviews with some of the participants.

government of India draws less pay than a brigadier, who may have ten years more service, but is equated with him in the Warrant of Precedence; even the relative status of the military in relation to the police has been downgraded, and officers deputed to quasi-military organizations such as the Border Security Force may find themselves under the command of police officers with less pay, less service, but a higher rank.[5]

All these organizational changes had the effect of reducing the military's role in the decision-making process. The military was thoroughly indoctrinated with the principle of civilian control and never protested against the reduction of its own powers, or at least never protested to the point of resignation. Indian officers were relatively inexperienced and were reluctant to test their authority against that of the government. Unfortunately, neither civilian politicians nor civil servants developed the expertise and skills necessary to understand and meet the Chinese threat which emerged full-blown in 1959. Even today, the personnel of the Ministry of Defense is relatively inexperienced in defense affairs; out of fourteen officers of the rank of joint secretary and above, only four have risen from the rank of deputy secretary in the Ministry of Defense itself; the rest have entered directly at the level of joint secretary.[6] The record of the political leadership of the Ministry of Defense is no better. Very few ministers of defense appointed since 1947 had any previous defense experience or recorded interest in defense affairs; many were not even politically influential. Krishna Menon (appointed in 1957) was an exception.[7]

This paucity of talent reflected the small number of Indian politicians who were seriously interested in defense affairs.

[5] For an army officer's view of these changes see Brig. S. K. Sinha, "Career Prospects for Officers in Armed Forces," U.S.I. Journal, LXXXXVIII, No. 412 (July-September, 1968), 263–269.

[6] Review of S. S. Khera's book by K. Subrahmanyam, Hindustan Times, Feb. 16, 1969. Subrahmanyam notes that the period of tenure of civilian civil servants in the ministry of Defense is usually only five years, two of which are spent learning their job. Defense affairs alone does not suffer from this approach. It reflects a faith in the "generalist" civil servant, capable of handling any kind of job.

[7] Khera presents a brief and frank survey of the various ministers of defense since 1947. See Chapter IV, "Defense Ministers of Independent India."

And, of these, many had been in non-Congress parties. The liberals as a political force had virtually vanished from India years before World War II, and their political descendents were able to mount only token opposition in Parliament.[8] The slate of the Congress leaders was clean with regard to defense matters (they paid little attention to improving the military administration of the British, but did not attempt to subvert or infiltrate the military, either). Yet the Congress leaders decided early that defense was not a high priority as long as the only likely enemy was Pakistan. In effect, the decision was made over a period of years to keep military administration and defense matters out of the main stream of politics. An information policy was formulated which in many ways was more restrictive than that of the British, and continues to impair intelligent criticism of defense policy.[9]

The Indian defense decision-making process is, as it was during the years of British rule, largely an administrative process, closed to outside scrutiny. If anything, the process has become more decentralized and more compartmentalized than the British Indian system. The military has sensed the difficulties of this arrangement and has frequently made proposals for the increased centralization of defense policy making, usually by the creation of a chief of the Joint Chiefs of Staff. They have not, however, gone beyond this proposal and presented a scheme for the thorough integration and reorganization of higher strategic decision-making which would take into account defense interests in several ministries. The present system is fragmented with several decision-making centers, none of which are adequately staffed or equipped to consider a broad range of security issues. For example, India has no

8 Pandit H. N. Kunzru was an active critic of the government's defense policy for several years in the Rajya Sabha (upper House of Parliament). He has also, on occasion, served on special committees to examine various aspects of defense and security problems, the most recent being The Kunzru Committee on Physical Education, which examined several quasimilitary youth programs for the Ministry of Education. See the Committee's *Report* (New Delhi: Ministry of Education, 1964).

9 Critics of the government, opposition parties, and newspapers, have not been enterprising in putting together available information from Indian and foreign sources. The Institute of Defense Studies and Analysis (New Delhi) is presently doing this with great effectiveness.

single department or institution adequately equipped, either intellectually or politically, to make decisions or even to study such an important issue as nuclear weapons procurement.

Part of the difficulty of the government of India during the past twenty years in managing its security policy stems from an inadequate conception of civilian-military relations. The attitudes inherited from the British have turned out to be a crippling legacy, providing neither theoretical nor practical guidance.

Krishna Menon's formulation of the proper relationship is widely shared:

It is wrong for the army to try to make policy; their business is to be concerned with military tactics. Military planning and arrangements and things of that kind must remain in the hands of the Government, and even inside the Government these questions are largely conditioned by finance. I believe the statement that was made recently, that strategy was left with the army, was due to misuse of terms. The Government is not going to say that it wants one company here or two companies there, but the Government will certainly say, "we should attack Pakistan" or "we should not attack Pakistan" or "we should accept trainees from Indonesia and Malaysia," or things of that kind; these are all matters of policy....
Of course, military matters are merely questions of expertise; strategy includes considerations that are related to our political orientation.[10]

Except for the implications of the final sentence, even the military would agree to this statement. Yet, Menon's own actions as Defense Minister indicate the many gradations between military affairs and policy affairs, and, as in the Kitchener-Curzon dispute and other civilian-military clashes in British India, much depends on who defines precisely the meaning of "military" and "political." Menon found it difficult to adhere to a restrictive formula. During his tenure as Defense Minister he initiated many reforms in hitherto "purely" military affairs. He widened the base of recruitment of the officer corps, tried to make the military more aware of its social obligations, and greatly expanded the range of military

10 Quoted in Michael Brecher, *India and World Politics* (London: Oxford University Press, 1968), p. 260.

items manufactured in India, laying the groundwork for relative self-sufficiency in the late 1960s.[11]

But Menon's most significant departure from his own theory of civilian-military relations occurred during the prolonged confrontation with the Chinese along the Himalayan frontier. During the months before the outbreak of hostilities in late 1962, Menon and Jawaharlal Nehru directly supervised the placement of individual brigades, companies, and even platoons, as the Chinese and Indian forces engaged in mutual encirclement of isolated outposts.[12] Neither Menon nor Nehru had any earlier military experience, and the Indian Army still harbors an extraordinary amount of bitterness at their use of troops as essentially political pawns. As far as the military was concerned, peace had turned into war and the politicians were still meddling.

The military's own approach to civilian-military matters is hardly more sophisticated than the civilians'. The British tradition of separate spheres of military and civilian activity has carried over. Even today Indian officers like to boast that politics and the military do not mix; that the two are immutably different and separate, and that the military is, and should forever be, outside (some say "above") politics. Junior officers in the Indian Army are taught to be political illiterates, and are content to remain so, concentrating on "purely professional" matters. Those few generals who have earned a reputation for political expertise (or at least familiarity with politicians), such as B. M. Kaul, have not been popular with their colleagues.

Yet, India's strategic environment, particularly her sensitive borders, makes it impossible for the military to avoid political questions in time of peace, let alone during hostilities. As officers are promoted beyond the rank of brigadier, they must demonstrate an understanding of politics. Whether politically

---

[11] See Khera, pp. 49–50, and also T. J. S. George, *Krishna Menon* (London: Jonathan Cape, 1964).

[12] See Khera, pp. 195 ff., Lieut.-Gen. B. M. Kaul, *The Untold Story* (Bombay: Allied, 1967), and especially Brig. J. P. Dalvi, *Himalayan Blunder* (New Delhi: Thackers, 1969). These three books are accounts of individuals personally involved in the NEFA disaster. Other versions are to be expected.

sensitive officers tend to be promoted, or whether they are sensitized in their new roles is not clear. It is also difficult to tell the ratio of "fighting" generals to "political" generals. One must assume that the Indian government is concerned with the problem, for it has established an institution, the National Defense College, solely for the purpose of broadening the background of promising officers of brigadier or equivalent rank. The officers are exposed, for the first time in their service careers, to a wide range of political, economic, and strategic issues. The effectiveness of such training is uncertain, although Chinese-Indian politics can hardly be understood without it. Indian politicians and the military quickly grasped the motives and actions of the Pakistanis. The Indians and Pakistanis had common cultural and institutional origins, and frequently personal links. The rules were understood by both sides. The Indians discovered, however, that the Chinese challenge was different, both in substance and style, and the events of 1962 are remembered in the army with much bewilderment and bitterness. The legacy of the British was to keep the military politically neutral. The Indians learned, however, that it was necessary to equip the military with political understanding.

Pakistan—The Loss of Legitimacy

British political legitimacy in India (in the eyes of the military) was established in the figure of the Viceroy who was the direct, personal representative of the Crown and Home government. He was often a man of great personal distinction and competence. The new Indian and Pakistani political elites which came to power after independence inherited the trappings of soverignty from the British and added to them the aura of legitimacy which derived from the struggle for freedom. The military in both states was content to acknowledge this legitimacy, and was at any rate too young and inexperienced to challenge it seriously. The military devoted itself to professional matters. In Pakistan, however, the military demonstrated that professionalism may, in fact, contribute to intervention in politics, if civilian authority decays. Professional corporateness curbed one potential coup, and several years later insured the success of another coup.

In 1951, a few officers of the Pakistan Army plotted the assassination of the Commander-in-Chief (a Britisher), the Prime Minister, and other high officials. This attempted coup (the Rawalpindi conspiracy) was quickly crushed, although it shook the officer corps to its roots. The plotters violated an old tenet of the British Indian Army which was supported by most Pakistani officers: as gentlemen and as colleagues, officers should "stick together" and not violate the chain of command. In the eyes of the more moderate and apolitical generals, such Ayub Khan, violating the trust of their fellow officers was as great a crime as acting against the legally constituted government.[13] When the military did intervene in Pakistan, a prime motive was its revulsion at the incompetence of the politicians and the corrupt civil service; its weakness and venality was harming Pakistan externally and internally, and, above all, threatened the integrity of the military itself.[14] In 1951, the corporate spirit of the military had the effect of rallying most officers behind the government and their British commander. In 1958, it insured the unity of the military behind Ayub Khan. Last-minute attempts to divide the officer corps failed.

Pakistan demonstrated that professionalism does not prevent military involvement in politics. Threats to a democratic-competitive system can come from too much professionalism as well as from too little. In former colonial states the military might be said to be "too professional" because it is technologically and temperamentally more modern and capable than the rest of the political system. Impatient for results, and fearful of a decline in its resource base (or its reputation),

---

13 Col. Mohammad Ahmad, *My Chief* (Lahore: Longmans, Green and Co., 1960), pp. 37 ff.

14 Fazal Muqeem Khan, pp. 176–186. In the eyes of the military the symbol of their potential deterioration was Maj. Gen. Iskander Mirza, who was President of Pakistan at the time of the *coup*. Mirza had left the army for the civil service. Although a personal friend of Ayub and other generals, he was exiled to London permanently.

the military steps into politics in order to save itself by saving the nation:

It may take longer in underdeveloped countries than elsewhere for military leaders to realize that modernization of the army is possible only if the society modernizes as well, but when this realization comes the army often tries to topple the old system and impose a new one more to its liking.[15]

Professionalism may help curb militarism by giving the military an organizational outlet for its ambitions and energies, but the gains may be lost to "reactive" militarism, such as that in Pakistan, where the military feared for its careers and its services.

The critical element is the perception of the officer corps of the strength and legitimacy of the political process. The British controlled the outlook of young Indian officers by highly selective recruitment and promotion procedures, isolating them from the political currents of Indian society, and by impressing them with the sheer weight of the history of British rule in India. Few of these devices are available today, and civilian elites must continually supervise and dominate, especially in areas where civilian and military interests overlap. Not only must the military be *taught* that civilian control is the norm, civilians must demonstrate their own *effectiveness*. According to the original Clausewitzian justification of civilian control, political considerations were so important in war that the purely military outlook was insufficient. The same consideration applies to all defense-related problems, especially in systems in which power is legitimized by rational-legal norms, for in these, performance is likely to be the ultimate criterion. The magnitude of an external or internal crisis alone does not determine a realignment of political forces in a nation, but the relationship of such a crisis to the will and determination of key elites.

The importance of legitimate and effective political leadership as a prerequisite for civilian control cannot be overem-

15 A. F. K. Organski, *The Stages of Political Development* (New York: Knopf, 1965), p. 52.

phasized. Relative power is not the decisive factor. If it were, military governments would be far more widespread today. The importance of authoritative political leadership derives in large part from the military. First, professional soldiers are generally obsessed with the maintenance of organizational integrity. They are paid to think and worry about the next war. Since they never quite know the capacity of potential enemies, they tend to ask for additional arms, men, equipment, and power. Political leadership which cannot manage the affairs of the nation is despised by the military not only for aesthetic reasons but because the military fears it may not be able to secure its proper share of resources. Inadequate transport, raging famine, poor production, uncontrolled demonstrations, and weakness in policy, are important hints to the military that it is under the authority of a political body whose competence is to be doubted. In time of war will civilian bungling affect the military?

A second reason for the importance of clear-cut legitimate civilian leadership derives from the special function performed by professional soldiers: they take human life and destroy property in the name of the state. Professional soldiers *learn* the special justifications for these acts. They learn that the moral responsibility for their killing lies with the government, and that decisions concerning life and death are morally neutral if they are politically legitimate. If the legitimacy of political leadership deteriorates, the officer must reassess the morality of his own actions, a difficult and painful task. A government which lacks legitimacy can no longer presume to be the arbiter of morality; those who perform tasks on the margin of moral behavior—the military and police—rapidly develop symptoms of anxiety when they are burdened with unaccustomed moral decisions.

RECRUITMENT AND REPRESENTATIVENESS

The organizational format of the British Indian Army had been particularly criticized by Indian politicians before independence, but was defended by those with close ties to the military. As we have seen, recruitment by class and caste was especially subject to attack, and World War II demonstrated clearly the irrelevance of much of the martial-races theory. Indianization of the officer corps had been another subject of hot debate, although the expansion of the army from 1939 to 1945 had led to the Indianization of most units. The role of the Indian officer was a related and still relevant question.

Few Indian politicians have articulated the deep, nonmilitary stakes behind the issue of recruitment, but many sense the importance of the question. The nature of recruitment is important to the whole issue of national identity and nation-building, especially in a democracy. Democratic states have always had difficulty in relating equalitarian, democratic values to the values of the military whose main purpose is to kill and destroy. Should this task be left to those who volunteer for it, or should it be one of the obligations of citizenship? The alternatives become more critical if the volunteers are an unrepresentative group, reflecting regional, class, or caste predispositions, or all three at the same time.

Representativeness is closely related to the spirit of a military organization. In any army individuals fight for several reasons—because of the pay, because of regimental or unit loyalty, because of personal loyalty to a civilian or military commander, and because of emotional identification with the larger political unit. Modern nationalism has emphasized the latter motivation—patriotism. Politicians who are trying to build or maintain a nation-state have always sensed the importance of using patriotism as a fighting motive. The spirit of patriotism increases political leverage over the military. It also increases national awareness in that part of society which is most likely to adopt purely professional, regional, or parochial bonds of loyalty. Politicians thus become concerned with the degree of equalitarianism within the military—the rank structure, officer–troop relations, pay, service conditions, and criteria for promotion. They also become interested in training and indoctrination programs having political content.[16]

16 Indian political leaders interested in developing an Indian nation were on firm ground in their criticisms of the Indian military system under the

After independence, Indian and Pakistani military and political elites turned to the problem of reshaping their military systems to reflect more closely their views of what an Indian or Pakistani army should look like. Both successor states are still—after more than twenty years—fundamentally reflections of the British Indian Army, although there has been considerable change since 1963.

The Officer Corps

Despite some desultory talk, neither army has changed the relationship of the officer to the other ranks, nor abolished the position of junior commissioned officer.[17] Both armies still are class-bound in the sense that officers are generally drawn from higher strata of society. They must be able to use English as their medium of communication, and aspire to a life style which clearly imitates the British Indian Army commissioned officer. Visitors to the subcontinent often conclude (as have many Indians and Pakistanis) that the military remains the last outpost of the British Raj. As in other former colonies the military is often regarded as the most "modern" sector of society. The military has a brusqueness of manner and a routinized method of problem-solving which often passes for

---

British. In the West, the rise of the modern nation-state was closely associated with the development of an equalitarian and representative military. See Alfred Vagts, *A History of Militarism* (rev. ed.; New York: Meridian Books, 1959), Samuel P. Huntington, *The Soldier and the State* (Cambridge: Harvard University Press, 1957), Quincy Wright, *A Study of War* (Chicago: University of Chicago Press, 1942), and Hans Speier, "Militarism in the 18th Century," in *Social Order and the Risks of War* (New York: Steward, 1952), p. 243. An officer corps recruited on representative and equalitarian criteria may contribute to nation-building, but not necessarily to the strengthening of democratic politics. See Gaetano Mosca, *The Ruling Class* (New York: McGraw-Hill, 1939), and Morris Janowitz, *The Professional Soldier* (Glencoe: Free Press, 1960), p. 254.

17 The JCO continues to play an important—if altered—role in the Indian Army. He still serves as a father figure for the other ranks, although less so in units which recruit from the educated sectors of Indian society. He may serve as the cultural bridge between commissioned officers and other ranks if the officer comes from a region different from his soldiers. Except for this situation, his mediatory role has been reduced, and Indian officers know their troops at least as well as their British predecessors. The relatively advanced age of JCOs has been a problem recently, in terms of physical condition and absorbing new ideas. However, there is no serious proposal to do away with the JCO.

development. Much of the recent optimism in Western intellectual circles (particularly American) concerning the great potential role the military might play in nation-building in the third world was based on this image of competence and efficiency.

Yet, behind the facade, even Indians and Pakistanis drawn from the most highly Westernized sectors of their societies have, as a group, transitional or intermediate personalities and outlooks. Individuals in the officer corps whose childhood and upbringing did not include a strong traditional component are rare. They have "honeycomb" personalities, and must shift rapidly from one role to another: from a purely technical encounter to a traditional home or personal life. They may present one face to a professional colleague,[18] another to a Western visitor, another to their family, and still another in a nonprofessional indigenous context.

Two important trends are under way (especially in India) which make the contrast between traditional and modern modes of behavior even stronger in the officer corps: a changing base of recruitment, and a changing professional context.[19]

For many years after independence it seemed as if nothing was being done to alter the composition of the officer corps in either India or Pakistan. A sampling of the cadets in the National Defense Academy (India) in the mid-1950s indicated a continuing preponderance of Punjabis, who comprised on the average a third of the cadet corps.[20] Delhi, which is adjacent to the Punjab, supplied about 15 percent of the cadets during the 1954–1956 period, while Madya Pradesh, Madras, Mysore, and Kerala supplied less than 5 percent each.

[18] Even in their professional life they may occupy a number of subroles and interact with a wide range of phenomena. An officer must learn to deal successfully with things—equipment, weapons, logistics problems—and with people. The latter will range from highly traditional *jawans* and camp followers to highly Westernized senior officers and civilians.

[19] Precise data are unavailable. The following is based in large part upon personal observation, biographical and autobiographical accounts of South Asian military professionals, a survey of professional service journals in India and Pakistan, and accounts of other observers of the military in South Asia.

[20] India, Parliament, Estimates Committee, 1956/57, *Sixty-third Report, Ministry of Defense Training Institutions* (New Delhi: Lok Sabha Secretariat, 1957), Appendix VII.

West Bengal and Andhra supplied less than 1 percent in some years. In Pakistan during this period virtually all army officers were recruited from the West Wing.

Yet, at least for India, these figures are not only obsolete, but they are misleading. They do not reflect important changes which have occurred in the social and geographical sources of the officer corps, and they do not reflect a rethinking of the problem of recruitment, especially after 1965.

Although precise data are unavailable, the status of the officer seems to have changed considerably, at least in India. Since 1939 the pay schedule of the lower ranks of the officer corps has remained the same while the value of the rupee has declined 80 percent. The attractiveness of officers in the marriage market (admittedly an indirect indicator!) has also suffered.[21] Housing has become unusually difficult for the Indian officer corps, and since 1962 increased deployment in the Himalayas has led to a more rigorous pattern of life. The military has lost its attractiveness for the old elites of Indian society, and is becoming a more popular career for India's growing middle class.

The doubling of the Indian Army after 1962 (and large increase in the size of the air force and navy) has speeded up this process. The number of officers in technical and support branches has increased greatly, and these officers usually have an abbreviated professional military training. Some fighting officers are engineers or communications and logistics experts as well, and have dual professional loyalties. Unlike the infantry officers, they do not participate as intensely in the mystique of comradeship of arms based on ethnic or caste loyalties. Many officers, particularly the engineers, were not even interested in the military as a career, but were unable to find suitable jobs in civilian life. For them the military is a good,

[21] *Times of India* (January, 1963): "Wanted a bridegroom for a very rich, beautiful, talented and highly educated young girl. The groom must have prestige and good social standing. Army officers need not apply." Quoted in: Brig. N. B. Grant, "A Soldier Fights—A Matter of Prestige," U.S.I. *Journal*, LXXXXIV (January–March, 1964), 21. Grant's entire article laments the officer's declining prestige. See also Lloyd I. and Susanne H. Rudolph, "Generals and Politicians in India," *Pacific Affairs* XXXVII (Spring, 1964), 5–19, and Brig. S. K. Sinha, *op. cit.*

secure if somewhat arduous job, rather than a faith. These men are obviously more representative of Indian society than their pre-World War II predecessors, although there is no reason to doubt their quality as officers.

A second important modernizing trend has been the shift in the nature of the professional officer's purpose and function since independence. Although for many years after 1947 little changed in the Indian and Pakistani military establishments, the Pakistan *coup* and the advent of V. K. Krishna Menon as Defense Minister in 1957 radically altered the traditional self-image of the officer corps. In the *coup*, the Pakistani military was thrust into the role of protector of the state. As for Menon, a powerful political figure initiated a series of reforms which stirred the political and social consciousness of some officers. The Indian military was further shaken by the advent of Communist China as a serious military threat.

These two trends—a gradual shift in the social base of the officer corps, and the rapid and increasing confrontation with a variety of new military tasks—produced a reexamination of the nature of the officer corps in India. The articles of the various professional Indian military journals—but especially the broad-gauged *Journal* of the United Service Institution of India—ask many of the same questions which were raised during the final years of British rule. "Officers for the Twenty-First Century" argues for a more scientifically trained officer candidate; "Our Military Tradition," savagely attacks all remnants of British customs in the Indian Army, and a letter rebuts it; "If Another Trial Comes" suggests the militarization of Indian society along Israeli lines; "Officer Like Qualities" describes the proper professional attitude of officers at each level of the hierarchy, and "Academic Recognition of Military Education" argues that military training and society have merged to the point where graduates of the various service academies should be given general societal recognition of their accomplishments.[22]

---

[22] These examples are taken from the U.S.I. *Journal* since 1964. Articles dealing in whole or in part with the ethos of the Indian Army and the officer corps regularly constitute a quarter to a third of the contents of each issue.

Reconciliation between an increasingly middle-class officer corps, the proud, aristocratic traditions of the Indian military, and the growing military threat is the common theme of these articles. The problem is not simply to turn Indian youths into proper gentlemen, but also to turn them into effective officers. Considerable disagreement exists (especially between generations) about the degree to which a gentleman is automatically an effective officer. Thus, senior officers lament the radical changes that institutions such as the mess have undergone. This instrument of social indoctrination and professional control becomes increasingly irrelevant and ineffectual when young officers are already married, posted to distant operational units, or both. Conversely, younger officers are less enchanted with unit traditions of martial valor and are increasingly interested in the more mundane problems of service conditions, pensions, housing, and perquisites.[23]

This extended and complex debate within the Indian military is a measure of the considerable—if belated—progress toward reconciliation of traditional, British, and contemporary modes of military and social organization. As the social composition of the officer corps continues to change, and as the military remains under external pressure, the debate will continue. The fact that it occurs at all—with considerable sophistication and apparently with no official approval or disapproval—is remarkable.

The officer corps of both successor states are examples of institutions whose members are successfully engaged in bridg-

---

If anything, their number has increased during the past few years, as has the quantity of popular fiction and professional books dealing with the military. "Technical" professional articles are published in one of the many branch journals (Infantry, Armour, and so on), and the U.S.I. *Journal* specializes in strategic, political, doctrinal, and theoretical subjects. The only equivalent Pakistani publication that this author has examined is the *Pakistan Army Journal*. The scope of its articles is somewhat narrower; the main theme of many articles is the exploration of ways by which a numerically inferior army can defeat a larger, but less dedicated one. In recent years two solutions have emerged: the adoption of guerilla warfare and the maintenance of a fierce Islam-based martial spirit.

23 An interesting attempt to explore the clash between several models of professional behavior (particularly political vs. apolitical and neoBritish vs. neonationalist) is found in Manohar Malgonkar, *Distant Drum* (Bombay: Asia Publishing House, 1960).

ing the gap between past and present. Intellectuals in developing states are aware of the internal schisms in their society.
Edward Shils notes that the alienation of the intellectuals in
transitional societies is a state of being cut off from their indigenous culture: "the experience to which the allegation of
being 'cut-off' refers is not to any serious extent a real result
of the intellectuals' acceptance of the 'foreign,' modern culture. It rests rather on their own feeling of distance from the
rest of their fellow nationals. . . . "[24] Two paths are open to
those whose aspirations and perceptions have been expanded
through modern education: they may seek a "transcendence
of concrete individuality," through communism, terror, and
anti-authority movements, or they may adjust to a modern institutional role, become an individual within their own sphere
of personal and private relationships. For an intellectual, this
means becoming a gadfly of the existing social order without
hostility for that order: criticism with affinity.

Military officers in India have been successful in following
the second path of adjustment to their society. Although they
may be deeply entangled in professional problems and debates,
their commitment to the system which they criticize is firm.
They do not display the symptoms of ambivalence and anxiety
toward authority so often found in intellectuals although they
criticize that authority. Probably no other group in South
Asian society is so critical of politicians on particular issues,
and yet is so strong in its support of the political system.

Caste and Region in the Ranks

India and Pakistan have chosen to emphasize different components of their joint legacy, and recruitment to the two
successor armies is based upon different principles. The Indian government made an early policy decision to terminate
the creation of new single-caste regiments.[25] The regiments

[24] "The Intellectuals in the Political Development of the New States," *World Politics*, XII (April, 1960).

[25] "In January 1949 orders were officially issued to abolish recruitment by classes in all arms/Services. Recruitment was thus thrown open to *all* Indian nationals. . . . For administrative reasons arising out of previous commitments and locations of troops, it was not possible to implement this decision immedi-

which it raised were mixed, such as the Parachute Regiment. Since 1963, and the doubling in size of the army, an attempt has been made to broaden the base of recruitment of existing regiments.[26] Although they bear the caste or class name of the older regiment, many are no longer single-caste or single-class. The Indian Army has, at present, three types of infantry battalions: "pure," "mixed company," and "totally mixed" heterogeneous units. The Gurkhas typify the pure unit; they are recruited primarily from Nepal, although some of their troops come from India (usually the relatives of former soldiers). Similarly, the Sikh Regiment recruits only Sikhs, and the Sikh Light Infantry Regiment recruits only scheduled caste Sikhs, who are segregated from higher-caste coreligionists. Some regiments, however, contain two or three "classes," and segregate them on the company level. The Punjab Regiment contains several classes organized in this way, as does the Rajputana Rifles, which has separate Jat Hindu and Muslim companies. The Rajput Regiment is composed primarily of Rajputs, but has several battalions of Bengalis who are enrolled as Rajputs in name only. Finally, and most interesting, is the third type of infantry battalion—that which is thoroughly mixed. The Madras Regiment recruits any eligible Indian from the southern states. It contains Christians, Hindus, Sikhs, and Muslims in the same section. They also mix Indians from all southern states in the same sections. The Parachute Regiment is similarly totally mixed, drawing from all of India. Some regiments bearing caste names draw, in fact, from all castes and classes in a particular region (for instance the Dogra Regiment, which recruits from Kangra and adjacent areas). Others bearing caste names have also expanded their base: the Mahar Regiment, which formerly recruited only untouchable Mahars, now takes in Indians of many castes,

ately in the case of the Infantry and the Armoured Corps. Regiments composed of particular classes, through several decades, developed a certain kind of cohesion and while steps are taken to broadbase their composition, it is essential to ensure that the sentimental attachment arising out of such composition is not suddenly disturbed." Venkateswaran, p. 188.

26 The following is based upon personal observation of several Indian army units and regimental training centers in 1964 and 1968–1969, and discussions with senior Indian officers responsible for recruitment.

(but especially other scheduled (untouchable) caste groups seeking a place in the army.)[27]

The Indian Army considers mixed-caste units as effective as pure units if they have been allowed to mature as a fighting force for a long period. Long-recruited classes have ready-made traditions and legends of martial valor. Newly recruited classes take some time to "settle down" and develop their own martial myths. One critical factor is the development of loyalty and affection between officer and soldier. Many officers have now come to regard mixed units with greater pride and respect than the old pure martial units. They do, more truly, symbolize the Indian nation.[28]

The Indian government has annually found itself attacked from two directions with regard to the caste composition of the army. Every debate over Defense Ministry funds produces demands for new, single-class regiments. (The Chamars and Ahirs have been particularly vocal.) Other groups press for the total abolition of caste and class as principles of recruitment, in name and in fact. Since the government has not yet released any figures on the actual composition of individual regiments the debate is somewhat unreal, for it is impossible to calculate the actual rate of change in the composition of the military. The government is correct when it claims that any Indian citizen is free to join the army, but the critics are equally correct when they point out that certain regiments are reserved for certain classes.

These marginal but increasingly significant changes in the social composition of the military have been accompanied by

[27] There are many Chamars in the Mahars, according to responsible officials. The demand in Parliament for a separate Chamar regiment (as in World War II) has been repeatedly rejected by the government. For further details of scheduled castes in the Indian Army see Stephen P. Cohen, "The Untouchable Soldier: Caste, Politics, and the Indian Army," *Journal of Asian Studies*, XXVIII, 3 (May, 1969), 453–468.

[28] Another factor which determines the stability of a unit (in terms of discipline and eagerness for combat, for example) is the attitude of the villages in the region in which the unit is recruited. Villages (or castes) with developed ties to the military serve as agents for recruitment and are important in maintaining discipline. To keep up their reputation they will return to duty any defectors, or informally punish soldiers whose actions might damage the group's reputation. Soldiering is not an anonymous profession for most Indian or Pakistani Army *jawans*.

the development of a new recruitment rationale. This rationale has had to serve several purposes. It had to be acceptable to the military and meet their manpower requirements, it had to take account of the democratic environment of the military, and it had to justify equal access to the military and equal obligation for all citizens. At the same time it had to account for the fact that the military was and is largely dominated by north Indian castes and classes.

This "secular theory of the martial races" was succinctly summarized by a recent Minister of Defense, Y. B. Chavan. He frequently declared, for example, that " we are all Kṣatriyas now," and that when it comes to the defense of the Indian nation, all are equally martial, whatever caste or class label they may wear.[29]

The consequence of this new theory is to stress the individual martial characteristics of each class. Thus, in a book recounting the martial traditions of the Indian Army (published under official auspices), the gallant traditions of the Bihari and Madrassi soldier were recounted along with those of the Rajputs, Sikhs, and Dogras.[30] Its author advises the reader to pursue the study of the Indian Army in the works of such theoreticians of the martial races as Lieutenant-General Sir George McMunn, but provides an account of those martial races and martial heroes who had been ignored by the British. The source of fighting efficiency is seen in loyalty to the regiment and loyalty to the nation.

The secular martial-races theory attempts to combine aspects of the nationalist view and the martial-races theory. It is a melding of two popular views, and should grow in strength over the years with or without continued official patronage.

---

[29] Also: "everyone has to become a Kṣhatriya to defend the country's honor. The blood that was shed . . . belonged to Muslims, Christians, Sikhs, and Hindus. This awakening and sense of unity and idea of secularism [sic] has to be sedulously fostered in the interests of our nation's well being." Speech at Poona, October 3, 1965. *The Statesman* (New Delhi), October 4, 1965.

[30] Dharm Pal, *Traditions of the Indian Army* (Delhi: Ministry of Information and Broadcasting, Government of India, 1961). See also, Brig. Rajendra Singh, *History of the Indian Army* (New Delhi: Army Educational Stores, 1963), pp. 256 ff.

Its attitude of compromise and its reconciliation of opposing theories of recruitment is strikingly similar to what Wilfred Cantwell Smith has termed the "Hindu view of secularism."[31] Just as Hinduism permits a wide variety of beliefs and practices within its diffuse structure, the secular martial-races theory permits the continuance of strong martial traditions within a broad equalitarian framework. In both instances compromise is essential. Hinduism has had great difficulty absorbing a particularist, aggressive religion such as Islam. The secular martial-races theory has the same difficulty in dealing with a class or caste which insists on its superior status as a martial race. Some may want to be "more equal" than others. The various groups must compromise with face-saving devices for those not yet up to standard. Great care is taken to insure that minority communities are well represented in awards lists, and that the most favorable image is projected to the public.[32]

The revised theory of the martial races is important to India because she is facing an opponent (Pakistan) who makes frequent and overt challenges to her secular underpinnings. To some extent, Pakistanis attempt to perpetuate the British image of an India composed of many discrete social bodies, destined to spin apart as a result of communal tensions.[33] An expression of this image occurred during the height of the 1965 war when considerable Pakistani propaganda was directed at the Sikh community, supporting demands for a separate Sikh state.[34]

India has used the Chinese invasion and the conflicts with Pakistan to blunt external and internal efforts to divide her and to encourage national integration. During each recent

---

[31] Wilfred Cantwell Smith, "The Problem," in the issue titled "Secularism," of *Seminar* (New Delhi), March, 1965, p. 4. See also Donald E. Smith, *India as a Secular State* (Princeton: Princeton University Press, 1963).

[32] In the 1965 conflict between India and Pakistan a large number of medal winners were Indian Muslims, and one *jawan*, Ayub Khan, was especially feted for his skill at destroying Patton tanks. After the battle many explicit references were made to the fact that Indians of all castes and religious beliefs died for the same cause.

[33] This image was implicit in the "Two Nations" theory.

[34] A separate "Punjabi speaking state," a euphemism for a predominately Sikh state, was created shortly after the fighting ended.

conflict a systematic, deliberate attempt was made to point out the variety of the military, to list the communities of individual soldiers and units which have performed heroically, and to give special attention to members of minority communities or religions. This policy is a great change from British practice which tended to stress the fragility of the balance in the military, and the great danger of tampering with it. Contemporary Indian political leaders have not yet had serious conflict with their military, and can safely exploit for integrative and other political purposes the diversity that exists in the services. If the trend of the past few years is indicative, the stress on diversity will grow as an organizational doctrine.

Pakistan encompasses almost as diverse a social system as does India. Consequently, although Islamic doctrine is available as an organizing principle, Pakistan has as much, or more, tension in relating theory to practice as India. Pakistan was founded and survives because of two basic assumptions; one negative and one positive. Negatively, many thought that the Muslims of the subcontinent were culturally and socially backward, and were vulnerable to Hindu exploitation through the latter's greater numbers and Westernization. Positively, Islam provided a doctrine through which the Muslim community could identify and separate itself from the Hindus, thereby purifying and raising the community to a social and cultural level in which competition would be equal.[35] When Pakistan became a state, these assumptions were applied to the new nation's military organization.

The Islam religion in Pakistan overrides all cultural and historical differences:

The soldiers of the Pakistan Army . . . are drawn from many different tribes and people—from the Pathans of the North-West, from the Punjabis, Sindhis, and Baluchis and from the Bengalis of East Pakistan. All share a sense of pride in their past and a de-

[35] Because of the great diversity of Indian Muslims, Pakistan was first envisioned as constituting only the northwest portions of India, and perhaps adjacent portions of Afghanistan, a region bound together by cultural, historical, social and religious ties. When East Bengal was included, it became obvious that many of these ties were not really shared, and that even the call of Islam did not hold out the same attraction for millions of Muslims.

termination to serve Pakistan loyally and well in the future. Uniting them all is the bond of Islam with its straightforward belief in the one and only God and in the prophethood of Muhammad; a faith which transcends all barriers of geography and language.[36]

Officially, all Muslims, because they are Muslims, are equally entitled to bear arms. This belief leads to the corollary that Muslim soldiers are more effective because for them religion and state are united in purpose.

Theoretically, there should be no great imbalance in the composition of the Pakistani military, either in terms of numbers, or distribution among units. In fact, however, the Pakistani military (especially the army) is more unbalanced than the British Indian Army or the contemporary Indian Army.[37] Two explanations present themselves. First, many Pakistani officers regard Bengalis as particularly unsuited for military life. They argue that a great deal of time, patience, and training will be necessary before a military tradition can be established in East Bengal. Second, and perhaps crucially: Can East Pakistanis be trusted to remain within Pakistan once a separation, already geographical, becomes militarily plausible and East Pakistanis can manage their own defense. Until the time comes when suitable recruits are available in adequate numbers, when political pressures for a more equalitarian recruiting system become greater, and when the integration of Pakistan has reached the point where the East can be fully trusted, it seems likely that the imbalance between the two wings will continue to be politically embarrassing to the military whose leadership is drawn almost entirely from the West.

[36] Maj.-Gen. Fazal Muqeem Khan, *The Story of the Pakistan Army* (Karachi: Oxford University Press, 1963), pp. 2–3.

[37] Seven Pakistan Army divisions included only one Bengali battalion. The strength of the Army is now being increased to ten divisions (February, 1966) and the number of Bengali units is being increased to two or three, "but still that is not much more than a gesture; the army can get all the volunteers it needs from the people it knows best, the old marital races of Punjabis and Pathans." Dispatch from "Our Special Correspondent," *The Times*, February 26, 1966. In July, 1956, the quota of East Pakistanis in the Army was fixed at 2 percent; there is no available information whether this figure was reached. See the debates on defense in the Pakistan National Assembly, June 25–26, 1964. The air force and the navy do not seem to have a quota system. Bengalis comprise up to 30 percent of the members of these services.

The military claims to be an all-Pakistani organization. However, East Pakistanis represent only 2 percent of the army, and racial, cultural, and political antagonisms have already produced separatist movements in the East. The official rationalization, that Pakistan is indivisible and the East should not mind being defended largely by units drawn from the Punjab and West Wing, does little to ease the concern and pride of East Bengalis. They have vivid memories of tough Pathan and Punjabi police and military units imported by the British for law enforcement and suppression of nationalist agitation. Continued inequality in the army keeps that memory fresh.

In summary, in both India and Pakistan, a considerable gap exists between equalitarian theories of recruitment and the actual composition of the military. If no effort is made to interfere with the system of recruitment already in operation (voluntary), then the armies of both nations tend to recruit from the classes, castes, and regions which already predominate. It is effective, cheaper, and coincides with the predispositions of many military men who believe in some variation of the martial-races theory. Since all Indians and Pakistanis now have the legal right to serve in the military, the military to that extent has come to reflect nationalist and equalitarian doctrine. But since recruitment to some units (especially the prestigious infantry units) is restricted to specific ethnic groups, the military has not abandoned its ties to traditional Indian and British patterns.

THE ARMY, ITS LEGACY, AND THE FUTURE OF INDIA

The legacy of the British Indian Army has been to limit the nonmilitary activities of the present Indian and Pakistani military. The present military plays no civic-action roles, and only limited "aid to the civil" roles, which are rapidly diminishing through the creation of paramilitary security forces. Although new tasks have been taken up by the two armies— road construction, weapons production, and, in the Himalayas, community-development projects—these are directed toward clear-cut military objectives. Indians have no interest in a "people's army," mass conscription, or use of the army for explicitly social-welfare ends. More surprisingly, there is no pressure from politicians, intellectuals, or the press for such an expansion of the military's role. The professional ethic of the old Indian Army dictated that the army's value stem from high standards of training and the unique mystique of the relationship of the officer to the other ranks. The standard of training remains high, and the mystique, though declining, is still present. To officers (in the Indian Army at least) profession comes first, and "politics" finds no place.

This relatively limited role was eminently compatible with the political system of India after independence. That system was dominated by a highly Westernized elite, intent upon establishing a parliamentary democracy based upon Western models. The military had no internal political role in their plans, and was to be confined to external defense activities.

However, even as this parliamentary democracy was being established, a mass political culture emerged, which took full advantage of the new political and technological innovations. The growth of this culture in India has been thoroughly documented.[38] Modern technology has been introduced to local or regional groups which were previously isolated from the mainstream of political life. Paradoxically, regionalism and provincialism may grow proportionately faster than nationalism.[39] The focus of public issues shifts from a nationalist orientation to the regional question of distribution of re-

[38] See Lloyd I. Rudolph and Susanne H. Rudolph, "The Political Role of India's Caste Associations," *Pacific Affairs*, XXXIII (March, 1960), W. H. Morris-Jones, "India's Political Idioms," in C. H. Philips, ed., *Politics and Society in India* (London: George Allen and Unwin, 1963), Lloyd I. Rudolph, "The Modernity of Tradition: The Democratic Incarnation of Caste in India," *American Political Science Review*, LIX December, 1965), and Rajni Kothari and Rishikesh Maru, "Caste and Secularism in India," *Journal of Asian Studies*, XXV (November, 1965). The term "mass political culture" is used as Myron Weiner used it in "India: Two Political Cultures," in Lucien Pye and Sydney Verba, ed., *Political Culture and Political Development* (Princeton: Princeton University Press, 1965).

[39] For a pioneering study of the differential rates of growth of regional and national languages in India see Karl W. Deutsch, *Nationalism and Social Communication* (Cambridge: The M.I.T. Press, 1953), Appendix III.

sources in a system of scarcity, especially such resources as jobs, profits, and status.

This vigorous growth of a mast political culture indicates that the revolution of modernity will not be led by the Westernized elites but by these newly powerful groups. Technology, and its frequent companions, democracy, are the keys to such groups. This postindependence development is probably the second phase of political change in many new nations. It is as important as the replacement of the Western colonial power by a Westernized indigenous civilian elite, or by a Westernized military elite.

What role will the military play in such a transformation? Given the continued growth of the scope and influence of the mass political culture, and no change in India's relationship to the great powers,[40] three developments seem possible. They are not mutually exclusive and may occur simultaneously. In decreasing order of probability:

1) The military stands as a deterrent to regional fragmentation, seperatism, or secession. Observers have often suggested that the intensification of provincial politics poses a threat to Indian unity.[41] However, just as India's diversity acts as a deterrent to military designs on political power, a unified military acts as a deterrent to regional politicians eyeing separatism. Whether the claim to independence of such politicians is based upon regional, linguistic, or ethnic distinctiveness, they will ultimately have to face the question of military viability. Presently, no region seems close to having the military resources to sustain its independence.[42] To any politician

---

40 Some alternative paths of Indian political development are provocatively listed and discussed in Nirad C. Chaudhuri, *The Continent of Circe* (New York: Oxford University Press, 1966). But see also Selig S. Harrison, *India: The Most Dangerous Decades* (Princeton: Princeton University Press, 1960) pp. 297 ff. and, more optimistically, George Rosen, *Democracy and Economic Change in India* (Berkeley and Los Angeles: University of California Press, 1966).

41 See Harrison for a careful presentation of this view.

42 Even the Punjab—once again partitioned in 1967 into Sikh and Hindu components—seems to have neither the administrative nor the political cohesiveness required of an independent state. The old British fear of the Punjab terrorizing the rest of India is increasingly less likely as the military is ever more dependent upon a decentralized industrial defense base.

contemplating separatism it should seem clear, after brief reflection, that military weakness is a powerful argument for remaining within, and supporting, the Indian Union.

2) The fact that the military of modern India recruits from all groups and has a national perspective, makes it especially sensitive to, and scornful of, political parochialism. As a group, the officer corps is critical of the disorder and unparliamentary behavior of groups newly "recruited" to the political system. The outlook of the officers remains that of the elite political culture, and they stress adherence to parliamentary procedures, in form as much as substance. The emerging mass political culture offends their sense of propriety and challenges their paternalist approach to social relations. The military could intervene in the political system as a result of their misperception of the significance of this growing mass political culture. Severe parliamentary instability in the center, or social and political instability particularly in several border states, would increase the military's disposition to intervene. Such intervention would probably come through the President and might simply demand a "cooling off" of political activity, or the elimination of particular groups from the political process. Without major social changes such reform would hardly have anything but a marginal impact upon the increasing politicization of India, and might in fact hasten that politicization.

3) A final development might be the emergence of the military or of military symbols as a common denominator between the two political cultures. If, as it has been argued, the relationship between the growing mass political culture and the elite political culture of India becomes more tense in the next few years,[43] a major elevation of the military as a model or as an object of veneration may well provide at least a temporary political solution on which both political cultures can compromise. The Westernized elite has often indicated its admiration for the way the military teaches western virtues such as self-sacrifice, loyalty, and discipline. Many of these same virtues

[43] Weiner, *op. cit.*

are deeply embedded in Indian culture, which is laden with martial traditions and military heroes. If present military pressures continue, Indian society might be rallied around a quasi-militaristic ethic with a spirit drawn from traditional martial India and manipulative techniques drawn from the United States and the Soviet Union. This new ethic would justify the financial sacrifices necessary for economic development and the perpetuation of security measures necessary to meet political opposition.

Evidence indicates that this process has begun on a symbolic level. Political integration is ultimately a collective state of mind.[44] It implies a group of people reacting together to common stimuli: a flag, a leader, a name, or—most relevant for our interests—a threat to a boundary. The military is a potent symbol because of its link to defense. Reaction to the military in times of crisis is a measure of national integration.[45]

The military has always been a cathetic object to the classes, castes, and religions which have historically contributed heavily to its ranks. Since the military is closely related to the concept of a political unity (especially after its transformation from an imperial to a national force) presumably there is some intergative by-product. This integration is of great concern to the military, which is preoccupied with the task of maintaining a stable and reliable recruiting base.

For the general population, and for many civilian elites with no earlier attachment to the military, the military can only serve as a symbol of what they would like the "new" India or Pakistan to be.

Through independence the leaders of the nationalist movement redefined the nature of the armed services and created a potential national symbol. Before 1962, Indians (for political

[44] Henry Teune and James V. Toscano, ed., *The Integration of Political Communities* (Philadelphia and New York: J. B. Lippincott, 1964), p. 256.

[45] One of the few polls designed to measure such reactions however, has, shown rather discouraging results from an integrative viewpoint. However, the poll was taken during the first of a series of crises, in an early stage of the learning process. See Albert H. Cantril, Jr., "The Indian Perception of the Sino-Indian Border Clash," *Public Opinion Quarterly*, XX (Summer, 1964), 233–242.

reasons) had been reluctant to use the military as a symbol of nationhood, although the process began earlier in Pakistan. The first war over Kashmir,[46] and the limited conflicts with neighbors kept the military alive as a minor symbol of nationhood, but its role was carefully circumscribed by Nehru. The Chinese invasion, the death of Nehru, second Pakistan war, the further shock of Lal Bahadur Shastri's death, and the apparent misdirection of economic priorities culminating in serious famine in 1966 have all contributed to a gradual shift in this role. Indians increasingly see existence as a matter of military might. A natural elevation of the military has occurred,[47] and the employment of the military as a symbol of integration has been rapidly speeded up.[48] Military symbolism is consciously and explicitly being taught to those hitherto unaware or unappreciative. Those most skilled in the dissemination of such doctrine—politicians, and communications elites—have undergone a cram course in military matters.[49]

If the military develops new roles and new relationships with Indian society, important new differences between India and Pakistan may result. Not only will there be two different system types (assuming India retains a democratic government, a form perfectly compatible with a sophisticated or

[46] K. M. Panikkar claimed that the army did not become a "national" army of India until the first battles in Kashmir. See K. M. Panikkar, *Problems of Indian Defense* (Bombay: Asia Publishing House, 1960). Yet, it was possible to write in 1966 that the general public attitude toward the military underwent a "sudden change" from casual indifference only in 1965. "The Essence of Military Personality," *The Hindu Weekly Review*, July 11, 1966.

[47] "There is a common tendency to think of expenditure on defense as expenditure which is not fruitful, which does not add to the wealth of the country and which if carried on for a number of years acts as a drag on the economy. This is not correct. Defense and development are indeed complementary to each other. . . . Defense expenditure does play an important part in taking a country forward." Y. B. Chavan, *Sainik Samachar*, March 3, 1966.

[48] Even the film industry has assisted by producing several war movies, e.g., *Haqeequat*. Such films are modeled after American classics such as *Bataan* and *Guadalcanal Diary* and serve the same function of communicating and developing stimuli based upon the military as a national symbol.

[49] The government of India actively encourages this educational process with its flow of information about the services and its expansion of the public relations apparatus.

moderate militarism), but the relationship between army and society will be different. Pakistan may find its military more powerful politically but less powerful socially and ideologically. India will not find its military politically more powerful, but socially more pervasive.

APPENDIX

A Note on the Indian State Forces

The British never claimed sovereignty over the numerous princely states of India, although they were careful to regulate the size and power of the military establishments maintained by the princes. Many princely states contributed forces to the British during World War I. These were placed under the jurisdiction of British officers.[1] After that war the government examined the role of these forces, and in 1922 instituted the Indian State Forces scheme. The rulers were invited to indicate the number of units they wished to maintain, and these were then classified into three types: "A" class units followed the organization of the Indian Army and were comparably armed; "B" units did not follow the organization of the Indian Army and were equipped with inferior .303 rifles; "C" class units were police-type units. The government of

[1] For the British attitude towards the state armies see: India Office Library; Political (Internal) Collection, Collection 2, File 8, Part 1, Indian State Forces Annual Reports and Reviews, 1932–38. The Annual Review for the year 1935/36 contains a brief history of the scheme. For a sympathetic Indian view, which includes a very brief history of each state army, see H. H. The Maharaja of Jaipur, *A History of the Indian State Forces* (Bombay: Orient Longmans, 1967).

India provided free arms to A and B class units and many states joined the scheme. After 1931, however, financial considerations led the Army Department to halt the distribution of free arms. It also halted efforts to upgrade units from class B to A class. During the 1930s the Indian State Forces numbered from 50,000 to 60,000 as states joined or left the scheme.

Some state units were good. The Jammu and Kashmir State Forces comprised more than three brigades, and were of excellent quality. (They were primarily Dogras, with some Muslims, Gurkhas, and Jat Sikhs.) Hyderabad had cavalry units of superior quality, although its infantry was rated poor. Patiala and Bhopal were rated fair. Most state forces, however, were of dubious military value. Many were glorified palace guards whose major task was ceremonial display or performance as beaters on shikari expeditions. They were unfit for internal security duties, let alone active combat. The chief difficulties were the lack of competent officers, the high incidence of guard duty (which restricted training opportunities), and the frequent ceremonial functions which had an equally disruptive effect on training. Marriages and deaths of members of the ruling family necessitated the use of large numbers of state troops, and demonstrated the personal nature of the relationship between the military organizations and the political authority. The British were not reluctant to indulge the ruling families, but did step in to correct occasional extreme incompetence, disbanding state "armies" on the advice of the local British military advisor.

The British exercised formal control over the state armies through their military advisors, who were responsible to their Military Advisory Staff, headed by a Military-Advisor-in-Chief, Indian State Forces (usually a brigadier or a major-general). The local resident military advisor assisted in training and in part determined the supply of vital Indian government funds. Informally, the state forces were controlled through their incompetence and small size. Their officer cadres were so tiny that little opportunity existed for promotion, and able officer candidates were not attracted. Those Indian state officers who were seconded to the Indian Army, or who underwent training at the Indian Military Academy, Dehra Dun, were markedly inferior to Indian officers of the Indian Army. In some years, the state officers did not even fill their quota at the IMA.

In World War II, the state forces were once more used by the British, but were placed under British control, and became part of the Indian Army. Their identity was wiped out after independence; none proved strong enough to resist Indian or Pakistani absorption.[2]

[2] See A. L. Venkateshwaran, *Defense Organization in India* (New Delhi: Publications Division, 1969).

BIBLIOGRAPHICAL NOTE

This book has relied more heavily on interviews than the footnotes might indicate, but many important published and unpublished sources should be given special mention.

Although the impact of the military upon Indian—and particularly Punjabi—society is universally acknowledged, few scholarly or analytical studies have been written on this subject. Two recent ones may be noted: M. S. A. Rao, "Caste and the Indian Army," *Economic Weekly*, August 29, 1964, describes the attempts of one caste to obtain a foothold in the military, and Stephen P. Cohen, "The Untouchable Soldier: Caste, Politics, and the Indian Army," *Journal of Asian Studies*, XXVIII, 3 (May, 1969) discusses similar efforts of several recruited castes.

No satisfactory history of the Indian military exists, recent Indian efforts being no more reliable or comprehensive than earlier British attempts. However, several histories of regiments and of presidency armies are outstanding. Patrick Cadell, *History of the Bombay Army*, London: Longmans, Green and Co., 1938, contains social data; Amiya Barat, *The Bengal Native Infantry, 1796–1852*, Calcutta: Firma K. L. Mukhopadhyay, 1962, contains excellent material both on officers and sepoys, but draws comparative conclusions unwarranted by a single-presidency study, and Lieut.-Col. W. J. Wilson compiled the massive *History of the Madras Army*, 5 vols., Madras: The Government Press, 1882, 1883, 1888, 1889. Regimental histories deserve, and have received, their own bibliographer: R. A. Myers, *Regimental Histories of the Indian*

Army, A Bibliography, (unpublished M.A. thesis, University of London), 1957. These histories are of considerable breadth but uneven quality. They were usually written by some literary-minded officer in his spare time, and are often simple paeans to his colleagues' valor and the regiment's history. A few contain important data. Also useful are the dozens of *Handbooks of the Indian Army*, published between the late nineteenth century and the beginning of World War II. These guides written for the officers of various units. They described the location, traits, temperament, and other qualities of the various castes recruited to the army. Many went through three editions, and much can be learned by comparing early and late versions. Some of these handbooks are genuine contributions to ethnographic literature; some merely repeat contemporary cliches and impressions, but are thus useful in their own special way. A few of these handbooks are scattered in university libraries around the world (especially the Ames Library of the University of Minnesota, which has a unique collection of books and materials on South Asian military history), but complete sets can be found in the Ministry of Defense Library (India) and the United Service Institution of India library. Somewhat less useful are the various one-volume compilations of descriptions of the "martial races": Saint Nihal Singh, *India's Fighters*, London: Sampson Low, 1914; P. D. Bonarjee, *A Handbook of the Fighting Races of India*, Calcutta: Thacker, 1899; Maj. D. Jackson, *India's Army*, London: Sampson Low, 1940; Lieut.-Gen. Sir George MacMunn, *The Martial Races of India*, London: Sampson Low, 1933; and Edmund Candler, *The Sepoy*, London: John Murray, 1919.

A valuable source of information and a true measure of the development of military professionalism in India is the quarterly *Journal of the United Services Institution*. The early issues contained primarily technical information, but after World War I the social and political content increased substantially. Under the capable guidance of Indian editors, it has provided a forum for much imaginative thought. A nearly complete set is on file at the Ames Library in Minneapolis, and at the institution's premises in New Delhi, which also houses an excellent military library. To celebrate its hundredth anniversary the U.S.I. is planning to introduce a series of publications dealing with various aspects of recent Indian military history. In addition to the U.S.I. *Journal* several Indian military journals of narrower professional interest (for instance artillery and ordnance) exist, as well as the popular soldier's weekly, *Sainik Samachar*, which is published in many Indian languages and English.

Biographical and autobiographical works are a rich source of data. A classic Indian Army autobiography is Lord Roberts', *Forty-One Years in India*, London: Bentley and Son, 1897. Almost every other Commander-in-Chief, Indian Army, at one time or another has authored his own autobiography. Kitchener and Curzon are represented by contemporary and favorable biographies, Sir George Arthur, *The Life of Lord Kitchener*, London: Macmillan, 1920; and Lord Ronaldshay, *The Life of Lord Curzon*, London: Earnest Benn, 1928, and also by later, critical biographies: Leonard Mosley, *The Glorious Fault*, New York: Harcourt, 1960, and Philip Magnus, *Kitchener: Portrait of an Imperialist*, London: John Murray, 1958. More recent autobiographies include the excellent pair by John Masters, *Bugles and a Tiger*, London: Michael Joseph, 1956, and *The Road Past Mandalay*, London: Michael Joseph, 1961; Lieut.-Gen. Sir Francis Tuker's intemperate *While Memory Serves*, London: Cassell, 1950; and John Connell's exemplary biography of *Auchinleck*, London: Cassell, 1959. Indian and Pakistani generals continue the great tradition with F. M. Ayub Khan's autobiography, *Friends Not Masters*, New York: Oxford, 1967; Lieut.-Gen. B. M. Kaul, *The Untold Story*, New Delhi: Allied, 1967; and Lieut.-Gen. D. R. Thapar, *The Morale Builders*, Bombay: Asia Publishing House, 1965. Gen Mohan Singh has written but not published an account of the Indian National Army. Kaul's account of the 1962 NEFA debacle has resulted in rebuttals of varying quality. Significant among these is the highly detailed analysis by Brig. John Dalvi, *Himalayan Blunder*, Bombay: Thacker and Co., 1969. Other accounts of this traumatic episode are to be expected.

Because few Indian leaders have had any direct contact with the military, only a small "civilian" literature dealing with defense or military problems has been written. The autobiographical writings of Bose, Nehru, Gandhi, and other important nationalists is often the best source of information on their approach to military matters. Indian National Congress annual sessions contain occasional references to military problems, before and after independence, as do debates in the Legislative Assembly. Today the *Lok Sabha* and *Rajya Sabha* (House of the People and House of the State) are sources of attitudinal data. A few civilian Indian military experts have published works, notably K. M. Panikkar, a diplomat-historian, whose *Problems of Indian Defense*, Bombay: Asia Publishing House, 1960, is a useful survey, and whose *Strategic Problems of the Indian Ocean*, New Delhi: Indian Institute of International Affairs, 1944, was influential. A similar strategic study was done by the Indian Council of World Affairs, *Defense and Security in the Indian Ocean Area,* Bombay: Asia Publishing House, 1958. Earlier studies include the excellent book by D. H. Limaye, *Some Aspects of India's Military Defense,* Bombay: New Book Company, n.d. [1941?]; and Brij Narain, *Post-War Planning of the Indian Defense Services,* New Delhi: Indian Institute of International Affairs, 1946; K. B. Vaidya, *The Naval Defense of India*; Bombay: Thacker, 1944; and the perceptive and detailed economic study by C. N. Vakil, *Financial Burden of the War on India,* Bombay: University of Bombay, 1943. The able P. S. Sivaswamy Aiyer published *The Self-Defense of India,* Madras: Methodist Publishing House, in 1924.

Since 1962 there has been a new burst of interest in defense and military affairs. Much of this literature is propaganda, but one can detect the rise of a new breed of defense experts, particularly after the beginning of the nuclear debate in 1964, and the Second Kashmir War of 1965. The government-subsidized Institute of Defense Studies and Analysis (New Delhi) produces a quarterly journal, several military-political digests, and occasional papers written by its staff. A survey of postindependence Indian defense policy can be found in Lorne J. Kavic's *India's Quest for Security,* Berkeley and Los Angeles: University of California Press, 1967. A comparable study by a leading Indian military writer is Maharaj K. Chopra, India: *The Search for Power,* Bombay: Lalvani, 1969. Of unique value is the collection of newspaper columns written anonymously by Gen. J. N. Chaudhuri (who ultimately became Chief of the Army Staff), *Arms, Aims and Aspects,* Bombay: Manaktalas, 1966.

For the bureaucratic and administrative history of the Ministry of Defense since Independence A. L. Venkateshwaran's *Defense Organization in India,* New Delhi: Publications Division, 1969, is valuable, as it is designed to serve as a popular history of the Defense Ministry, and a guide for the use of Defense Ministry personnel.

Comparable defense literature dealing with Pakistan is lacking. The few studies that have appeared are published under official or semi-official auspices. See Aslam Siddiqui's provocative *A Path for Pakistan,* Karachi: Pakistan Publishing House, 1964, Ayub's autobiography, noted above, and the important book by Maj.-Gen. Fazal Muqeem Khan, *The Story of the Pakistan Army,* Karachi: Oxford University Press, 1963. A long review of this book is found in Stephen P. Cohen, "Arms and Politics in Pakistan," *India Quarterly,* October–December, 1964. Other studies of the Pakistani military include Wayne A. Wilcox, "The Pakistan Coup d' Etat of 1958," *Pacific Affairs* (Summer, 1965), and Raymond A. Moore,

"The Army as a Vehicle for Social Change in Pakistan," *Journal of Developing Areas*, October, 1967. *The Pakistan Army Journal* publishes articles of strategic, social, and political interest, but is not publicly circulated—copies can be seen at the Royal United Services Institution, London.

Through the years numerous official studies of the military in India have been undertaken and published. The Peel Commission (1859) and the Eden Commission (1879) are especially valuable. Later official studies of significance were the Esher Committee (1920), the Indian Sandhurst Committee (Skeen Committee), 1927, and the unpublished Indianization Committee (1939). The complete files of the latter committee including written and oral testimony are held in the Ministry of Defense Archives, India. The Indian Round Table Conferences on occasion dealt with the military, as did the *Report* and *Supplementary Report* of the All Parties Conference, 1928.

A wealth of military and administrative data is contained in the archives of the Historical Section, Ministry of Defense, India. In the course of producing an official history of the Indian Armed Forces in World War II, much of this material has been published by the "Historical Section, India and Pakistan." This joint agency was created to write the military history of the war. All archives are located in New Delhi, and the Pakistanis have not contributed to the numerous volumes already published. The World War II series is complete, and work has begun in Delhi on the official Indian accounts of various postindependence military operation.

Stimulating conceptual and theoretical approaches to the military and society can be found in S. Andrzekewski's remarkable *Military Organization and Society*, London: Routledge and Kegan Paul, 1954 (republished in 1968 by the University of California Press): S. E. Finer, *The Man on Horseback*, London: Pall Mall Press, 1962; Samuel P. Huntington, *The Soldier and the State*, Cambridge: Harvard University Press, 1957; Morris Janowitz, *The Professional Soldier*, Glencoe: The Free Press, 1960, and his *The Military in the Political Development of New Nations*, Chicago: University of Chicago Press, 1964. A classic study is Quincy Wright's *A Study of War*, Chicago: University of Chicago Press, 1942; and Hans Speier, *Social Order and the Risks of War*, New York: Stewart, 1952, and Alfred Vagts, *A History of Militarism*, New York: Meridian, 1959 are valuable. Useful case studies of other nations can be found in John J. Johnson, ed., *The Role of the Military in Underdeveloped Countries*, Princeton: Princeton University Press, 1962, and William Gutteridge, *Military Institutions and Power in the New States*, New York: Praeger, 1965, and

Wilson C. McWilliams, ed., *Garrisons and Government: Politics and the Military in New States*, San Francisco: Chandler, 1967, which reprints an excellent study of Indian civilian-military relations by Lloyd and Susanne Rudolph.

INDEX

Ahirs. 44; in W.W. I, 69; in W.W. II, 142; demand own regiment, 189
aid to the civil, 97, 127–130, 194
Aiyer, Sir P. S. Sivaswamy, 85, 111; resolutions on Indianization, 78ff.
Akali movement, and Sikh unrest, 95
Ali, Aruna Asaf, and R.I.N. Mutiny, 98
Ambedkar, Dr. B. R., military background, 59–60
Amritsar Massacre, 93–94, 128n.
Auchinleck, F.-M. Sir Claude, 131, 156n., 162, 163n.; on civilian control in India, 28, 110n.
Ayub Khan, F.-M. and President, 120n,. 122n., 130, 178; on martial races, 48n.

Barlow, Sir George, and White Mutiny, 19ff.
batta (field allowance), 11–12
Bengal: and Lord Curzon, 89–90; British ridicule of, 99. *See also* Bose, Subhas Chandra; Bengalis
Bengal Presidency Army, 9, 11, 17, 33–34, 37ff., 44
Bengalis: in military, 37, 44; Lord Roberts on deterioration of, 46; non-martial nature of, 48; de-recruited after W.W. I, 76; seek equality in army, 81–82; interest in officer corps, 112; success in military ex-

ams, 118; in armored corps, 141; in NDA, 184; in Rajput Regiment, 188; in Pakistan military, 192–193
Biharis, martial exploits of, 190
Birdwood, F.-M. Lord, and aid to the civil, 128
Bombay, mutiny in, 5. *See also* Royal Indian Navy
Bombay Presidency Army, 9; recruitment in, 34, 36, 40, 44; Mahars in, 59
Bose, Subhas Chandra: career and interest in military, 99–102, 112, 138, 154, 157; ideology of, 162–163. *See also* Indian National Army
Brahmins: in Indian Army, 35, 37, 38, 44; Maharashtrian, seek re-entry into army, 61; Deccani, 70; Punjabi in W.W. I, 72; in W.W. II, 142
Briggs, Lt.-Col. J., urges promotion of Indians in 1836, 63
British: presence in India, 4ff.; legacy to India and Pakistan, 2–3, 29–31; and Mutiny of 1857, 35ff.
British Army, table of organization and Indian Army, 42–43
British-Indian Army (1680–1947), early problems, 4–14; reform, 14–18; legacy of civilian control, 29ff. *See also* Indian Army; Pakistan Army
Bucher, Sir Roy, advises Indian officers on politics, 166–167

211